649
WE

Westin, Jeane

The coming parent
revolution

DATE		
MAR. 3 1 1982 JY 14 '99		
JUN. 2 1982		
OCT. 1 2 1982		
3/26/83		
OCT. 1 9 1985		
AP 2 3 '92		
JAN 1 0 96		
JAN 2 4 96		
FEB 1 3 '96		
FEB 2 8 96		
MAR 1 8 96		
SEP 2 2 97		

© THE BAKER & TAYLOR CO

THE COMING PARENT REVOLUTION

The Coming Parent Revolution

JEANE WESTIN

RAND McNALLY & COMPANY

CHICAGO   NEW YORK   SAN FRANCISCO

Library of Congress Cataloging in Publication Data

Westin, Jeane Eddy.
   The coming parent revolution.

   Bibliography: p.
   Includes index.
   1. Parenting—United States.   I. Title.
HQ755.8.W45   649'.1   81-13073
ISBN 0-528-81112-6   AACR2

First printing, September, 1981

Second printing, October, 1981

TO ALL MY FAMILIES — the one into which
I was born, the one I helped to create,
and the one to follow

CONTENTS

ACKNOWLEDGMENTS

Many people helped in the creation of this book — so many that I cannot mention them all, which in no way lessens my appreciation for their contributions.

A special word of thanks must go to those who gave significant assistance: parents around the country who trusted me with their deepest emotions; Kate Pemberton, who typed and retyped my manuscript and went beyond her duty to give me valuable comments; Shirley, Jeri, Ebba, and Michon, who Xeroxed the manuscript, reading it as it came from the machine and giving me on-the-spot encouragement; my editors at Rand McNally; Jane Jordan Browne, my agent, whose expertise was critical at every point; and my husband, Gene, whose shoulder never tires.

This is the true nature of home —
it is the place of Peace;
the shelter not only from all injury,
but from all terror, doubt, and
division.

— *John Ruskin*

THE COMING PARENT REVOLUTION

INTRODUCTION

During the almost three years I researched and wrote this book, hardly a day passed when I did not fear that my views might be construed as anti-child or negative toward my own child. At the least, I thought, an important issue might be dismissed as the frustrated ravings of a "failed" parent.

I have decided to speak up because I believe that what I have to say is more important than my private fears, that it will serve a forgotten group of which I am a member—average parents in middle-class homes, mothers and fathers who are being deprived of society's support in truly tragic fashion.

This is a book about parenting, written for today's harried two-parent families, by a parent, in consultation with other parents. It is not a book specifically for single parents, although many single parents are trying to raise their children according to age-old values. It is not a book for the homosexual parent or the parent in a multifamily communal experiment or the feminist parent; they either have their own books or soon will.

Rather, this book is for the majority of parents, the eight out of ten parents who are married mothers and fathers devoted to the ideal of the family imperative, parents who want to know if there is any possible way to raise responsible, loving children in an anti-parent, anti-family, youth-bedazzled culture.

There is a way. This book is a passionate advocacy of that single cause—a solution I call the New Traditional Family. I concede at the outset that I will not deal with the big picture, the environment or world affairs as they affect families. The focus here is on the trap that has ensnared all those parents who, like me, swallowed the bait of the last quarter-century's progressive child-rearing practices.

My daughter reached adolescence the product of almost religious adoration and careful child-rearing methods based on the democratic family principles of Rudolf Dreikurs, the feminist movement, and a continually updated assortment of psychological techniques that advocated listening—really listening—to your child. In practical application this meant that if my daughter was sitting in her father's favorite chair (carefully *not* called Daddy's chair lest parents seem to have special privileges), she did not have to relinquish it when he came home from work. To have insisted on such favored treatment for an adult would have violated her equal rights and, even worse, in the early 1970s, might have promoted sexism.

I encouraged and instructed her in the human potential movement's concept of self-love, believing completely that more lives were ruined by lack of self-regard than by any other destructive force. I practiced understanding her behavior. What was her motivation? What were her stresses? Remembering the painful exclamations of "wicked," "bad," and "shame on you" from my own more traditional upbringing, I subscribed to the psychologists' injunction against even mentioning such archaic and guilt-producing words. Most of all, I tried to protect her from emotional pain. I thought this would keep her safe.

At 13, then, my daughter was bright, articulate, assertive, self-starting, ambitious, dynamic, filled with a sense of self-worth, a splendid example of successful, modern child-rearing—and impossible to live with.

In her adolescent years that followed, I was to run a gauntlet of emotion, a parental grief experience that sped from disappointment through hurt and anger to desperation and depression. Most distressing of all, I lost confidence in my ability to be a parent.

As a writer, I discovered long ago that my experiences, my feelings are not unique. This time was no different. Mine was a familiar tale, I found, the more I talked with other parents. The same child who has been lavishly loved and psychologically indulged by this generation of middle-class parents suddenly withdraws from family life, rejects parental affection, and institutes what can only be called a reign of emotional blackmail. In a desperate effort to reestablish communication, parents remove any remaining pressure on the child to achieve. Far from earning the longed-for return of the estranged child, this capitulation seems to be perceived as final permission to live only for self.

Finally, we parents see in our children's eyes that being loved is all they know. We taught them to owe us nothing. We based our child-rearing on psychologically correct principles of regard for their worth, but we refused to consider *our* worth, *our* needs. We rejected the ancient commandment of owed honor for parents, believing that we should earn it, not understanding that unconditional loving, without expectation, earns only youthful contempt. We accepted as our guiding star the dictum that by our example they would learn, not understanding that example without guidance is not always instructive.

My journey in search of my daughter and myself soon widened to become a search for an answer to what has happened to middle-class parents who put their hearts and minds into child-rearing. Statistics show us that parents today are the best educated, most affluent in history. Observation indicates that they are caring. Why is it that well-educated, prosperous, loving parents are having so much trouble with their children? Why, in short, has family life become so painful?

At first, I looked for answers among the experts. That is standard journalistic procedure. With some notable exceptions, I found either parent-survival techniques that characterize parents as helpless victims, or methods that purport to be aids for parents but in reality only teach them more ways of "understanding" their children's problems. The hallmark of all these expert answers was an almost complete lack of understanding about how parents really feel today, their hurt, frustration, and yes, even rage.

What mothers and fathers must have, I thought, is a book that supports parents, parents whose child-rearing abilities have been downgraded by experts, parents who have been ignored by their young. To write such a book, I planned two thrusts to my research: to discover what was behind the tragic loss of parental self-esteem and then to find how it could be restored. I believed that when I found these answers, they would show me the way to the New Traditional Family, one that would be modern enough for the 1980s without sacrificing parents' rights on the altar of psychologically progressive child-rearing.

I began by interviewing parents I knew, people I considered good mothers and fathers, who tried hard, read the "right" books, and took the latest parenting classes, but whose children were family drop-outs. One mother told me her 16-year-old daughter had maintained a punishing silence at the dinner table for two years; a father talked through held-back tears of a 14-year-old son who rejected his affection and sneered at his offers of help. These parents had more than family breakdown in common. They felt dreadfully alone with their problems and were crushed by guilt. I wondered: Could groups of parents help each other?

My next move was to organize parent-to-parent talkshops, six to 12 parents meeting to discuss the problems of parenthood in the 1980s. At the very first talkshop, one embittered father walked out, saying, "I don't even want to talk about my children." But most parents wanted to talk. Once they started they could scarcely stop, so that sessions scheduled to end at 10:30 p.m. often were still full of energy past midnight. My first impression was that parents, given permission to talk about their feelings without fear of being regarded as bad parents, acted like initiates at an Alcoholics Anonymous meeting. They were overwhelmed with relief that they were not alone. The atmosphere at the talkshops was much like that of a good self-help group—concerned, supportive, and honest.

As a result of these parent talkshops, I began to ask myself a question. Since these parents, who had heretofore met all the measures they believed essential to good parenthood, were now experiencing serious problems with their children, were there forces in today's society that were negatively affecting parenting and family life? Over and over again, talkshop parents mentioned four forces they perceived as hostile influences: the confusion wrought by parenting experts, government intervention, the chaos of education, and the infiltration of everyday life by anti-family messages via the entertainment media.

To gain broader understanding of the ways in which these forces affected parents across the country, I devised a 42-part parent-attitude questionnaire and wrote to 150 newspapers, asking for their readers' help. More than 500 parents asked to participate, of whom 293 completed and returned their questionnaires, many including long, sad, mad, proud letters. Of these 293, I chose 117 for a second, even more detailed questionnaire. Eighty-one of those responded, 31 of whom I later telephoned or visited for in-depth interviews.

In all, including individual interviews, parent talkshops, and questionnaires, I collected the opinions and personal experiences of mothers and fathers in 402 families. These individual opinions and

experiences are referred to throughout the book. The collective pro-
file of these parents is as follows.

Geographically, 33 percent live in the West, 24 percent in the
Midwest, 23 percent in the East, and 20 percent in the South.

Mothers make up 69 percent of the parents responding.

Parents vary in age from 18-year-old mothers to an 83-year-old
father (who has an adopted high-school age son at home), with the
majority—64 percent—between ages 30 and 40.

Altogether they have 1,022 children, 51 percent female and 49
percent male, which meets precisely the national norm. The largest
family in my sampling has nine children.

By age, 14 percent of the children are preschoolers; 11 percent
are 5 to 10 years old; 9 percent are 10 to 13 years old; 26 percent 13
to 18 years old; and a whopping 40 percent are older than 18 and
living at home.

In religious preference, 53 percent of the parents claim to be
Protestants, 27 percent are Catholic, 6 percent are Jewish, and 14
percent list no religion.

Ninety-two percent are currently married, 6 percent are divorced, and nearly 2 percent are widowed. Only one parent (a
19-year-old mother) is living with a lover.

These parents proved to be highly educated, with 21 percent
holding graduate degrees, 27 percent having college degrees, and 28
percent having attended some college. Of the rest, 22 percent have
high-school diplomas, while only 2 percent have less than a high-
school education.

Forty percent of the mothers have full-time careers outside the
home, with 14 percent working part-time. But 46 percent are full-
time homemaker/mothers, many of them making a special point to
list this as their occupation. Every father is employed, except the
83-year-old, who only recently retired.

Many trades and professions are represented. Teaching was the
most often reported, at 14 percent of the total. Others listed themselves as physicians, nurses, farmers, clerical and factory workers,
engineers, police officers, and there is one former nun, a belly-dance
instructor, an actress, a school-board member, and a state legislator.

Statistically speaking, my 402 families may not have been selected as scientifically as Gallup-poll interviewees, but all of them
are concerned parents responding to the question, What are the con-

cerns of average parents in the 1980s? Many of them are heartland Americans, middle-class parents who feel left out of the process that shapes national attitudes about parents and families. One Nebraska mother wrote to me, "Since I don't live in a big city, I didn't think anyone was interested in my opinions." But even a Los Angeles mother told me, "It seems to me that the sensible voice of average parents has been lost in the media's chase of every far-out group that holds a rally or chants a slogan at the top of their lungs."

As I talked with these parents and read their letters, I became convinced that my sampling represents the spiritual center of the American family. Their opinions matter. Their questions matter. But most of all, it matters very much to all of us that the traditional values of these average, middle-class parents—call them what you will—be carried forward into our future.

This book is divided into three sections. In the first I show as briefly as possible why parents are angry, how they have been driven up against the wall, who or what has pushed them there, and what they can do about it. In section two I explore in some depth the four negative forces outside the home interfering with child-rearing today as they have been reported by parents and according to reports I have assembled, sorted, and assessed from myriad sources. The final section offers parents proposals on ways to found their own New Traditional families and take control of their homes. Throughout the book, I have delved into many social areas that affect parents and their families negatively, not as an expert viewing these phenomena with scientific objectivity but as a parent to whom these things happened.

A word to those with an aversion to neologisms: In this book the recently coined "parenting" is used as the new generic word for carrying out parentlike activities. It was commonly used by the parents I interviewed. "Where shall we look for standard English," said Henry David Thoreau, "but to the words of a standard man?"

PART ONE

FAMILIES UPSIDE DOWN

*"What did we ever do
to deserve this?"*

CHAPTER 1

demoralized, alienated, angry parents

From one end of the country to the other, within every middle-class sphere and suburb, parents are talking about their children. Once they boasted about good marks in school or a hit clean over the right-field fence. Not today. Today they commiserate, sometimes with tears. They exchange examples of their children's awfulness, their rejection of family standards, their strange lack of affection for loving parents. "Why are our children doing this to us?" parents ask each other.

Unbelievable? Aren't parents supposed to love and support their children, no matter what? To speak ill of offspring has always been considered bad form. Parents with problems acted brave and tried to cover up. But never before in our history have the young managed to generate so much bitterness and alienation in parents.

The problem is all the more poignant because it is most intense among caring parents, the ones who tried so hard to measure up to almost scientific perfection.

A Maine mother, describing herself as educated and a WASP, recites a tale I heard from parents many times over:

> *I have long felt the anger of lovingly raising a pair of children who seem to feel their only purpose in life is the pursuit of their own pleasure. I thought they would learn to be loving and kind and sensitive to others through the good example their father and I tried to set. But the older they got, the worse they got. Although we offered them a college education, our daughter, the eldest, stayed two years in two schools, gave up on an art career, took a dog-grooming course, hitchhiked around the country, and is now back—living at home, studying bartending. She doubts she will make the commitment of getting married, never intends to have children, wants to live only for the moment. What has happened to ambition?*

The boy lasted two weeks in college and has since had a variety of jobs, none requiring more than minimum effort and producing little more than minimum wages. He only recently left home to live with four other young people, but he has at least four meals a week at home, rides to his job with his father, brings home his laundry and his Doberman when she goes into heat. He has perhaps untied the apron strings, but won't let me take off the apron.

This mother has described two members of what has been termed the narcissistic or Me generation. I believe many of today's youth should more properly be labeled the Peter Pan generation. No other term so precisely fits the desperate, self-absorbed search for their shadows (read *feelings*) among today's "I want to be Me" mob.

How do I define this new breed of child? They are most easily characterized by their needs and their attitudes: (1) every effort must result in fun; (2) obstacles must give way to immediate satisfaction; (3) they must be the center of family, classroom, or group; (4) they are takers rather than givers; (5) they deny all authority; (6) they see themselves as not needing improvement, and thus are unable to change their behavior if corrected; and (7) they blame others, particularly parents, for their problems.

parent burnout

There are signs of parent burnout everywhere. A sense of betrayal compounds the normal angst of raising children—never easy, but never harder than today. Some families, it's true, seem to be coping beautifully, especially those with religious or extended family supports. But others report classic burnout symptoms: feeling empty, exhausted, trapped, ready to give up. This California mother of four is scraping along, her parental morale at rock bottom.

Anger is not really what I feel. It's alienation. Turnoff. I feel, in a kind of sad, resigned way, that the past 20 years were a total waste. My husband and I have nothing to show for it. It's not that we're sitting around crying. We have jobs, travel, full lives, but the child-raising part of our lives was a waste because the kids are nothing, just nothing.

But parent burnout, no longer private grief, has gone public in recent years. The full significance of the tax revolt, especially when it affects schools, has never been recognized by social observers. The increasing numbers of rejections of school tax levies, even those designed to keep schools from emergency closures—while reflecting inflation, school failure, and reduction of the urban tax base—could be a covert sign of parental disenchantment with their young.

Another development that indicates the mood of fed-up parents is the phenomenon of the Goodbye Mother, which gained momentum in the 1970s. Today more mothers than fathers are running away from home. Of course, some mothers have always gathered up their children and run away; but the significant difference is that today's Goodbye Mother is leaving her children behind. Family experts look on this as a new type of marriage problem brought to boil by the women's liberation movement. It may be, instead, an angry reaction of mothers to their offspring.

Disinheriting their children in favor of friends or even neighbors is a trend among older parents. When questioned, they say they have already given their children too much and received little or no appreciation in return.

A further sign of parent unrest surfaced in the 1970s when columnist Ann Landers asked readers: If you had it to do over again, would you have children? After 70 percent of the 10,000 respondents wrote that they would not have children again, even the unshockable columnist was shocked.

In interviewing parents for this book, I found that 68 percent would have children again, but 21 percent of these parents said no to having the same number of children again, or said, "Only if I could choose which ones I wanted." True, some parents added unsolicited and loving remarks, such as "With my children I'm everything I ever dreamed of being" and "they're my joy." Yet many comments were not so rosy; some parents wrote such things as: "took all my life," "crushing burden," and "too much emotional stress." Oddly, in an escalating inflationary period, few parents mentioned the financial strains, but it was the rare parent who didn't mention the emotional stress of parenthood.

When asked why they had had children in the first place, 80 percent of the parents I talked with had only two reasons: to create a close family and to love and be loved. Most of them say they feel cheated.

Too often, parents told me, the reality of family life didn't match the dream, especially when children reached adolescence. A Wisconsin father of three said:

It's normal for teenagers to want to be with their peers, but my children think their rights are being violated if they are asked to participate in any family occasion. My son told me "old people" make him nervous. They seem to be unable to tolerate any time at all away from their own age group.

For other parents the idea of reciprocal love has proved to be a cruel trap. One Georgia mother echoed the hurt feelings of many mothers:

Mothers are supposed to give unconditional love, but instead of following the example, my children exploited an opportunity to get everything for nothing.

Mothers more than fathers may be victimized by the demands of parental loving in the modern family. For 2,000 years the Madonna and child have been the ideal religious picture of mothering in Western culture. The image of the eternal, loving mother has not diminished in an era influenced by psychology but has grown even more intense.

Far more than financial problems, the feeling of rejection by their own children plagues many parents. "She is completely indifferent to our views and feelings," and "Our kids don't respect us; they feel they know more about everything than we do" are common threads running through their conversation. One mother put this ironic twist on the youth-culture dictate that everyone, especially parents, has to *earn* love:

I taught my kids they didn't have to love me just because I'm their mom; I thought they would love me for the good person I was and for how hard I tried. But they no longer respect that; they think that's dumb.

Another example of parent alienation is the "I lost my turn" parent. Many of today's mothers and fathers were raised in traditional adult-centered families in which the parents' needs were met and the children taught to do things to make their parents proud of them, to give something in return for parental care, if only their own obedience. These sons and daughters, now grown to be parents themselves, are raising their offspring in child-centered families in which the child's needs are primary. While this generation of parents was growing up, the rules of the game changed. They are the generation in the middle.

A Wisconsin mother says:

> *I've been married for 30 years and haven't had my turn yet. My oldest son, a lawyer, is married and has an 18-month-old son. I'm "too stupid" to have input on child-raising, but not too stupid to baby-sit night after night. My second child, a daughter, has a master's in English; she brings her laundry home for me to do on weekends. My third, a college graduate and flight attendant, is having a ball; she never even writes. My fourth, a daughter, is a college freshman studying World Culture, whatever that is. My whole life has been spent jumping when one of them yelled "Jump!"*

These are a few of the signs of parent burnout. Their stories don't mean that, at some signal, parents will rebel against their children en masse. They do indicate that parents are seriously questioning modern concepts of child-rearing (sometimes called permissive) that demand so much of the parents and so little of the child.

the love-machine mother

During most of human history the family worked together. Father was at home and he was the authority figure, the disciplinarian, while Mother was all love and affection. She liked that role. Everybody likes to be loved. But then about 1920, when the nation made the shift from an agricultural to an industrial economy, the majority of fathers had to leave home and farm to find outside work. This caused Mother to play dual roles: She was supposed to be a "love machine" on the one hand and a disciplinarian on the other. The roles created a natural conflict, and today's mother is presented with this dilemma. She asks herself, Am I going to be loved, or am I going to be obeyed? Most of the time she opts for love. The pop culture supports her in this decision; it says that love is the one simple cure-all to every problem between parent and child.

"Mother has been doubly victimized by the culture," said Dr. Tony Campolo, head of the Sociology Department at Pennsylvania's Eastern College, in an interview.

> Not only has she been told that love is the answer to parenting problems, but she's been told that if her children don't love her back, she's a failure.
>
> Today we see the Love-Machine Mother working overtime to get her kids to love her, because the culture has her convinced that if they just love her enough that will solve everything. And, of course, it doesn't.
>
> Have you ever watched mothers with children in supermarkets? They are afraid to discipline them, not because they are weak people, but because the whole culture has said, "This is not the thing that you do; you love them, and if you love them right, you reason with them."

Campolo has articulated the main message our culture sends to mothers: If you love your children right, they'll turn out fine; if they fail, it's a fault of your loving. Young people are very aware of this today. The young have been indoctrinated with the same psychology, which says if anything is wrong with them, it's because their parents didn't love them enough.

No wonder, then, that so many parents pull back, not only from punishing their children, but from inflicting the slightest emotional pain or discomfort. Dr. G. J. Fruthaler, a New Orleans pediatrician, addressed this problem in a letter he wrote to me after reading a newspaper article about this book.

> Yesterday I had in my office a 2-year-old child with a problem of some duration whose mother could not bring herself to take the clothes off the child so that I could examine him. To establish my point that she was afraid to allow the child to cry, I went off and saw several patients until she finally disrobed the youngster after about 45 minutes of screaming and fussing. He quieted down within a minute and allowed me to do a very thorough physical; he was smiling and cooperating completely at the end. I see many mothers who apparently believe the first priority is to keep the child from crying at them, and everything else, particularly their own decisions, is subsidiary.

The love machine grinds exceedingly fine. Many women whom I interviewed for this book described the results of trying to be mother and love machine, like this California mother, alienated from her daughter:

> *I have a running argument with my oldest child. She claims that no matter what she does, I am supposed to still love her. There is this big split in her mind between her actions and my moral judgments about her actions. Her complaint with me—after she does one appalling thing after another—is that it shouldn't make any difference in my love for her.*
>
> *She feels very hurt that she can't get me to feel the way she wants me to feel about her and still do whatever she wants to do.*
>
> *At the same time I feel guilty. I consider her point of view over and over again, wondering what is wrong with me that I can't come up to what she expects of me.*

A Maine mother's admission exemplifies this confused thinking among parents:

> *A good part of the time I find myself doing what the kids want. First, I reason with them, but they can play that game better than I can so I give in. That makes me mad and I yell at them. But then I feel guilty for yelling, for being such a lousy mother, and give in again. They get too much; I do too many things for them.*

More than two-thirds of the parents I questioned admitted to me that theirs was a child-centered family. Most said they thought parents today might be fed up with this arrangement, but that they themselves were too afraid of alienating their children to do much about it. One West Coast mother confessed:

> *I adore my kids but I'm their handmaiden. My children feel as though adults should drop everything when they beckon. We have made them the center of everything. It's grossly unfair for me, as Mom, to be Z on their consideration list. But I'm afraid to withhold attention because the quality of my love might affect them for the rest of their lives. I realize my responsibility, but I can't stand this guilt trip or this constant giving.*

Although fathers certainly suffer from the loss of their children's affection, mothers often feel the loss more acutely. Many sense a kind of undertow tugging at today's mothers.

In his *Generation of Vipers* (1942), Philip Wylie coined the word "momism" to describe the emotional domination of children (and society) by mothers. This time around we have "kidism," the domination of mothers by their children. When the social order is upset and the young are worth more than adults simply because they are young, the controls on youthful narcissism break down. The result is this sad mother's story:

> *My girls don't care about my feelings. They expect everything to go their way, and I am here to serve them. My rules, morals—everything having to do with my authority—is outside their lives, and unobserved.*

These parents all admitted to me that they resent having *their* feelings ignored. Why are they so angry? It seems that too many children in their frantic pursuit either of independence or of some grandiose dream of self-worth, choose to ignore or manipulate the emotions of their parents. It is no wonder parents are angry enough to overthrow a system that promotes such a poor payoff for two decades of parenthood.

Is giving your child more love the real answer to child-rearing problems? Historian Christopher Lasch in his book *The Culture of Narcissism* thinks not. "Recent evidence suggests," he says, "that American children, far from becoming overly dependent on their mothers, form strong attachments to neither parent, acquiring instead, at an early stage in their lives, a cool, detached . . . outlook."

In this age of Peter Pan, more and more young people are growing up in a youth-centered, narcissistically inclined culture that seeks to make obsolete the standards of the past 2,000 years. In such a society, heaping more and more love on children and withdrawing discipline can have devastating effects on families. Briefly, this is the scenario: The father works away from home, and the mother must dispense both affection and discipline; she opts for love over discipline and becomes afraid of incurring the resentment of her children; the children take over the family. Why? Because our children have the love to give that validates every mother's existence; they've got all the power.

Is this just another pat theory, or is this story being played out in countless homes every day? Let's hear what parents, especially mothers, have to say—a mother of four in Kansas, for instance:

> *My children have a maddening power to hurt me. The more I give, the less they care. I think I have to lower my expectations of their love.*

Or this New Orleans mother:

> *I thought my children would follow my loving example. They didn't. Nobody believes that an unloving kid can come from a loving home. They can.*

Finally, an adoptive father of a 15-year-old boy:

> *I am really angry when I hear that children should be loved endlessly, while psychologists label parents neurotic when they need affection.*

Mothers, discussing their shifting position over the last two decades, feel that motherhood itself is being challenged in the home and in society. They are faced, they think, with what amounts to psychic chaos. A Missouri mother of five wrote me:

> *I've come to the conclusion that no matter what I do or say or feel, when my kids grow up, they will blame me for everything— what I did and what I didn't do, as well.*

Many mothers feel that a double-edged sword of Damocles hangs over their heads, since half of society damns them if they go to work, and the other half condemns them if they are full-time mothers. Often economic realities offer them no choice.

One parent talkshop of stay-home mothers agreed that the term "equal opportunity" should be applied not only in the nine-to-five work context but to mothers as well. Those women especially who elected to be traditional mothers declared a change was needed in society's attitude toward motherhood. Most full-time mothers agreed with this San Diego mother of four:

> *Motherhood has been downgraded. I would be more fulfilled in the Mom role if it were "glorified" or at least dignified. I need to feel like a heroine and to be assured that I am essential in this world.*

Working mothers, on the other hand, feel that stay-home mothers tend to characterize working women as "bad mothers" or, at best, as materialists "working for steak so they won't have to eat hamburger."

There was a discernible trend among young mothers with whom I talked toward simplifying their financial needs so they could remain at home with their very young children. They had found that the rewards of one-paycheck parenting compared favorably with the affluence of two incomes.

Nearly all mothers, working or not, agreed that preschool children were worse off if their mothers weren't at home. The mother-child attachment, they felt, was a necessary antidote to today's casual disregard for duty and devotion.

the parent dilemma

While mothers are caught in a dilemma unique to this age, both parents today are faced with a confusing contradiction. Everywhere they are told that in their hands they have the power to shape their children for good or ill, yet they have been counseled endlessly to be cautious of corrupting their children's psyches by the use of that power. Thus, parents actually perceive themselves to be powerless, especially as their children grow older and bring the anti-family moral experiments of the sixties and seventies, now become custom, into the home.

For the last 25 years the parent-in-charge, traditional family has been seen as the corrupter of children's lives. But parent power didn't corrupt. Our intimidation by the youth culture and its promoters— the forces of expert advice-givers, government, schools, and the media—is what has corrupted our families and brought us to the brink of parent revolution.

CHAPTER 2

the forces of disorganization

It is true that parents have dropped the age-old prohibition against speaking ill of their children. They are too frustrated, angry, and hurt to keep silent. Yet they are still suffering a mental tug-of-war between the sense that, as parents, they owe their children everything and the awareness that, as human beings, they should naturally resist an increasingly unbearable emotional overload. How has such a dilemma come about?

Just a generation ago, parents were not involved with the care and feeding of their children's psyches. The word "psyche" had barely become familiar to the general public, let alone grown into a need. Children not so long ago were reared in a culture that respected hard work, authority, God, and country. In such an atmosphere the "self" had not assumed the importance it now has.

I asked parents in all sections of the country to rank, from a list I provided, the most important things in their adolescents' lives today. The following are the results: (1) self; (2) peer groups; (3) money; (4) rock music; (5) television; (6) telephone; (7) sports; (8) family; (9) education; and (10) religion. Sadly, such values filter down to even the youngest children. For example, in a 1979 poll, third-graders chose television over their dads and elected a jiggly TV celebrity their wished-for mother substitute.

An Ohio father has this perspective on the cultural difference between a generation ago and today:

> *The heroes they raise up would have been looked down on just 15 years ago; our entertainment scene is full of alcohol, drugs, sex, and violence; and commitment to family is sneered at. The personal value displayed everywhere is "me" not "thee." The number and variety of immediate dangers to my children stagger me. It takes a lot of courage to raise kids today.*

The roots of what I call the Peter Pan generation were planted in the 1950s, years that could be termed the psychological decade. The result in the 1960s and the 1970s was a culture to which every young person belonged and from which most parents were excluded. Unlike their predecessors, the flappers and the bobby-soxers, the members of this new generation never had to confront the realities of economic scarcity and hard work. They had what amounted to a guarantee of security until they *decided* what they wanted to do with their lives.

Out of the general "enlightenment" that followed the entry of psychology into child-rearing came the concept of the democratic family—an impossible dream. The search for a utopian family life in this age of individualism and thirst for personal independence led directly to the idea that one family member equals one vote. This misguided effort to encourage children to exercise their judgment equally with adults in family councils has resulted in families in which children are encouraged to help make decisions that they are not qualified to make. The questions of where Daddy should work and where the family should live are not problems children are equipped to tackle.

the philosophy of the right to happiness

Parents have trouble combating the current right-to-happiness philosophy, which is organized around either pursuing thrills or passively waiting to be filled up with rich experiences. A California mother in one of my parent talkshops talked about her drinking, drug-taking, violent 19-year-old son:

> There are stories about kids running away from home, but what I hear my kid saying is: "I don't like it here, but until I've had all the fun I deserve, I'm going to stay. I'm your kid and you have to take care of me."

Among the parents in my survey a surprising 40 percent listed children over 18 years old still living at home. Some of these children were staying because of their inability to support themselves; many were going to college; but, if parent complaints are any indication, too many were practicing their right-to-happiness doctrine at their parents' expense.

Add to this subtotal the Peter Pan generation's policy of self-glorification. The slogans of the youth culture tend to justify anything they might do. For example, "The world is beautiful because I'm in it" teaches the young to expect admiration and acceptance not for their accomplishments but simply for themselves.

Parents today sense that the passion to live only for the moment, only for self, is destroying their children. Most parents believe that entering adult life must include respect for predecessors, as well as for posterity. What parents really fear is the promotion of an autonomous youth culture that, in effect, prevents adulthood.

Only partly aware that there are forces outside the family disrupting age-old verities, parents practice self-blame and redouble their efforts. Laboring under the tyranny of a flood of advice-giving handbooks, they try to practice instant communication, total openness, relevant with-it-ness—a parade of pop-psych remedies that has fostered an external control of child-rearing, formerly the business of the parents. These parents are told again and again that they don't know what they're doing, and this well-intentioned, professional advice, given with the purest of motives, has eroded parental self-reliance.

Even the most dedicated parents no longer know what constitutes good parenting. They fear they are not meeting their children's needs, and yet, sometimes, they resent the enormous demands that parenting today obviously makes. The result: Being a parent isn't the most attractive job around. Witness the rejection of parenthood by some young adults who go as far as sterilization. In 1980, 750,000 females who had never had children voluntarily ended their chances of ever doing so!

Not many years ago, the payoff for parenting was there in dollars and cents. When we were an agricultural nation, everyone on the farm worked. Each child stood to make the family an equivalent of $10,000 richer by his or her labor. Children were expected to contribute—as they still are in traditional homes. Today, too often the only benefits to Mom and Dad come through emotional fulfillment, if they come at all. This fundamental change has placed inordinate power in the hands of our children. Parents today instinctively protect themselves from the loss of their children's affection, trying to preserve what may be their only reward. In striving to do the psychologically "right thing," we have suffered one real loss: *the loss of parental authority.*

what has gone wrong with our children?

"Practically every significant innovation in child-rearing over the past 50 years," says Henry Malcolm in his book *Generation of Narcissus,* "has had its greatest impact among the affluent class. The theories of John Dewey, Maria Montessori, and A. S. Neill have had enormous influence. The subtle and all pervasive impact of Freudian psychology has also left its mark."

What kind of children have been produced? Malcolm tells us that in a growing environment of immediate gratification and parental emphasis on self-motivation, "these children experience the so-called real world from a unique vantage point. It is a world that seemingly extends outward from their own bodies."

Parent after parent with whom I talked echoed Malcolm's analysis of today's young. One engineer father, who despite his harsh words had tears in his eyes, said:

> *I'm father to a sneering 14-year-old boy who totally rejects his mother and me. What I've taken in this past year is what I call a lot of bullshit! I don't know why it is, or where it comes from, but I do know the kind of thing that our family is undergoing is more than just adolescent rebellion. I call it self-centeredness. We've tried to work things out, but we're just able to tolerate each other.*

Many of our children have become a chore rather than a challenge. How did parents get into this deadlocked, no-win position?

Our entire youth-oriented society collaborates to bankrupt traditional family values. Parents are literally hostages to narcissistic forces that encourage their children to look into the family "pool" and see only themselves mirrored there. We are trying to pass on moral values in an era in which popularized nonconformity is a value in itself.

The cult of Peter Pan thinking has invaded the middle-class home and persuaded our children to fly to never-never land where they will not age, where no adults will remind them of the perishability of their youth or nag them about a future when they, too, must become responsible adults. Here they can live without boundaries of reality, without good and bad, guilt, traditions, and, best of all, without "evil" authorities. In this never-never land, the frantic consumption of pleasures can forever masquerade as the joy that eludes them in reality and can conceal the lack of meaning in their lives.

Sociology professor Dr. Tony Campolo says that today's students are likely to reply to the question "What are you going to do with your life?" by saying, "I don't know, I haven't found myself yet." Campolo shakes his head at this. "I try to tell them that the self is not an essence waiting to be discovered," he says. "It's an essence waiting to be created."

Parents know this philosophical truth. The only way to create identity and meaning is through commitment to something outside ourselves. Human beings become what they commit themselves to. That is why we urge our children to study, to work hard, to think of the future. Parents know that the way their children view the future to a large extent governs the way they behave in the present. We see a growing number of our children equating their lack of commitment with "freedom," when we know the opposite to be true.

the traditional family under assault

The continual extension of the concept of family to include every social fad and sexual fancy has resulted in the trivialization of the family and is one reason for the brittle relations between parent and child.

Religion and law—forces that used to check such trends—don't speak out, can't be heard, or feel compromised. Parents, the most concerned group of all, aren't organized and are busy blaming themselves for the family's problems. For the most part, the mainstream church is so anxious to attract and hold an audience that it sits on its traditional standards. And the psychological "helping professions" are forever busy discovering new life-styles that conflict with the purpose of the traditional family.

Oddly enough, in an era in which even the most pea-brained ideas become "concepts" overnight, the concept of family has become undefinable. The most noted "family experts" huddled together for a four-day conference in the late 1970s to answer the question, Who can define "family" in a way everyone would accept? No one pointed out that "family" has always been defined as parents plus children and that family experimenters can jolly well come up with their own concepts rather than asking the traditional family to move over.

To parents, society's assault on the traditional family seems to be rigged to a perverse double standard. Let only a rumor of a statistic of juvenile vandalism, drug use, or self-indulgence be published in any journal, and professional family experts swarm like film extras in front of cameras to scrutinize the dying traditional family. But let one kinky, alternative family experiment after another rise up and demand its right of recognition, and these same professionals view the situation as healthy and suggest that the already strained concept of family once again be broadened to include all comers.

All of these negative influences on the middle-class family helped to form a foundation for the Peter Pan culture, but they did not just appear all at once and full-blown. There were forces of disorganization (I like sociologist David Riesman's term "great complexifiers") growing in America during the last 25 years, forces that invaded the home, the last stronghold of real privacy, and superseded parental control. These same forces alienated parents from their pasts and encouraged in many children a disaffection, an indifference to family ties.

The first force to huff and puff at the family door was social science—psychologists, social workers, and cultural anthropologists with their formulas touting the triumph of parenting expertise over parental common sense. At first parents welcomed the new theories, but eventually they became afflicted with self-doubt; their natural instincts were swamped by the flood of permissive ideologies. Parents who would never have dreamed of spoiling their children with an excess of material comforts found themselves spoiling their children with an excess of psychological understanding. Christopher Lasch writes in *Haven in a Heartless World:* "The confusion of parents dependent on professional theories of child-rearing, their reluctance to exercise authority . . . and the delegation of discipline to various outside agencies, have diluted the quality of child care."

All too often the result of professional meddling in everyday parent-child relationships has been to cut the ties that bind and to alienate the affections of parents and their offspring.

The second force to invade family life was paternalistic government—the Great Parent in Washington, D.C.—whose intrusion has since become a metaphor for what is wrong with almost every aspect of contemporary society. Gradually, removing responsibility from those who should have it, government agencies—aided and abetted by energetic social scientists—have undermined the family's historical right to be the sole custodian of its children's destinies. Minors, as the result of legal decisions, have adult rights in contraception, abortion, school attendance, and many other areas, leaving parents no voice in decision-making but responsible for the outcome.

Big Mama Education was the third force to disrupt the family. Based on the argument that education was too precious to leave in the hands of inexpert parents (especially immigrant parents), a system was devised that would prepare our children for effective and literate functioning in a technological society. Now the system has ballooned into a specialized and unresponsive bureaucracy and has produced a generation of children who are *less* well educated than their parents, the first time this has happened in our history. For this dubious service, most middle-class, home-owning parents contribute about half their property taxes.

The fourth and final force to attain an astonishingly tight grip on the family in 25 years was that combination of television, movies, rock music, and books collectively known as the entertainment media. Few areas of contemporary life have received as much public attention in recent years as the study of media influences. Because their effect on children is still largely inscrutable (even to a multiplying coterie of media experts), the media provoke more uncertainty and fear among parents—and more passionate anger—than any of the other forces confounding parents today.

What has been the result of these forces chipping away at our basic parental rights? What has been the effect on families in which child-rearing authority has fallen more and more to people and agencies other than parents? It has thrown parents into what I call the Caring-Parent Predicament: Parents are being held responsible by society for indulgent, self-absorbed, poorly educated, and sexually adventurous children while being undermined in their value-training by powerful institutions outside the family.

Seventy-eight percent of the parents surveyed felt that forces outside the home had usurped much of their authority, either directly or indirectly. Here's how parents ranked a list of the four forces of disorganization pitted against them. First was *media/advertising*, which outdistanced its nearest rival *education* by nearly three to one. *Psychology* came third and *government* fourth, both with nearly identical percentages. The category *other* was included to discover additional negative forces perceived by parents. A significant number of parents rated their children's peers as powerful enemies of the family and usurpers of their authority.

Christopher Lasch comments in *Haven in a Heartless World* on the shambles of the "sanctity" of the home: "Most of the writing on the modern family takes for granted the 'isolation' of the nuclear family," he writes, "not only from the kinship system but from the world of work. It assumes that this isolation makes the family impervious to outside influences. In reality, the modern world intrudes at every point and obliterates its privacy."

parent revolution counterattack

If parents are going to change the future, to be able to get up in the morning with the belief that they can make a better life for their families, they will have to find ways to regain control of child-rearing. A utility worker, the father of two, puts it this way:

> *I'm tired of hearing that my kind of family is dying and that we parents should trade it in for a more modern model. As usual in this country, we tend to throw out everything that is giving us problems.*
>
> *If the traditional family is in trouble, let's fix it; and that means to me that we parents have to start believing in ourselves again and boot out all the experts who tell us they know what's best for our kids.*

Does that sound like the first rallying cry of the parent revolution? To strengthen the family through a new parent-led counterattack is, indeed, a social intervention of the first magnitude. In an age that has doted on youth for so long, parents could be the forgotten lever of social change.

It's time to reassess the advice parents are being given about raising their children. Most parents readily admit the need for psychological child-rearing information that helps them recognize developmental stages in their children. What angers them is the attitude that all areas of parenthood are too important to be left to amateurs—the parents. That viewpoint on the part of an entire range of experts, no matter how well-meaning, is one of the biggest hustles of our time.

In the long history of mankind, parenthood has been experienced billions of times, and instinctive reaction is based on acquired, if unconscious, wisdom. How can it be implied over and over again that parents are mere blank pages for psychologists to write on?

Psychological and child-advocacy concepts, which view parents as problems and not as responsible adults to be assisted, have infiltrated our national bloodstream. Sham scientific authority has affected the way we parent our children from the moment they are born. Such influence can no longer be accepted at face value, as author Martin Gross challenges in *The Psychological Society:* "Outside the purely medical . . . scientific aspects there's no substance to the expertise in psychology. You're dealing in pure speculation. Yet the world has bought it—in juvenile delinquency, education, therapy, the arts, business, parenting, crime. It's the greatest hoax of the twentieth century."

Parents whom I interviewed generally object to the child-rearing advice-givers for the following reasons: (1) the instruction weakens parents' confidence in their own judgment; (2) the information is so complex it cannot be mastered; (3) the advice changes from expert to expert; and (4) the guidance is subject to the whims of psychological fashion. Unfortunately, all the advice has also caused parents to focus an inordinate amount of attention on the psyches of their children and not on the real victims of this preoccupation—themselves, and the family in general.

Many parents recognize that a sense of their own impotence grows when they use outside experts to validate their parenting. But this helplessness was learned—and can be unlearned. Parents need to know how they came to feel this way. Parents need to know the sources of their symptoms before they will be able to cure them. And parents need to know why they feel alienated from their own children. Such awareness is the first step in a positive parent revolution that will restore self-esteem and bring parents and children together again in a newly created traditional family.

In the 1980s, the priority for parents is to recreate a family ethos that will act as a fortress against outside disruptive forces. Although sociologists have long told us that the child-centered family is inward-turning, I believe the opposite is true: Child-centered families turn *outward* to experts, children turn *outward* to peers. What we need is the family-centered family that turns inward to its values for strength.

Parents of the parent revolution must offer this society the working model of a family-centered family carrying forward the traditions of the past—not as a millstone, but as a stepping-stone to a better, happier future for parents and children alike.

CHAPTER 3

toward a new traditional family

Gradually, from parent talkshops I organized, out of the survey of parents from across the country, from in-depth interviews of parents, and finally from my own mothering experiences, the shape of the model, right-side-up, post–parent revolution family emerged, an ideal that can only be called the New Traditional Family. Although most parents rejected the social tinkering that produced the failure of the child-centered family, they also repudiated the authoritarian "children should be seen and not heard" model of pre–World War II times. Out of these rejections came a new vision for the 1980s, indeed for the rest of the century, a vision that would recognize the primacy of parents, nourish the spirit of the child, and give a sagging society strong families on which to rebuild.

What constitutes the New Traditional Family? Simply this: It is neither parent-centered nor child-centered—it is *family-centered*, with parents at its head.

All good families provide love and mutual aid, and act as buffers to human isolation. But the New Traditional Family is also a fortress that keeps at bay anti-family forces which enslave our children under the pretext of freeing them. In that respect, it is a haven from an external society in a mess.

The family has so often been trivialized by sentimentality that we forget what practical, even indispensable, functions traditional families perform for all of us. It is the basic economic, educational, moral, protective, and recreational unit. It is the one place in a pluralistic society where shared beliefs give us comfortable rituals to fall back on when society becomes too tense. It is a place where we can grow old with those we love and where our elders can grow old with us. The New Traditional Family honors its parents of whatever generation.

Unlike "do your own thing" individuals, family-centered people define themselves through belonging to others. They find their identity in being part of a family network; they are aunts, cousins, mothers, sons, brothers, and wives. They are never alone, never completely "I." As James Hitchcock, professor of history at St. Louis University, said in *The Family: America's Hope*, "One can be one's true self only in the community of others. The family is, for most people, the crucible in which their humanity is forged."

It is no surprise that our young resist the pull of family, preferring the romantic search for their own special meaning. The entire symbolic function of the family today, as philosopher Michael Novak reminds us, is to make us realistic. Therefore, our children perceive family as a threat to their own liberation, because realism ultimately means that each of us is destined for only a brief presence in this world—a short time in which to pass along our particular human essence. Unlike most contemporary liberation, the kind that frees people from work, vows, and duties, family-centered people find true liberation in involvement with their families. Only when we submit to this discipline, when we bind ourselves to one another in dutiful relationships, are any of us truly free to develop our individuality. In other words, an individual can come from the institution of family; a family can rarely come from the self-fulfilling individual.

Families in the 1980s provide their members with their best route of escape from the results of culturally rampant individuality. A North Dakota father of five writes:

> The growth of an impersonal society is having the effect of bringing families closer, if only in self-defense.
>
> The people who will have the best time of it in the 1980s are those who make earnest efforts to work and play together; to stay close emotionally, and work toward common family goals. In today's increasingly rootless existence, everyone needs all the family he can get.

the new traditional nurturer

During the 1980s, I believe the issue of whether mothers should or should not work will be thrown into high contrast for New Traditional families. Economics and personal preference may not be the primary concerns. Certainly no one wants to be the stereotypical "barefoot and pregnant" woman, but few traditional mothers want to exchange the old stereotype for the new one of "organization woman." Says one mother who calls herself a "woman of today":

> *One parent should be at home with a* primary commitment to family and hearth. *It could be the father, but I think the family that recognizes the immeasurable importance of motherhood has an advantage. I'm not a sexist; women should be able to have careers. But raising children is a full-time career and should be so considered at least until children are in school. I think we women have to give up the feminist notion that having children doesn't mean we have to make a sacrifice. We must make up our minds that we can't have it all until we've given our children a good start in life. Why balk at the word "sacrifice"? That's neither an obscene nor an outmoded word.*
>
> *Of course, making a conscious sacrifice isn't being a martyr; it's making a choice, and we should be respected for it. If present-day mothers and fathers start demanding some of the respect and recognition they've had in the past and still desire today, then maybe parents in the 1980s will still have something going for them.*

On several home fronts, even with self-acknowledged "liberated mothers," there is a growing awareness that it may be necessary to make different career choices at different times in one's life. Notwithstanding necessity, mothers in traditional families deeply believe that the essential bond of child-to-parent suffers from their absence, and they reject the impersonal atmosphere of day-care centers or nurseries. In the 1980s, we counterculture parents should stop defining the worth of a career by how much money it pays and instead judge how much that career contributes to society. If we can manage that, motherhood (and fatherhood) can be reestablished as the highest-status job in the culture. The false message that women can have it all—babies and a seat in the typing pool or in the boardroom—and no one will suffer is an echo of Peter Pan philosophy. It is not progress for women.

the "declining" traditional family—alive and well

The public continues to receive a steady parade of examples "proving" that divorced, never-married, homosexual, bisexual, transsexual, communal, and living-together units form the bulk of today's "families." The essence of this approach is to define "traditional" so narrowly that *all* variations, including women who work and families with adopted children, are thrown into the nontraditional category. This has been called the demographic-demolition approach to "nuking" the nuclear family.

The media to the contrary, the traditional family lives! The U.S. Bureau of the Census estimates that 81 percent (1979 figure) of our more than 69 million children under the age of 18 are living with two parents. That figure jumps to 98 percent if one-parent families are included. According to the Children's Defense Fund in Washington, D.C., there are estimated to be between 500,000 to 750,000 (1979 figures) youngsters growing up in foster homes. This is a truly sad statistic, but hardly one that proves the demise of the traditional family. The assumption that more children than ever before are growing up without their parents cannot be supported statistically or historically. The high death rates of earlier times and the mobility of the breadwinner during the westward expansion meant that a higher percentage of children in early America lived in one-parent or no-parent homes than do so today. "It is terribly important," says Professor Michael Novak in *The Family: America's Hope,* "to doubt every public image about us, every time we hear something said about the . . . American family . . . to doubt it, to believe deep in one's heart that the experts in such matters are generally wrong."

The truth is that while the divorce rate is up and all manner of experimenting with family structure has increased, the traditional mom-pop-and-kids family is still the family of majority choice.

If 81 percent of citizens voted for an issue in an election, it would be called a landslide and cause for exultation. Why does the same figure, when applied to the traditional-family structure, bring on doom and gloom hucksters? Statistics can perhaps be used selectively to make a media story more interesting, but in this case they serve only to undermine the position of traditional parents in our society.

The statistical and the pathological, or "the family is sick," approach to viewing the modern family has had an even more appalling result. It has helped to popularize and promote the culture's faddish affair with alternative types of families—from the "permanent date" to the union of lesbian mothers to that fashionable substitute for Mom and Dad, the urban communal "friendship circle."

We New Traditional parents represent the real majority. As you will see, it is the meddlers at the family gate who have demonstrably failed the family, not us.

In spite of the confusion fostered by sensationalized media reports, the majority of parents in the 1980s want to take charge of their families, to control the raising of their children, to pass along the best traditional ideas and values, which are never-changing. But some of these parents have provided formerly unheard-of psychological freedom for their children and ask, Isn't it too late for us? For parents who want to break with the age of child-centered families, that amounts to Chicken Little logic.

No one, certainly no parent in this less than puritan age wants to see his or her children burdened with false guilt, weighed down with imaginary shame, or so lacking in self-esteem that they are crushed by the world they live in. But the psychological message promoting self-respect has been garbled, and the misreading is flashing danger signals throughout the society. A healthy feeling of self-worth is much different from unwholesome self-involvement. The former enhances the ability to love; the latter kills loving. Self-esteem is not a tangible item parents can hand over to their children like a lollipop; it derives from a well-lived life.

It's true all of us are born narcissists, an attitude fostered by the total care babies require from their parents. As we grow up, we re-channel our narcissism into a progressive ability to love others. At least that is the ideal. In times past, we learned this rechanneling in the family, and our learning ability was enhanced by a society that did not suffer narcissists any more than it did fools.

The sky will not fall if parents give their children *more* than love and understanding, if they give their children the benefit of their experience as a guide to the future. This is the time for parents to remain true to their own roots. If we blindly follow the youth cult and its morality, we deny our own lives and our own experience. In essence, it would be like saying we have nothing worth giving future generations.

Many of the parents surveyed said, "It's time to take a firm hand." Most mothers and fathers believe that this hand need not clench the proverbial rod. But a firm and loving hand is desperately needed now to guide children back to the fundamental virtue that recognizes parents and their generation as having more to offer the young than the young have to offer themselves.

One major move toward change, as many parents see it, is to

reassume the right to pass on traditions, moral codes, and acquired knowledge—the fingerprints of civilization—to their children. An overwhelming majority of the parents queried thought this to be the most important job they have, even though less than half of them felt they had the "right" to buck the prevailing youth culture, and fewer thought their children would listen. But, uneasy with their response, they asked: Is having no expectations the answer?

The contrast between what parents today see as possible and what they remember their parents seeming to accept as right is cause for wistful comparison from a Texas mother:

> *My folks knew exactly what to do. They never questioned them-selves nor agonized over what was right, as I do. I'll never forgive them for making child-rearing look so easy.*

The questions parents face are not easy ones. How can children respect us for our achievements when they are reared in a pervasive atmosphere of flattery, flattery that comes from psychologists, teach-ers, the media, and even the clergy? How can children view adults as successful in a world in which material possessions and celebrity are most admired? What parents can compete with the glamor and glory of youthful peers when they can provide only shelter, food, clothing, and ever-present love?

take-charge parenting and the new traditional family

Many parents, when asked how they perceived a positive parent re-bellion, said it meant two things to them: (1) a return to the idea that parents are the primary child-rearing authorities in their own homes; and (2) the renaissance of take-charge parenting. Most par-ents think that their common sense is still in goodly supply and resent the implication in the plethora of how-to-parent guides that they can't deal with the "exotic" demands of these times.

Take-charge parenting for one Nebraska father means:

> *My children must respect my decisions. That's the one most basic of all child-rearing principles. I appreciate what experts are trying to do, but I won't be threatened by a "system" of book and talk-show warnings.*

The first step in the rehabilitation of parents in the 1980s, then, will have to be their absolutely clear understanding of what parents owe children and what children owe parents, thereby placing logical limits on permissive psychological parenting.

The second step, one that will help defuse parental anger, is for parents to cease being the scapegoats, the new "out group" of society. All scapegoats are used by society to explain its unexplainable troubles. The ill-conceived theory goes that if only the "offenders" could be converted, burned, enslaved, or cured, society's ills would be solved.

parent revolution—counterculture for the eighties

There was a youth revolution in the 1960s. The young—characterized by their anti-war demonstrations, new morality, creative clothing, Woodstock sound, and painted vans—were dubbed the counter-culture. The prevailing, or traditional, culture of that decade was imagined to be either sinister, stupid, or funny. The pliability and adaptability of American society is amazing. In less than a decade, a broad cross section of people had adopted the mores, manners, and novelties of the young until what had been a style of life that ran counter to the culture *became* the culture.

To save the traditional family from any further erosion, parents must become the new counterculture of the 1980s. Led by parent evangelists preaching the take-charge child-rearing gospel, they must rise in opposition to the excesses of the Peter Pan generation and its mob of apologists, who reject the authority of experience and promote the new morality. For the new counterculture of parents, family stability will be the fundamental goal. Every move that will foster, nourish, and sustain this goal must be supported by parents in their own homes and communities and in the country at large.

Parents have two choices for the 1980s—parent revolution or a new family dark age. It is clear to many parents that a basic battle must be waged to reassert their primacy as the experts on child-rearing and to regain the honor in society that the job deserves. At stake is not simply parental pride, nor even the reclaiming of our children, but the survival of our most precious resource—the family.

The majority of parents I talked with choose to fight this battle.

PART TWO

FAMILIES UNDER ASSAULT

*anti-family forces
at work*

the social engineers: helping professionals versus parents

Ever since the 1950s, mothers and fathers have been coping with the Great Falsehood: You are unfit to parent. The first move in the coming parent revolution is to recognize that many of the social-scientist healers bent so solicitously over the family "sickbed" are carriers of the same disease they diagnose.

In *Haven in a Heartless World*, historian Christopher Lasch identifies this professional elite, which includes psychologists, medical doctors, and social workers, as "agents of paternalistic social control." These "social engineers" set out to become professional stand-ins for parents, apparently believing that post–World War II parents were authoritarian and guilt-producing and therefore could not provide for their children's needs without massive doses of professional child-rearing advice. Says Lasch of these social engineers: "Some of them, indeed, had so little confidence in the family that they proposed to transfer its socializing functions to other agencies," such as schools, social welfare, and juvenile courts.

First the social engineers condemned the values of the traditional family. "They played on public fears of disorder and disease," observes Lasch in *The Culture of Narcissism*, "adopted a deliberately mystifying jargon, ridiculed popular traditions of self-help as backward and unscientific, and in this way created or intensified a demand for their own services."

If there is any doubt as to who really benefited from the explosion of the family "helping professions," just look at how they grew: The membership of the American Psychological Association soared from 12,000 to 48,000—a 400-percent increase—between 1954 and 1980; the American Academy of Child Psychiatry grew from 102 members in 1953 to 2,100 in 1980, an increase of more than 2,000 percent; and membership of the American Academy of Pediatrics increased by

400 percent—from slightly more than 5,000 in 1957 to more than 20,000 in 1980. During this same period, roughly the last 25 years, the number of families with children under 18 rose from 41,951,000 to 57,215,000, an increase of only 27 percent.

Is it any wonder that the "need" for parent education, family counseling, in-school counselors, youth-therapy groups, and parent-advice books increased so rapidly?

It would be wrong, however, to imply that all helping professionals are anti-parent. I've cited a number of pro-parent social scientists in this chapter and throughout the book. My quarrel is with those who advance a technical view of child-rearing and encumber parents with jargon, theory, and guilt.

the professionalization of parenting

Every mother and father knows that parent-child relationships differ from those relationships that exist between child and teacher, doctor, or even therapist. Nevertheless, parents have been brainwashed for a quarter of a century into thinking that the closer they can come to adopting professional techniques of dealing with their children's behavior, the better parents they are apt to be. One mother of four with a degree in psychology pinpointed the problem:

> *In a therapy relationship, the therapist can't let his ego get involved. He can't have any needs. A therapist learns to stamp out emotional involvement early in his career, but a parent never can. Yet that's exactly what parents are trying to do by being always supportive and understanding, never critical—even while suffering through an all-give, expect-nothing-in-return relationship with their children.*

Stanford psychologist Dr. Robert D. Hess—a critic of parent education—says in an unpublished paper that the parent-to-child relationship "calls for and justifies more direct, intimate interaction, including anger and discipline as well as love and support" than does the professional-to-child relationship. He goes on to say that most parent-education literature presses parents to adopt professional attitudes and behavior.

The result of assimilating such attitudes over the years, as so many parents report they have done, is often an inability to discipline or to recognize that their parental anger is justified. A Georgia mother of two says:

> *There were times when I actually believed I was* destroying *my kids if I became angry over bad behavior. Sometimes I just didn't confront problems, rather than do the wrong thing.*

Even though many parents I talked with were bluntly outspoken in their objections to professions meddling with their parenting prerogatives, they confessed a lingering fear of psychological damage to their children, no matter how they tried to dismiss it.

How did such a fear develop in the first place?

Sigmund Freud early pointed to the danger of a child becoming sexually maladjusted from overparenting. Consequently, psychiatric definitions of normal behavior tended to extol lack of inhibition as the absolute normal. Any teaching of good and evil, right and wrong—with its potential for inhibiting "natural" behavior—was seen as bad for a child's mental health. Taking their cue from Freud, the helping professions developed theories of child-rearing that were based largely on pathological samples from truly disturbed families in analysis. After a short time, all parents came to be defined according to the sickness of the very few; and by such a definition no conscientious parent, no matter how permissive, could pass a mental-health checkup. By the post–World War II period, influential Canadian psychiatrist C. B. Chisholm, speaking to the World Health Organization, could state flatly: "The training of children is making a thousand neurotics for every one that psychiatrists can hope to help with psychotherapy."

how parents are encouraged to depend on the social engineers

From everywhere during the past 25 critical years for the family, the word has come that parents need help. "What the social scientists have learned," declared a president of the National Conference on Family Relations, "must now be made available to larger and larger circles . . . through educational institutions, through churches and synagogues, community centers . . . press . . . radio."

So instead of keeping child-rearing theory and therapy in the medical office or on the therapist's couch, the social engineers exported it into all the social institutions that affect the family. Teachers began incorporating the ideas of Jean Piaget and A. S. Neill; ministers, according to one Baptist preacher I talked with, learned about Abraham Maslow along with the teachings of the Apostle Paul; and of course parents, eager to provide the very best emotional support for their children, began to depend more and more on professionals (as they were told to do) and less and less on their own experience. Many parents I talked with said, in effect, "I ended up mistrusting my own instincts."

Although a few parents claimed they received support from family counselors for *their* rights, most reported that they had sacrificed those rights for the sake of achieving communication with their offspring. A mother of three in Ohio had this experience:

> We were told we were too firm—that our daughter needed more freedom, that our morals were not the same as hers.
> True, counseling sessions resulted in opening up more communication between us; but we felt that the extra freedom brought dreadful results and that we as parents had made all the concessions while our child had made none.

There is apparently a large gap between the concerns of parents and those of the professionals who dominate family advice-giving. As parents see it, instead of representing the right of parents to instill a moral code that respects family standards and emphasizes a sense of responsibility and planning for the future, professionals all too frequently champion the "rights" of children to give vent to their feelings, to follow their own moral codes, and to live it up in the here and now.

It's worth repeating for the sake of parents who bought the tale of their own ineptness: A kind of psychological noose has been encircling the family since the 1950s. The greater the influence of psychologists and the social healers, the greater has been parental guilt and need for family-counseling services. From the beginning, professionals implied that parents needed more than on-the-job training for parenthood. They implied that child-rearing, like everything else, responded to proper technique, which, of course, they alone knew and they alone could teach.

Does that seem overstated? Listen to Dr. Robert Hess, himself an educational psychologist, who expresses reservations about advice from his colleagues in a paper on parent education: "They [the professionals] can impair family functioning by undermining the parents' sense of confidence," he says, "creating dependence upon external resources and diminishing the authority of the family as a socializing unit."

child-rearing manuals and how they grew

Although psychological child-rearing concepts have become as much a part of our atmosphere as smog, it is the self-help best-seller that has intensified the idea that parents are apt to make a mess of things if left to their own devices.

Baby and Child Care, Dr. Benjamin Spock's phenomenal seller (it has had more than 200 printings), was the first post–World War II parent manual. The good doctor offered some fairly straight advice with a minimum of "or you will do permanent damage" scare talk. (That phrase, or others like it, has surfaced in book after book during the last 25 years and is the greatest little guilt-producer ever written.) Spock's success was followed by a torrent of popular books written for parents by professionals, all more or less implying parental incompetence, if not downright stupidity. It would be unfair to single out a few of these books, since most are guilty, but they all have a somber tone. A typical pronouncement warns: "We believe it is quite easy for a parent to teach a child to develop problem behaviors." And this one: "Millions of new mothers and fathers take on a job each year that ranks among the most difficult anyone can have. . . . Yet how many parents are effectively trained for it?"

But professional-as-teacher and parent-as-student are not the only themes advanced in these books. Just as damaging to parental self-reliance, and perhaps even more debilitating, is the idea that parenting is really easy if parents learn the right technique: "Any parent should be able to change the behavior of his or her children by using the method presented in this book," said one. "We have demonstrated . . . that with a certain kind of special training many parents can greatly increase their effectiveness in parenthood. They can acquire very specific skills that will keep the channels of communication open."

Is it any wonder that parents feel guilty, stupid, harassed? The ultimate message of this deluge is that if parents are not successful *it is their own fault*. After all, they need only learn one simple technique or another!

An Indiana mother took this view of how-to-parent books:

They seem to say that you can parent by formula. I find that they only inhibit my own natural responses. Furthermore, I believe my children are aware when they are being manipulated, which is really what a lot of these systems amount to.

A mother of two in Pennsylvania found book formulas were not working in her family:

It sounds easy to use reasoning techniques when I'm reading them in a book. Yes, I listen to their side of every issue. Yes, I'm careful not to impose my authority in a manner that is disrespectful to their humanity. And we always try to arrive at mutually acceptable decisions.

But yesterday my 14-year-old son walked out the front door while he was grounded, and my 9-year-old girl has refused to eat at the table or go to bed on time for a week.

Now what do I do?

A practicing family counselor, himself a father of two girls, blamed parents, not his profession, for the increasing demand for child-rearing "cookbooks":

I think too many parents were raised to believe anything that appears in print. But there is no such thing as a magic psychological salve that can be applied by a parent in a given situation, at a given time. Yet this is what parents are looking for; and like the overweight woman who flits from one fad diet to another, parents flit from one psychological fad to another. There is no one answer. It doesn't exist in psychology.

This father has a unique perspective as both professional and parent. Most parents rarely hear such candid opinions from insiders.

A California mother of an only boy confesses:

For years I was on a seesaw with every new "recommended" child-rearing method, until I saw what a monster I was developing.

Parenting books—seems like I read hundreds. My husband never fell for them; refused to read them; never attended classes with me. I've come to believe he was probably right.

Sixty-four percent of the parents surveyed for this book had read some how-to-parent books, and most had tried more than one. Dr. Spock's book has been by far the most influential, followed by other best-sellers by such child-rearing authorities of the past quarter-century as Rudolf Dreikurs, Arnold Gessell, Thomas Gordon, and Haim Ginott.

An Idaho father of two, who has "read them all," says:

> *It's helpful to know that certain behavior is normal for a certain age, but I'm the one on the firing line. I have to go with my "gut feeling!" My kids are both different from each other. There is no one cure-all solution.*

In my survey, in the parent talkshops, and during my one-on-one interviews, anti-authority feeling was evident toward every kind of "expert." A mother/state legislator said, "Our society is overloaded with advice on all subjects." A father/engineer took me to task, saying, "Everyone is in the book business, even you." But most of the anger was aimed at self-proclaimed child-rearing experts. One Texas father put them down this way:

> *Most of these people become psychologists in an attempt to solve their own problems. What makes them think they can solve mine?*

On what evidence do the experts base their advice to parents?

Although there has been progress in family research, this progress is most often clinical. According to Stanford's Dr. Robert Hess, an understanding of the influence of family interaction and parent behavior on children outside the clinical setting is primitive at best. Although knowledge about family dynamics is growing, it is still in an elementary stage. That is why Hess, for one, finds it difficult to justify precise statements about the influence or long-term effects of child-rearing practices. "Much of the data on adult influences on children's behavior," he says in a paper, "is obtained from studies in which the adult who interacts with the children is the research psychologist . . . whose relationship to the children in the study is superficial and transitory. The consequence of such findings, while interesting, is certainly not as transferable to family situations as parents have been led to believe."

Hess, echoing many of the parents I talked with, sensibly concludes: "We know very little at the present time about how [parent] competence is acquired. Conventional wisdom is that teachers learn to teach in the classroom; I suspect that parents learn to be parents in their encounters with their children."

Everywhere parents are advised to seek psychological intervention in parent-child problems. Normally tough-minded personal-
help columnists often advocate "professional" help for misbehavior
that once might have been thought improper or discourteous rather
than "sick."

the family-therapy business

During the past 25 years, family therapy has become a new star in
the psychological firmament. Virginia Satir, the grandmother of family therapy, views the family as "the factory where people are made,"
and most of her colleagues see psychology for the young as next to
impossible unless the entire family climbs onto the couch. (In 1974,
Dr. Joseph D. Noshpitz, president of the American Academy of Child
Psychiatry, enthusiastically claimed that 24 million of the under-18
population—or one in three—suffered from emotional illness.)

We parents aren't dealing here with legitimate, battle-tested
techniques, but with mere theories. The state of family therapy is no
more a science than are its sister "arts" of marriage counseling and
individual therapy. In *The Family: America's Hope*, Michael Novak,
professor of religion at Syracuse University, says, "The psychology of
the family is awful stuff."

There isn't just one form of family therapy; there are many,
from high-tech video-playback of family arguments, to hypnosis,
to Esalen-type discover-your-body treatments, to office encounter
sessions. Which approach brings the best results? What theory has
the answer troubled parents need? Apparently none of them. A family
psychologist at a family-therapy conference in the late seventies said,
"Many therapists are trying to fit all parents to one type of therapy."
She went on to indicate that this was not a good idea at all.

What kind of ideal family will family therapy produce? "To be
successful therapists," said another psychologist, in the American
Psychological Association's *Monitor*, "we need good techniques and
a strong theoretical basis. *It is not necessary [that we] have a good
family ourselves; we don't even know what is a 'good family'!*" (My
emphasis.)

I'm not suggesting that all family therapy produces negative results or is a jumble of quasi-orthodox procedures. Although many of
the parents quoted earlier in this chapter felt their rights had been

sacrificed in therapy for their children's rights, one New Mexico mother found precisely the right help:

> *After months of trying to work things out by ourselves, we finally decided to consult a family counselor. I must admit that I was hesitant to do this, because it was like admitting failure. However, this psychologist turned out to be someone who recognized that we had lost our sense of what our needs and rights were. His technique was based on the firm philosophy that parents not only have the right to set limits, they have an obligation, morally and legally, to do so, and that children must conform to these limits. Once he had begun to restore our power to assert ourselves and had established that there were no underlying familial problems, he set out to tackle the everyday confrontations without a lot of psychological double-talk. Meanwhile, he talked with our child to get to the bottom of what was triggering her behavior. He recognized that she had needs too, but he would not allow unreasonable demands or behavior as a means to meet these needs.*

This family got the kind of counseling that supports parents' rights to set limits on children's behavior and upholds parents as head of the family.

The kernel of truth hidden in the theories of family counseling is that the family is recognized as the healing social unit. The lie is that all families need professionals to prevent them from breaking into antagonistic separate parts. Culture-countering parents of the new, family-centered family could make that idea unfashionable or, better yet, ridiculous in the 1980s.

a word about margaret mead

It is difficult for those of us who grew into adulthood in some awe of the accomplishments of social anthropologist Margaret Mead to now turn on some of her most cherished ideas for being anti-family. Nevertheless, it was this humanist-scientist who, in her desire to see every child raised in a home with psychologically "qualified" parents, laid some of the theoretical groundwork for state-controlled breeding.

The future predicted in *Brave New World* and *Logan's Run*, worlds where there are no parents, only assembly lines of fertility machines, is a chilling one. But an even more frightening prospect is a world in which only psychologists would train and license those few parents declared psychologically fit to raise our children.

Mead, in her extensive writing on the modern family, didn't see much hope for the current crop of parents. She proclaimed in 1970 that "There are no elders who know what those who have been reared within the last 20 years know about the world into which they were born."

What has been the result of her well-meaning and purely theoretical call for psychologically "qualified" parents to rear all the children born to society, leaving less qualified parents free to explore their inner selves and one another? What began as an exercise in Mead's mind, in just ten years has become an accepted psychological dictum that crops up regularly in magazine and newspaper articles aimed at parents. Here's one of the latest in the long string of such proposals, made by psychologist Jerry Bergman of Bowling Green State University, in Ohio: If you and your spouse have IQs above 80, earn more than $8,000 a year, have no serious emotional problems, and know how to care for children, you would receive a license from the government to have a baby. If you failed one of these requirements, you and your mate would not be allowed to become parents.

The idea of parent licensing is the final takeover of family by the professionals, a takeover that has already begun with the undermining of parental confidence. This loss of confidence is the most serious consequence of professional intervention in family life and has made it almost impossible for children to believe that parents have any authority in the first place. Thus the foundation for the child-dominated family and future Peter Pan generations has been laid.

psycho-babble and the old-time religion

An even more immediate threat to the family comes from an amalgam of social engineers called the human-potential movement. The philosophies of these therapies have driven a deep wedge between parents and children, between family and society.

By the time rumors of God's death reached the cover of *Time* magazine in 1966, an enormous moral vacuum had begun to open outside the family's front door. The support once given parents by organized religion was supplanted by human-potential therapies, which assumed the trappings of religion—rebirth, spiritual growth, salvation, and the power of love—without adding the essential ingredient of belief in something or someone beyond self.

The human-potential movement is a loose collection of spiritual-sounding humanist psychologies that, generally speaking, advocate personal liberation. Descended in a ragged line from the work of psychologists Carl Rogers, Rollo May, and Abraham Maslow and hawked to the consumer with the foot-in-the-door enthusiasm of salesmen, human potential is the pap that feeds the feel-good, "I want to be me" attitudes prevalent today.

Speaking in many therapeutic tongues, it has invaded the Judeo-Christian religious establishment and undermined a traditional source of help for many parents. Says sociologist Dr. Tony Campolo, himself a Baptist minister: "If you go to many churches today, you tend to get nothing more than the human-potential movement dressed up in religious terminology. What these churches are trying to sell is that religion is really just trying to help you become a self-realizing, self-relying person, which is not true at all. One of the basic tenets of Christianity is that one must forget self."

Psychological thinking rapidly infiltrated organized religion so that many clergymen and priests became pastoral counselors, scarcely distinguishable, in some instances, from therapists preaching self-awareness as the solution to all spiritual ills. Campolo believes that those in religion were just "going where the crowd was going" so they could say, "Look, we're doing that too."

Rather than attracting the young to psychologized religion, the blurring of the line between psychology and orthodox faith seems to have had the opposite effect: Religious young people are now turning to fundamentalist, no-compromise, Bible-based churches. Perhaps belief in a larger moral system outside oneself is, after all, the most attractive "therapy" for spiritual loneliness.

In choosing a minister/counselor, parents should be as careful as when they choose a heart surgeon. To safeguard the health of the family, they should seek those who support family-centered families with parents in charge. One such minister told me: "It's important for children to be able to make decisions and know their own minds; but it's equally important that they recognize the rights of their parents. Discovering yourself should not make you oblivious to everyone else. Young people too often seem to confuse freedom with irresponsibility."

human potential: a false agenda for the future

Much of what passes for psychological insight these days exploits everything that families have always stood for and that caring parents have tried to teach their children by example.

Those who advocate a philosophy of self send the young the good news of a "religion" of personal development: If studies are not fulfilling, then quit them; if relationships are not meaningful (whatever that means), then find someone who shares your life-style; if parents are quaint, old-fashioned, or repress you, then "split" to a new "family" of friends who will absolve you of duty, work, and mutual dependence.

Parents, even those of us indoctrinated with the ideal of psychological self-examination, have become increasingly uncomfortable with children who seem to have an insatiable lust for self-understanding as a life goal. Narcissism equals growth in the human-potential lexicon; our young call it growth when they reject all limits. Any caring parent knows this is not the formula for growth but its opposite.

The ultimate expression of the human-potential movement is that you must love yourself so much that you don't need to have others love you. The young have been carefully taught to throw off guilt and shame for antisocial behavior as inhibiting silliness.

Of course, caring parents want their children to discover all their potential. But many of us have begun to question the game of self-discovery so many of our young are playing. A young mother of two preschoolers, herself a graduate psychology student, told me:

> *I am sick and tired of hearing about "self" and "me" and how to get in touch with the "real me." I'm convinced that most of these people wouldn't recognize their "real self" if it jumped up and slapped them in the face.*

As parents of the new family-centered family, we see that openness limited to self is a false road to the future. Openness to family, and ultimately to the world, is the traditional goal of child-rearing. As Spanish philosopher Ortega y Gasset has said: "I am myself plus my circumstances, and if I do not save them, I cannot save myself. This sector of circumstantial reality forms the other half of my person; only through it can I integrate myself and be fully myself."

I believe parents are the certified experts of their own families. The social engineers have a place—as consultants to parents, not as primary authorities—and they should be put back into their place. We parents do need information about such things as immunization, the flammability of sleepwear, the importance of health examinations, and the presence of carcinogens. But we do not need social scientists' interference, however benign, in how we raise our children. A mother of three from Ohio says:

> *During our experience with our son's misbehavior, we sought counseling from three different agencies. They all told us to ignore it. "Shrug it off," one said. When we told them about our concern that our son was using marijuana, one said he would worry more if a boy* wasn't *smoking pot these days.*
>
> *We were at a complete standstill. We had had no help at all and were considerably shaken in our own judgment, but we finally decided to use our common sense and handle our son as a discipline problem and not worry that we might be destroying his "self."*

As we move further into the 1980s, the strengthening of the parents' role is imperative. The psychological fraternity's relationship to the family must change from that of master and slave to one of consultant and client. There may be a certain amount of comfort in relying on a "surefire" child-rearing technique, but it can't beat the pure pleasure of adult self-reliance, of knowing that you have the competence to nurture, teach, discipline, and interact emotionally with your child day to day. It's the kind of trade-off that parents of the coming parent revolution are ready to make.

CHAPTER 5

child rights advocacy: a good idea gone mad

This is the big question: Who knows what is best for children, the state or parents? In the 1980s, this once-unthinkable question will touch the deepest feelings of every parent because social engineering has inevitably led helping professionals to legal involvement on behalf of children's rights. Some of these child advocates have set themselves up as the arbiters of what is best for children. Parents are often seen as the enemy.

Who are the child advocates? The term includes at least three groups that hold different points of view about the rights of children. First are the *child savers*, who want to protect the child not only from abuse but from what they see as the ignorance and narrowmindedness of parents. These child savers believe they know what is best for every child. The second group is the *child liberationists*, who believe that the child should be able to decide what is in his or her own best interest on such issues as abortion or medical treatment. *Traditionalists*, the third group, view minors as not being mature enough to make decisions about medical treatment, education, marriage, or leaving home. This traditional group thinks that parents, as long as they are not negligent or abusive, know what is best for their own children.

Most parents I interviewed for this book, and I am convinced they represent the majority of parents, fall into the traditionalist camp. Most social engineers, on the other hand, can be identified as child savers or child libbers, mistakenly applying the theories of the civil-rights movement to children.

Child advocacy began as a high-minded idea. Between 1890 and World War I, child protection was a humane issue and child advocacy meant protecting children from real harm. It was an intense period of activism, when good people fought for the elimination of child labor, the establishment of a juvenile-justice system, mandatory education, and pasteurized milk. Indeed, there was so much work being done on behalf of children that early child advocate Ellen Key said the rest of the twentieth century would be exalted as "the century of the child." She was, as many parents know, prophetic in a way she never dreamed of.

Early children's rights were sensible, and easy for any caring parent to agree with. They included the preservation of life and health, freedom from premature toil, education, and care of dependent children. But what started out as a genuine reform movement soon spawned a number of professions related to child-helping. Enter the social workers, child psychologists, early-childhood education specialists, pediatricians, and all the rest of the social engineers.

The early child advocates and their modern-day descendants, in order to push through much-needed reforms, gradually created the mythical ideal child, one that is by virtue of youth more sensitive, creative, and knowing than an adult. What, then, was the explanation for children's cruelty to one another or for a sullen, self-involved angry adolescent? The child advocates didn't have to look far. The reason these children are "sick," they said, is that they have been raised in typically sick American homes where parents victimize their children by denying them their rights. The list of these "inalienable" rights began to grow as the helping professions grew, until today they have reached the height of silliness. The emancipation of minors whose "life-styles" differ from their parents' and the payment of minimum wages for household chores are but two rights that have been espoused. Indeed, today's child advocates view children so totally as the innocent victims of parents that had they come upon Lizzie Borden axing her father, they would have exclaimed, "That poor child. What he must have done to alienate her so!"

The lobby of professional helpers of children is so powerful today that it has penetrated almost every aspect of modern living; its antiparental influence is especially pronounced in government agencies. Mark this example from a 1973 book published by the Office of Child Development: "The problem of accountability is particularly difficult to solve in child advocacy programs, because the interests of children and parents are not always synonymous and parents are not always adequate spokesmen for their children." Parents may not always be adequate spokesmen for their own children, but who always is? It doesn't take much cutting through the smoke screen of jargonized "what's best for the child" talk to see that child advocates have long ago concluded that *they,* not Mother and Father, know best.

Have parents assimilated the social-worker attitudes of the children's rights lobby? A South Carolina mother of two wonders:

> *I am aware that I allow my children more choices over their personal affairs and that I seem to increase this freedom with each year. I try to reserve the right to insist on the values I consider important, but I have less and less influence as they have more and more freedom. I know that I have contributed to the excess of freedom that I see our young people practicing everywhere, but I don't think I can stop it.*

I understand what this mother means. I once considered granting the young more and more rights a hallmark of civilized parenting; I wrote magazine articles extolling it as a virtue and exercised the principle as a parent. But I have come to the conclusion that whenever children's rights, needs, or problems are treated separately from those of parents, a tear appears in the family fabric through which all manner of evil—no matter how good the original intention—enters.

the legal rights of children

Today, the rights of children to self-determination take precedence over parents' rights in some of the most emotional and physically important aspects of parent-child relationships. In far too many ways, the child advocates have succeeded in elevating immediate psychological " needs" over biological ties. They have lobbied effectively to reduce the age of consent for receiving contraception advice and devices, medication for venereal disease, and abortions—all without parental approval. This action is in keeping with the current fashion of equating all parental demands for involvement in decisions about their children with child abuse, or at least invasion of the child's privacy. The results have led to some sad and ludicrous scenes, such as this one reported by a New Mexico mother:

> *I received a bill for $46 from my gynecologist for treating my daughter. I asked her what it was for, but she refused to tell me. When I called the doctor's office, the nurse said she couldn't violate my*

daughter's right to health privacy. O.K., I said, then send the bill to my daughter. The nurse got real snippy, reminded me that I was legally responsible for my minor daughter, and said that if I didn't pay, the doctor would turn me in to a collection agency. What kind of world is it when parents have only obligations and no rights?

A father who discovered that his 15-year-old daughter had had an abortion told me with great bitterness:

This is so utterly wrong. My daughter can't even have an appendectomy without my consent. Where's the logic in this?

We parents are expected to assume unquestioned responsibility for our children, but we are not expected to know when they're in trouble—pregnant, suffering from a venereal disease, or using an IUD. Could anything make less sense?

In addition to being worried about their children's rights to medical treatment without their approval, parents are also expressing a growing concern about their children's access to psychological counseling. A Nebraska mother wrote that her two teenage daughters, angry at being grounded for disobedience, told their teacher that they had been physically abused. The teacher then called the local, state-funded family center, which obtained a court order to investigate the home.

Even though they found nothing wrong, they were ready to believe my daughters before they believed me. My girls are now receiving counseling at the Center and are practically impossible to live with.

We work hard, own our home, and have raised five children; but now our reputation in this small town is ruined. I can't even bear to be in the same room with these two girls—I know that sounds terrible for a mother to say, but I can't help what I feel.

This increasing advocacy of children's rights exacts a heavy price by separating children from their families. In light of recent trends, the following statement by a former director of the U.S. Office of Child Development sounds perfectly rational: "Children," proclaimed Edward Zigler, "do not belong to parents." Expanding upon this theme, Judge Lisa Richette of the First Judicial District of Pennsylvania says: "If there is a least detrimental alternative, remove the child and don't worry about the rights of parents. The child belongs to society. The parents were only biological producers." The sum of these arguments is that our children really belong to the community of professional child advocates.

premajority rights—the move toward ever-younger citizenship

Americans, it has been said, value certain tenets: freedom of discourse, the equality of ideas, the adversary system, objectivity. These ideals are properly cherished, but they are just that—abstractions, which are valuable when applied to adult citizens but misused in the tug-of-war called child-rearing. Of course, children have human rights, but the rights of citizens have always been awarded to those who have reached maturity. At least it was so until the child savers mixed up the idea of "guaranteed childhood" with the idea of the adult right to self-determination.

The argument advanced by the children's lobby is that, somehow, children's rights should be tailored to their stage of development. In other words, if a child is deemed mature by some authority at age 12, then that child could vote, have a credit card, or be granted whatever other rights are conferred by citizenship and adulthood.

Another vision of the professional child advocates is the right of children to participate in all decisions concerning their lives, here articulated by Pat Walk, an assistant attorney general of the United States, in a 1974 speech entitled "Making Sense Out of the Rights of Youth": "Perhaps the most basic right children should have in their relationship with all adults . . . is the right to know, to comprehend, to challenge and to participate meaningfully in all the decisions that vitally affect their lives."

It does not take mystical insight to see the machinations of the child advocates at work behind the 1979 California law that emancipates adolescents. This law allows 14-to-18-year-olds to become legally free from their parents if they are married, in the military, or *living apart from parents with their knowledge, but not necessarily with their approval.*

There has even been a Self-Skills youth program (how aptly titled) established in the Los Angeles area, staffed by the usual professionals, to help adolescents prepare for independent living under this law. The project offers classes, a manual, and counseling for young people thinking of becoming emancipated from their parents. Why counseling? Explains the Self-Skills coordinator: "Most young people are not ready for living independently."

Of course they aren't. Common sense and laws that make sense are the first casualties of modern child advocacy—a good idea gone absolutely mad. Such self-determination for our children, while masquerading as part of a brave new world of freedom and equality for all, actually makes parents little more than paying custodians.

I asked parents what they thought of the trend toward lowering the age of majority. Eighty-two percent felt 18 was too young and that 20 or 21 was more realistic. This Florida mother, for example, says:

> *I feel very strongly that a law which suddenly decrees children are adults at 18 has tied parents' hands. My children are not mature enough and don't even want to be responsible for themselves. They just want adult rights, while I take care of them.*

"tell it to my lawyer, mom"

Encouraged by a child-advocacy atmosphere that traces everything wrong with the child to bad parents, 24-year-old Tom Hansen brought a $350,000 malpractice suit against his parents in the late 1970s. Basically, he charged his parents with lack of psychological support during critical periods of his life.

As a legal concept, "malpractice" means a dereliction of professional duty. The interpretation that was bound to be applied to parents, considering the ongoing attempts to professionalize parenting, is nonetheless terrifying.

No question raised the hackles of the parents I interviewed more than "How would you feel if your adult child filed a 'parenting malpractice' suit against you?" Forty-one percent of parents understandably responded "deeply hurt," while 21 percent indicated they would be "madder than hell!" Others expressed such feelings as "surprised," "hated," and "betrayed," and 11 percent were ready to plead guilty.

Then I asked parents what their defense would be in such a suit. Some answered with saving humor, saying "I'd show the judge my check stubs," "I'd head for Mexico and let the kid try and find me," or "I'd plead insanity." But most parents took the question seriously: 55 percent said they would use an "I did my best with what I had at the time" defense, and more than 20 percent turned their brainwashing into a defense, saying they would plead "I was untrained."

One California mother of five seemed to sum up the feelings of many parents:

> *I would be devastated by such a suit. I can't even imagine such a thing. But if children are going to file parenting malpractice suits against parents in the future, perhaps I should start keeping tape recordings of all the times I beg my kids to study, to practice piano, to not eat so much candy or drink so many Cokes. I think their answers would absolve me before any jury in the land.*
>
> *Most parents I know do their best, and I've done my best. I keep telling my kids that so they won't blame me when they grow up and have problems.*

Tom Hansen's suit against his parents was thrown out of court by Colorado Judge Murray Richtel, who found Hansen's assertion that his parents caused "intentional infliction of emotional stress" wholly without merit. The parents, said the judge, used every possible means at their disposal to perform the task of parenting in a decent and reasonable manner.

However, it is only a matter of time—given the atmosphere of the youth culture—before other such weird suits surface. The increase in the number of self-involved youths, coupled with the greater number of available attorneys, practically guarantees it. After all, it is only a small step from the concept that parenthood should be professionalized to the concept that parents using improper professional techniques be forever legally responsible for their children's emotional shortcomings.

sweden—the child advocate's eden

As far as outside intrusion into parent-child relationships is concerned, Sweden is as close to George Orwell's *1984* as you can get. Ever progressive in children's rights, during 1979 alone Sweden outlawed spanking and considered legislation that would permit children to "divorce" their parents while parents paid "alimony." Chairman of the Government Commission on Children's Rights, Tor Sverne, explains: "It is not our intention that a 6-year-old who has a row with his parents should be able to just go out and divorce them.

But a 3-year-old child in a foster home could divorce his natural parents if they no longer showed any interest in him. Similarly, a 16-year-old who went to live with her boyfriend would have the opportunity to divorce her parents if they objected to the relationship."

And who's behind this never-never land for children? Listen to child advocate Ulla Jacobson, a professor of law at the University of Stockholm, in her book *A Child's Rights*, published just one year before the child-divorce law was proposed in the Swedish legislature: "I propose that a child should have the right to divorce his parents. My suggestion for legislation to that effect is as follows: *'Due to profound differences in personality or views between the child and his parents*, the court can, at the child's request, remove the parents from custody and—if there is reason—assign custody to a specially appointed custodian'." (My added emphasis.)

To be fair, in some ways Sweden appears to be a parent's paradise. Mothers and/or fathers get nine months' paid time off to care for a newborn, and they can hire a municipally trained and subsidized baby-sitter for their children for $200 a month. But oh, what a price parents pay for benefits that the government giveth and then taketh away.

The Directorate of Social Affairs is entrusted with almost absolute power over the custody of children. There is no fighting an order depriving a parent of custody of his or her own child. Due process for Swedish parents has become impossible. Why? Because bureaucrats, not courts of law, wield the power. In Sweden, child-welfare officials can enter a home to investigate family conditions; the officials also have power to order the police to force an entry and remove children without parents having recourse to the judiciary. This is so common that the press doesn't even report it unless something dramatic happens. Every birth is reported to the local child-welfare center, which sends a representative to assess home conditions. To resist causes suspicion of child abuse. Moreover, citizens are encouraged to report any suspicions of maltreatment to these child-welfare centers, where the informer is guaranteed anonymity. Opportunities abound for petty vengeance against parents in Sweden.

And what has this paradise of professional child advocacy wrought? In 1980, a film entitled *Sweden: Waiting for Spring* was screened on the American Public Broadcasting System. It showed ill-mannered, listless pupils paying no attention to their teacher, playing cards in class, complaining about their pointless lives. Later, these children were shown swilling beer, wine, and vodka at a house party while their parents upstairs paid no attention. Other adolescents were falling down drunk in the streets.

It is unfair to condemn an entire social system on the basis of one film, but it is not unfair to question a system that encourages alienation of children from their parents and creates a vacuum in which parents, having no real authority or support from society, give up on their children in frustration. Whenever outsiders, not parents, have primary authority over children, the family is hollow—a mechanical thing, without a soul.

I asked parents throughout America what they thought of the new law in Sweden that forbids parents to spank their children. Though they did not necessarily condone spanking, 86 percent of the parents I surveyed thought the law was "stupid and unenforceable." Said one Louisiana father:

Government makes a mess of everything, even good ideas!

A California mother of four answered:

Sweden must be rapidly becoming a nation of closet spankers.

The virtues or defects of spanking are matters that American parents have to decide for themselves. What is alarming and eye-opening about this new Swedish law is that Swedish parents so readily accepted *another* intervention by child professionals into parent-child relations. Not even the Soviet Union penetrates so deeply into family life.

What started out as the well-meant effort of Swedish reformers to protect abused children from bad parents has gone much further. The no-spank provision of the 1979 law also included a little-publicized (at least in this country) provision that forbids parents to subject their children to "humiliating treatment." Violations of this seemingly reasonable law include such punishments as sending a child to bed without supper, censoring mail, and not answering when he or she talks to you.

Even this, if treated like some silly archaic American laws such as not riding a horse into a mother-in-law's parlor on Sunday, might not cause too much family disruption. But Swedish child advocates, with the ink barely dry on the anti-spank, anti-humiliation legislation, began to busy themselves implementing it. Videotapes were churned out for schoolchildren advising them of the their "constitutional rights," and an ombudsman was hired to investigate children's complaints.

If there is a lesson for American parents in all this, it is that child advocates, backed by an unlimited, publicly funded bureaucracy, can become a real threat to all parents and to family life *if parents passively submit* to escalating intrusion. Although Sweden may be a very long way geographically from the United States, philosophically its children's-rights advocates are cut from the same cloth as ours.

a child libber's manifesto

When American psychologist Richard Farson wrote his book *Birthrights* in 1974, he immediately went to the head of the child libbers' class. Farson sees children as just one more oppressed minority denied the right of self-determination. Among other things, he calls for the right to a single standard for adults and children. He suggests that truly liberated children should have the right to "alternative home environments"; in other words, they shouldn't *have* to live with their parents. Farson wants children to have the right of freedom from education, or, as he sees it, freedom from a system that sacrifices youthful individuality. He also advocates the right of freedom from physical punishment, the right to work at any job, and the right to political power—including the vote. Perhaps Farson's most controversial "right" is the right to sexual freedom for all children, including free access to birth control. Oddly enough, this right is the one that has been realized.

This ultrapermissive assault on middle-class parents and values—from what author Paul Johnson in his *Enemies of Society* called "the Fascist Left"—continues into the 1980s, promoting lists of rights for children, a new one popping into the headlines every year.

School psychologists who gathered at the International Colloquium in 1979 made up their own list for the International Year of the Child, calling it the "Declaration of the Psychological Rights of the Child" and giving it wide media distribution. Here's a short version of what they think a child's psychological rights should be: (1) The right to love, affection, and understanding; (2) The right to freedom from fear of psychological and physical harm or abuse; (3)

The right to protection and advocacy; (4) The right to personal identity and independence and the freedom to express these; (5) The right to opportunities for spiritual and moral development; (6) The right to satisfying interpersonal relationships and responsible group membership; (7) The right to formal and informal education and any necessary special resources; (8) The right to full opportunity to play, recreation, and fantasy; and (9) The right to optimum physical and psychological development, and encouragement toward this.

Of course, the validity of some of these handsomely wrought phrases, although couched in psycho-babble, could scarcely be denied by loving parents. Naturally, we want our children to have love, affection, and understanding; we don't want them to be fearful; and we hope they have fun on the playground. However, "optimum . . . psychological development, and encouragement toward this," translated into the vernacular, obviously means lots of employment opportunities for phalanxes of future professional child advocates.

the child-abuse/neglect/incest cudgel

In late 1980, a 14-year-old New York City girl was snatched from her home and kept in a children's shelter for 11 days, even though she insisted the anonymous child-abuse charge against her father was a cruel hoax.

The story of abuse had been hatched by Julie (not the girl's real name) and her girlfriend after Julie's father had refused to allow her to go out with "a bunch of bad girls." No effort had been made to check out the complaint telephoned to a child-abuse center by the girlfriend; Julie's parents were not even notified of her whereabouts for two days.

After two Family Court hearings, Julie was allowed to go home, but the family still receives frequent unannounced visits from social workers, and mother, father, and daughter were all ordered by the court to undergo psychiatric examinations.

This story is not meant to imply that all parents accused of child abuse are innocent victims, nor that social workers and courts are all this insensitive. But such incidents should sound an alarm in the ears of parents who prize their basic rights and question the enormous legal power that professional child advocates can unleash.

One thing is clear. Child abuse, be it physical, mental, or sexual, is an abomination that violates every moral ideal sacred to the concept of family. No decent parent would argue about that with the child's rights people for a minute. But something else is afoot that does need to be challenged so that parents are aware of yet another assault against them, whether one is intended or not.

The growing public emphasis on child abuse has become a club to use against parents, another manifestation of the raging among various child advocates who make policy in the gamut of government agencies and commissions. As is typical with their descriptions, the picture of child abuse unveiled to the public is overblown and sometimes semihysterical. In a conversation I had in 1980 with Dr. David Sears of the Children's Bureau of the Department of Health, Education and Welfare (now the Department of Health and Human Services), he admitted that no one knows the exact figures on child abuse and neglect. Yet I had newspaper clippings, quoting one expert or other, that claimed there might be as many as 4 million cases each year. Sears said he thought these figures were very high, suggesting that the actual incidence of abuse and neglect was more like 400,000 cases annually, which is twice the bureau's official estimate of approximately 200,000. I also reported a magazine article that stated flatly that child abuse was increasing 15 to 20 percent every year "according to government estimates!" Sears didn't know if abuse and neglect were increasing. "In fact, they might be on the decline," he said, "since there were no reliable early national statistics."

Dr. Murray A. Straus, director of the Family Violence Research Program at the University of New Hampshire, confirms the decline in a letter to me. "My estimate," he writes, "is that violence of all types within families has been slowly declining and continues to decline. The seeming increase in the rate of child abuse is a function of new standards, not new behavior."

In seeking to right one wrong—the horror of child abuse—another is being committed. The logic of the experts, as filtered through the media, is: Abuse is bad; parents are abusers; therefore parents are bad. This represents the last straw for parents under assault from every corner of a youth-loving culture. It is outrageously unfair to cast doubt on millions of loving parents based on the nebulous estimates of professionals who stand to gain in government study grants for every red flag they manage to wave. Where is the proof that more parents every year are abusing their children? Has child abuse become the "national disgrace"? As dreadful as the crime of child abuse is, it is not rampant. Parenting has come a long way since Pilgrim fathers could legally kill a disobedient son.

The majority of the parents I surveyed were willing to give up a cherished freedom in order to protect children against abuse: When asked, "Do you think governments should ever regulate the way you parent in your own home?" two-thirds of them spontaneously replied, "Yes, in case of child abuse." Of the 33 percent who said no, almost all did so on constitutional grounds. "Other ways must be found to protect children" was the consensus of this minority. "The cure of state intervention between parent and child is worse than the sickness of child abuse."

There is abundant evidence of the love of parents for children. Our labors and our lives are organized around this affection. To treat all parents as a class on trial because there are instances of child abuse is to create a prejudice that eventually justifies taking over the family. Regarding parents with that kind of suspicion suggests that somebody else ought to take charge of the situation and subordinate parents. This can mean nothing less than giving ultimate authority to the child advocates working through the state.

If there is one thing that history has taught us, it's that governments are not more kindly to human beings than are parents.

the parent-child legal relationship

As long as there have been laws, the right of parents to speak for their children in all matters has been held supreme to any other laws governing the child. From earliest times, parental rights have been ordained, sustained, and reaffirmed. At least this was true until the 1960s. Recent judicial opinions, legislative enactments, and administrative rules—all influenced by cohorts of professional child advocates—have significantly reduced traditional parental power in a number of areas. The professionals' emphasis on individual rights for children has in many ways divested parents of power and turned it over to the children. Before the age of Peter Pan, the treatment of a minor by a physician without parental consent would have constituted battery and possibly have led to a lawsuit.

In courts, even younger children are acquiring the power to speak for themselves through professional child advocates, who are gaining the power that parents are losing. "In some situations, the parents are replaced by others as decision-makers in questions involving their children," says Boston University Law School's Henry A. Beyer. "More often, the parents continue to decide for their children, but . . . an independent party reviews their decision."

The professionals have not always won. In 1972, *Wisconsin* v. *Yoder* brought a pro-parent decision from the U.S. Supreme Court, which ruled that Amish parents have a right to keep their children out of the public schools since they consider them harmful to their way of life. "The child is not the mere creature of the State," the majority of the court said; "those who nurture him and direct his destiny have the right, coupled with the high duty, to recognize and prepare him for additional obligations."

Nevertheless, this same court decided just four years later that minors could obtain abortions without parental consent. The movement toward greater self-determination for children and less power for parents, although suffering minor setbacks, has marched inexorably on.

the hodgepodge laws

Child liberation has spawned some strange legal contradictions. In *Planned Parenthood* v. *Danforth*, 1976, the Supreme Court held that girls under the age of 18 could receive abortions without parental consent. In that same year the Federal Trade Commission, responding to a complaint filed by Action for Children's Television, ruled that a drug company must stop advertising its product as a "super-vitamin." This decision (*Goodman*, 1976) was based on the belief that "children are unqualified by age or experience to decide themselves whether or not they need or should use" the advertised product.

Does it make sense to believe that our children haven't the maturity to choose vitamins, but do have the maturity to decide on abortion without family support and guidance? Does it make sense to protect children from their inexperience in a consumer matter and not in a life-threatening one?

The injustice of child's rights laws carried to their logical extreme can probably best be illustrated by the experiences of parents caught in bureaucratic machinery. In Minnesota, for example, a court ruled that two parents must support their unmarried adult daughter and her two children. The parents, who had both worked to raise ten children, were ordered to pay not only for their own grown daughter but also for her two children until *they are 18.* By that time, the grandfather—if he can survive a heart condition—will be nearly 80 years old.

Would minors leave home so readily and would young unmarried girls have so many children if they were not, in fact, subsidized by the government to do so? I think not, and the majority of parents I talked to in every part of the country and of every economic class do not believe they would. A Vermont mother of five said:

> *My children know they can leave home anytime by going on welfare. Kids today are smart. They pass this kind of information around at school. My daughter signed up for food stamps right out of high school and moved in with a commune of other young people. She didn't listen when we begged her to come home and go to college. Now she's pregnant, but she tells us she doesn't need us.*

children's medical rights versus parent rights

For many years courts have ordered medical treatment for children over parents' objections. It is clearly a lesser evil to give a child a blood transfusion than to protect the right of parents, however sincere, to allow him to suffer. But many issues in which parents and government are now wrestling for control are not as black and white. Take the tragic Chad Green case of the late 1970s. Three-year-old Chad, a leukemia victim, was placed on chemotherapy. It is a devastating treatment for parents to administer to a toddler. After a time, Chad's parents discontinued it, saying, among other things, "If God is going to give him just a short time with us, then we want it to be a good comfortable time."

But Chad's doctors protested and the boy was made a ward of the state of Massachusetts, which *ordered* the parents to continue chemotherapy. They complied, but added a Laetrile-based metabolic treatment of vitamins and enzymes. Again the doctors went to court, where the parents were prohibited from administering anything except doctor-prescribed treatments. (Even the boy's diet was controlled by hospital nutritionists.) The distraught parents, without a shred of control left, took Chad and ran for Mexico, where the boy eventually died.

I hold no more brief for Laetrile than I do for Dr. Feelgood's Magic Brain Elixir. But here the doctors argued for *total* control, when, according to National Cancer Institute studies, only one of four leukemia chemotherapy patients survives for three years. With such dubious results—certainly incomparable with clear-cut blood-transfusion cases of the past—the courts still intervened to take away the Greens' parental authority and, in a way, some of every other parent's as well. In a case like Chad Green's, where there are powerful moral arguments on both sides, I believe the parents' decision should have prevailed.

Another area in which child-advocate experts have stepped between parent and child is in the admission of children to institutions for the retarded or the mentally ill. Traditionally, parents have been able to apply for the "voluntary" admission of their children if the institution agreed that it was in the best interest of the child. During the 1970s, this situation began to change. Today several states have ordered each case to be reviewed before the child can be admitted. Granted, in the past mistakes have been made by both parents and institutions. But critics of this new policy point out that judicial review often delays needed treatment and forces parents and children into adversarial positions, further straining already tense relationships. Of course the child savers see this review as a necessary protection from ogre parents just waiting for the opportunity to push their perfectly sane children into asylums.

I do not find it surprising that parents in general have not heretofore objected to the loss of their rights. The forces against the family, which portray parents as either inept or tyrannical, have done their propaganda work well. Many parents I talked with, while knowing themselves to be good parents, thought other parents were not. The chain of thought went like this: I know I'm a good parent, but there's so much talk about bad parents, it must be true; therefore other parents are bad parents.

the juvenile-justice question

Did you know that the law can blame you if your child commits a burglary? This fact is echoed by a psychiatrist who specializes in child criminals: "Kids who burgle," he says, "come from families that don't play straight with them." But is it families or juvenile justice that is not playing straight? Chicago lawyer Lori B. Andrews found that middle-class children, once in court, are judged "sick" and are quickly packed off to psychologists. The courts usually decide that such children need treatment—understanding—rather than punishment.

Christopher Lasch interprets this trend as a campaign to empty law of moral content, to banish the ideas of right and wrong and replace them with the ethic of human relations. The juvenile-justice system, Lasch says, illustrates in the "clearest form the connections between organized altruism, the new therapeutic conception of the state, and the appropriation of familial functions by outside agencies."

According to the FBI, 48 percent, or nearly half our violent crimes—murder, rape, and aggravated assault—are committed by youths under 18. And the cost to taxpayers and to victims of this juvenile crime is skyrocketing—$11 billion a year, according to 1978 estimates. But that is not the total bill for youth crime that taxpayers end up footing. During the same year, $53 million was spent on research and evaluation by the middlemen—the social engineers. Their escalating outlays, it seems, are matched only by the increase in the crimes they're studying. In California, for example, the number of violent crimes committed by children has jumped from 15 percent in 1966 to 41 percent in 1979, prompting Judge Art Gilbert of Los Angeles to warn that a "children's army" is prowling city streets, willing to kill. Says Gilbert: "I've even had defense attorneys say to me, 'What on earth is going on?' "

It's not as if the social engineers and juvenile courts haven't had their chance to reform juvenile justice. Seventy-five years ago Jane Addams was extolling the new attitude toward youthful offenders: "The element of conflict was absolutely eliminated," she wrote, "and with it all notions of punishment." By the mid-1920s, a social worker/ author was advancing the argument that even the "best families" turned out bad kids and that "a specialized agency had better take over the whole matter of child-rearing." It is amazing how quickly social reformers decide that their philosophies should be put into practice at the expense of parent rights.

For more than 70 years, the objective of the juvenile-justice system has been treatment, not punishment. But the great objective has never been realized. In case after case, dangerous youths who commit major crimes are released only to commit yet more serious crimes. Terrorism in today's America is synonymous with the name of youth. This from one Pennsylvania mother of two:

> *We live in a good neighborhood, but all around us are kids, some as young as 10, who are beating up the elderly and handicapped, committing armed robbery—even rape. I hear them talking, and they sneer at the law. They know they can get away with "murder" because they can con the judge and all the psychologists at juvenile detention.*

Many parents agree with this mother. Moreover, they worry about the influence such young people have on their own children. "There is a kind of perverse status to committing a crime and getting away with it," several parents observed. One father, a state police officer, said in a parent talkshop:

> *These kids aren't ostracized, as you and I would have been; they are thought to be "cool."*

Another father remarked:

> *Years ago there was a humorous explanation for the Yiddish word* chutzpah. *It's when a kid kills his parents, then expects the court to show mercy because he's an orphan. That's no joke anymore.*

Juvenile crime is certainly no joke to adults. Many parents admitted that they were afraid to report criminal acts against their own homes, fearing retaliation. A parent in suburban Chicago had this perspective:

> *How come there's so much vandalism in a nice suburb like I live in? Why are kids from middle-class homes with big money in their pockets riding over my front lawn, performing senseless acts of vandalism almost every Saturday night? I'll tell you why. They want the excitement of doing something risky. After a time even this bores them, so they look for something worse. When kids have no moral limits, at home, in society, or in the law, anything goes when they get together.*
>
> *What happens if I complain? What if I turn some kids in? Their friends will come back and really get me!*

Some parents say harassment by gangs of youths is so terrible they must act as vigilantes, organizing neighborhood patrols, supervising children in open fields and parks. One Los Angeles father told me his neighborhood was like a "war zone."

There has been too much understanding of criminal behavior by the courts, a circumstance that has helped confuse today's young people about right and wrong. Unless we return to a culture that rewards good behavior and punishes bad behavior—in other words, a culture that makes value judgments—some youths will never fit into an orderly society.

the new parent-child legal relationship

Most parents I talk to agree that stringent new laws should be passed, laws that treat *serious* juvenile criminals as adults. These parents reason that you could be just as dead from a 15-year-old's bullet as from an 18-year-old's. With lesser crimes, they think, the offender's age can be taken into account and restitution provided.

Several communities around the country have passed parental responsibility laws that make parents liable for their children's behavior. Many parents I surveyed thought that the young people *themselves* should pay their fines or make financial restitution to their victims by "working it off," either directly or by doing community work. A father, the state police officer quoted earlier, suggested:

> *If a kid steals a motorcycle and wrecks it, he should have to pay for it himself. If he vandalizes school property, then sentence him to clean up the mess and repair the damage. It wouldn't be so "cool" to spend your afternoons scrubbing or repainting. Kids should be forced to confront their acts and take responsibility for putting things right. If they aren't straightened out the first time, chances are good they'll wind up in big trouble.*

The startling increase in juvenile crime parallels the emergence of the Peter Pan generation and its concept of normless values. Youthful criminals, once characterized as angels with dirty faces, have taken a less romantic, more violent turn. The formerly permissive social engineers now respond with a different twist—blaming family for lack of discipline, while teaching parents they have no skills— their usual parent-as-scapegoat argument.

Many parents are angry with the juvenile-justice system and what they perceive as its permissiveness. Nevertheless, I would hate to see the juvenile court lose its power to support the authority of parents in so-called status offenses, such as incorrigibility and truancy.

The helter-skelter pattern of the parent-child legal relationship is a problem that must be addressed in the 1980s. Wherever the rights of the family are in conflict with the state or its "agents," the social engineers, the law should come to the aid of the parents. Otherwise, it's virtually a no-win situation: The state loses with weakened families, the parents lose necessary authority, and children lose meaningful structure in their lives. Only the social engineers, scrambling for research grants and justice-system jobs, "win."

The professional child advocate, once an aid to families, has helped turn the family upside down. Instead of assisting parents, child advocacy as practiced by professionals in the 1980s tends to smother our historic parental authority. Parents who think they are safe simply because they receive no direct welfare payments should recognize that when there is intervention in any family, there is the potential for all parents being gradually brought under state control.

It is not too farfetched for me as a parent to wonder if I might someday find at my door a well-meaning child saver, backed by a sympathetic government and court system, come to "protect" my child from my old-fashioned moral standards.

Considering this alternative, it becomes imperative that parents in the 1980s take action by working for the proper separation of family and state. That means supporting the valid legal rights of the young, which protect them, but opposing the ever-extending rights of "choice," which pit parents against children.

CHAPTER 6

big daddy government
and the family

You would assume that if a family is not on welfare, the government cannot have direct control over it. Government intervention, you would think, is something that does not affect a middle-income family—it hits only the very poor or the handicapped. Frankly, I thought so too, until I discovered how child-advocate social engineers had insinuated themselves into dozens of government agencies. I now believe that tax dollars are used by the federal government to support a morality and philosophy that are tearing our families apart. The tale of one California mother dramatizes how an average parent can get caught in the machinery of government-financed child advocacy:

My daughter, Linda, ran away when she was 16. She complained that I didn't understand her. You see, I insisted that an adult be present when her friends visited our home—primarily because when they went out the door, they carried our belongings with them. I wouldn't allow her to drink or smoke pot. In other words, I wouldn't let her "do her thing."

One night she said she was going out to visit a friend. By eleven o'clock I was worried. I sent her brother to get her, but no one knew her at the address she had given us.

I spent the night frantically searching for her—driving around, telephoning, getting neighbors and her friends' parents out of bed. Finally I called the police and reported her as a missing person. I didn't know if she had run away, been raped, or was dead. A few days later the police asked me to identify a dead teenage girl. The body at the morgue fit Linda's physical description. The girl's face had been blown off, and it wasn't until our dentist had checked the teeth that I really knew for sure it wasn't my Linda.

I never stopped looking for her. About a year after Linda had gone, I received a summons from the district attorney's office telling me to appear in court for "willful failure to provide for your minor child."

I guessed it was the welfare department that was going to sue me, although the district attorney wouldn't tell me, since the information was "confidential." Likewise the welfare department said their information was "confidential." I finally called the police to find out what was going on. Later that day, the police called. They had found Linda and were holding her as a runaway.

I rushed to the station. I saw my daughter for the first time in a year. Linda was obviously pregnant.

She revealed that she had been living on $420 a month, plus free medical care, plus food stamps. She and her boyfriend had been granted Aid to Families with Dependent Children and been listed as a common-law family.

I told her she didn't have to go on welfare—she still had a home and family—and that I would take care of her and her baby when it was born.

But Linda decided to get married. The next day she and her 18-year-old husband applied for and went on the welfare rolls again.

Despite everything I've tried to do, I am being sued by the county to recover the money they foolishly paid Linda while she was a known runaway.

What a paradox! The welfare department hands out money to a minor without bothering to check if she is a runaway. Then they hold parents legally responsible for their negligence.

There is no way of knowing how many times this parent's experience has been repeated across the country. Laws that were set up to protect children and help troubled families all too often have been used to pursue parents and subvert their authority. By in effect paying Linda to stay away from home, the welfare agency was financing a runaway and contributing to the delinquency of a minor. In some cases they might even be supporting sexual activity by children, since the only requirement for receiving Aid to Families with Dependent Children is that young girls be pregnant.

Linda's mother, caught in the tangled web of welfare policies, decided to fight the suit in court. She will spend in legal fees ten times what the welfare department says she owes. But some rights are worth fighting for, no matter what the cost.

how federal programs affect families

Government controls are not bad things in themselves. For example, we rise to an alarm clock set to a government-regulated standard of daylight saving time; brush our teeth to music played on a federally assigned radio frequency; and drink coffee made with water that meets government standards of purity. I could go on to include almost everything we eat, the medications we take, and the transportation we use. Indeed, almost every aspect of our lives is touched by some kind of government regulation.

But some government controls, especially those aimed at families, are not so benign. "Government policies are not neutral to families," A. Sidney Johnson, director of Family Impact Seminar at George Washington University, told the Smithsonian's Family Forum in 1976. "Many public policies in this country have direct effects on families and many others have indirect effects. Just because these effects may not be intended or ignored does not mean that they do not exist."

By 1978, according to the Institute for Socioeconomic Studies, 268 federally financed programs directly aimed at helping the family were costing more than $55 billion annually. Why should this figure interest you? Because the first rule of economics says that you, the taxpayer, ultimately pay for everything. A Wisconsin dad couldn't agree more:

> *The government has increased my taxes to help other people's children to the point where I can't do for my own children as I would like.*

It would be foolish to condemn all government programs for families. Children are fed, parents are job-trained, and families are held together by some of them. But far too often, well-intentioned programs are perverted by a bloated bureaucracy of professionals.

After talking with parents of 402 families, I feel that many parents today are afraid that government intrudes into their private lives in ways they don't know; some are just vaguely aware that government is "tinkering"; a few traditionalists are worried that the liberal-sounding altruism of government has had a dampening effect on the traditional family.

More than one-third of these parents reported that government had, to some extent, legislated against their family in everything from inadequate tax deductions to education to family planning. These parents thought that excessive federal meddling in families amounted to what one father called "destroying the family in order to save it." Several parents asked, "Why can't I be in control of the 'help' my family gets?" Some of these parents used vague and hopeless statements such as "The government never did anything worth a damn," but some complaints were specific.

A Maine father "talked back" to government injustice:

> *The federal government—state and local too—acts in response to vested interests. Until parents are one of these interests, government can stay to hell away from my family.*

Other parents asked hard questions. Why, they said, should I trust a government to help me when it is riddled with people who push radical children's rights that call for giving free legal, medical, or psychiatric care without my consent and allow my child to remain in runaway centers even if I want him home?

Why have we allowed—even at times encouraged—government to meddle in family life? A New Mexico minister, himself a father of five, points to inattention brought about by our changing economy as a possible cause:

> *We are a society in which machines have replaced humans, causing job dissatisfaction and unemployment. Fathers and mothers often work far from home, and their employment is rarely related to family values. The joys of life don't seem to come, these days, from such virtues as Christian commitment, creative work, family life, and community participation. Rather they center around things bought with dollars and cents.*

But some parents, such as this mother, disagreed with this anti-government stance:

> *Our handicapped son benefited greatly from government programs. We praise those federal dollars that made it possible for him to be placed in a special school.*

It is only natural to like those programs that help us and to dislike those that cost too much or do not share our values. The question is: How do most parents, especially the ones who don't gain directly, know which of the government programs they're paying for are truly beneficial to some or all and which are not?

Milton Friedman, the conservative economist, feels no such ambivalence. "I believe," he was quoted as saying in the *Washington Post*, "that almost all government spending in the name of innovative programs has done great harm to society, to the public at large, and particularly to the lower income groups. . . . Personally, I believe that a very large number of our so-called social problems actually . . . are the result of too much government." Friedman goes on to argue that because of the political vigilance of special interests, it's almost impossible to halt a program that has outlived its usefulness or has been proven unworkable.

In the 1980s the bulging bureaucracy has reached an all-time peak of meddling in family affairs through growing and well-meaning attempts to "help" children and families. Nevertheless, it is inaccurate to hold the bureaucracy responsible for the bureaucracy. The trail of blame leads inexorably to the Congress of the United States, which controls the nation's purse strings. Senators and representatives, sitting on the 333 subcommittees, have let themselves be co-opted by the social scientists, who see mental sickness behind every social problem and who want to dip their fingers into every mental-health pork barrel. These professional helpers demand continuation of the old, worn-out programs, cherished projects that limp along from year to year, often with few beneficiaries except for the number of "helpers" they put to work. Former Health, Education and Welfare Secretary, Elliot Richardson, admits that only a handful of people in Washington even began to comprehend the 300 grant programs in force during his HEW tenure well enough to weigh the claim of one against the other. The problem is compounded, says Richardson, at the state and local levels, where the programs are actually administered. Their profusion "makes a responsible, democratic system impossible . . . because of the piling up of report requirements . . . and creating new agencies regardless of whether they make sense."

How can too much money hurt family programs? Because it invariably brings too much bureaucratic paperwork, a pyramid of paper that requires ever-growing contingents of paper-shufflers to keep it moving. Even though parents are supposed to be involved in many government programs at local levels, their involvement is often merely a meaningless ritual performed to comply with the letter, not the spirit, of the regulation.

the illicit union of the federal government and social science

The federal government got into the family-helping business back in 1909 with the First White House Conference on the Care of Dependent Children, out of which came the establishment of the Children's Bureau three years later. The bureau's original function was to "investigate and report upon all matters pertaining to the welfare of children and child life." This research gave rise to the publication of *Infant Care*, which first appeared in 1914 and was revised and reprinted for 50 years. Before 1950, *Infant Care* gave advice on thumbsucking and toilet training along with the need for parental firmness. But the old themes were forgotten after 1950, and a dramatic shift toward more permissiveness was apparent. Mothers were urged to avoid battles by manipulating the home environment instead of directly confronting their children's wills.

Also in 1950, at the mid-century White House Conference on Children and Youth, the federal government embarked on its long career as a consumer of psychological expertise. Gone was the emphasis on the pragmatic problems of infant care. This conference focused on how to provide each child with a fair chance to achieve a healthy personality. Unbeknownst to parents, this was the traditional families' first foray in the battle against the social engineers who, backed by federal policy, saw parents as tyrants and children as victims in need of liberation. Within two decades, we had traveled a mighty distance: In 1971 the White House Conference on Youth was able to assert (in the language of the Peter Pan generation) "the right of the individual to do her/his own thing."

The federal government has created a bureaucratic Frankenstein's monster within a startlingly short time. Since the formation in 1952 of the cavernous experimental laboratory called the Department of Health, Education and Welfare (now the Department of Health and Human Services), social-welfare expenditures increased from 9 percent of the gross national product to about 20 percent in 1977. The expropriation of parental expertise by the government-backed mental-health and welfare professionals has inflated the cost of social-service programs faster than the gross national product has grown. The social engineers self-perpetuate. They diagnose the family as diseased and prescribe large doses of mental therapy and research, funded by tax dollars and administered by themselves.

"There is a huge family establishment through all the family-service agencies of the government," says Professor Michael Novak in *The Family: America's Hope*, "with a strong interest in understanding the family in a certain way. It is quite able and willing to smother us with statistics of a certain sort and to propound official views of the family."

Today, the federal health-and-welfare empire employs more than 150,000 people and has the third largest budget in the world. All 50 states combined do not spend as much in one year as does this one bureaucracy. Understandably, no other institution, private or public, has more impact on family life, especially when at the state and local levels the current bureaucracy balloons to more than 7,500 government and 47,500 private agencies. The birth and growth of this giant precisely corresponds to the emergence of "the troubled family."

Since the inception of HEW and especially since 1960, Congress has expanded its duties by passing a storm of social legislation aimed at helping families. In 1961, the law authorizing Aid to Families with Dependent Children was amended to allow payments to families with a live-in unemployed father who is physically able to work. This marked the first departure from the practice of providing federal welfare assistance only to deserted mothers or to women with handicapped husbands. Since this time, the number of second- and third-generation welfare families has increased in California alone from 15,000 to 130,000 families in 1980. Some legislators see the increase as a direct result of this policy change. A general war on poverty was declared in 1964, which further liberalized income-support programs. And in 1974 all states and counties were required to adopt a food stamp program, originally initiated as a pilot project by executive order in 1961.

The list is long, and even though the enacting of new programs has slowed since the 1970s, expenses for maintaining existing programs continue to mount as relentlessly as the inflation they fuel. A few voices of caution began to be heard in the late 1960s, such as James L. Sundquist from the Brookings Institution: "There are many signs that the capacity of the United States government to make policies and establish programs in the domestic field has outrun its capacity . . . to finance and administer them." But such voices had no real power to force a reevaluation.

The social-science bureaucracy now dispenses some $400 million each year to outside researchers for work touching on the family. This is more money than is spent to protect our environment and almost as much as is spent by the Department of Agriculture; yet this figure represents only about one-fifth of the total federal social-science research expenditure, which, from an accounting by the consulting firm of Wakefield Washington Associates, amounts to $2 billion annually. The result of that beneficence is that federal grants and contracts now come from a welter of different agencies and constitute a mother lode for social engineers mining such research. Take, for example, such nuggets as "The socioeconomic meaning of family garbage"; "The need for sibling interaction" (a study about whether or not brothers and sisters should have anything to do with each other); or, "Did family poverty contribute to the number of bums in the 1700s?"

I am by no means implying that all social and mental-health studies are puffery. Those that investigate the problems of the handicapped and juvenile justice, for instance, give us vital information that can make positive contributions to family and community life. I quarrel with economic social-science opportunism, which steals our tax dollars and provides fluff or "we know best" expertise that, when disseminated at our expense, supports the fabrication that our families are declining because parents don't know what they're doing.

Nothing short of a social-science explosion has taken place in the past 25 years. The National Association of Mental Health is now a highly influential lobby that keeps such a close watch over state legislators, governors, Congress, and even the President that few souls are hardy enough to speak out against any mental-health program lest they be accused of advocating a return to Bedlam.

But there is a great difference between the eighteenth-century guards who chained the mentally ill and the gang of social scientists who think federal largess and militant mental health can march parents lockstep into the future. Washington columnist Nick Thimmesch says, "Now the anti-traditionalists are well-meaning. They are convinced that if only enough federal programs are funded—Eureka!—

the age-old problems of families will be diminished to a manageable level."

What did the parents I surveyed think of this governmental interference? Generally, they felt: (1) too much government concentration on the problems of children undermines parental authority; (2) too many government programs giving away too much money increases family dependence on Washington; and (3) the intrusion of government bureaucrats, whether in the form of directives or social workers, alters the basic character of family relationships. A South Carolina father of three said:

> *So many government pronouncements about troubled parents become confusing. I think it often puts parents and children on different sides.*

And a thoughtful Maine mother said:

> *I realize that the government's desire is to "do good" for my family, but I don't know where they can draw the line between real help and interference.*

A California mother I interviewed told me this:

> *The more government takes responsibility for child-rearing decisions away from families, the weaker becomes the government. Strong families are the best strength any country can have.*

federal family policy—the dismal record

Evaluating public policies is almost impossible. Objectives are multiple and conflicting; performance is difficult to define, measure, and interpret. What most parents I talked to agree on is that there has been a progressive softening of real government support for parents. This Indiana mother/teacher told me:

> *I see too many government agencies trying to substitute for the home and social workers substituting for mothers and fathers. The laws of our land should be structured so that they support parents and families, not replace them.*

As we have seen, the social scientists who control so much federal policy-making for the family don't think much of parents' ability to raise children. In fact, many of the social engineers in government don't think much of anybody's ability to care for themselves. They've come up with what they call the continuum-of-care concept, which, as explained in 1979 by Arabella Martinez, assistant secretary for Human Development Services at HEW, provides for "interventions which can be designed to meet the range of predictable human needs throughout the life cycle."

In the same year, at the National Council on Social Welfare conference, Dr. Cecil Sheps, professor of social medicine at the University of North Carolina, asked those in attendance this question: "Who but the social workers with their expertise" can advise and direct the changes the society needs?

This attitude of superiority engulfs parents and children in the concept of cradle-to-grave government care. Federal policy, rather than coming to the family's defense as agencies maintain it does, often invades family territory when it undermines parent resourcefulness.

The late 1970s brought families into the social-service spotlight. Families were deemed to be troubled and in need of "saving," and the analysis commonly turned up statistics reflecting family stress, marital breakup, teenage pregnancies, and rising welfare dependence. Most of these troubles were generally laid at the door of poverty, racial and sexual inequality, inadequate health care, unemployment, and bad parenting. The solutions to family problems, according to the experts who defined the problems in the first place, run virtually the full length of the social-service agenda—guaranteed income, full employment, wider opportunities for minorities and women through affirmative-action programs, more and better sex education for young people, and training for incompetent parents. The "answer," then, is not new at all, but is the same old solution of throwing at families more federal programs and tax dollars, all supervised by the social engineers in government.

As the arguments about family policy crossed into the 1980s, experts still couldn't decide the question: What exactly is a family? Is it two or more people related by blood, marriage, or adoption, or is it anyone in any kind of communal or sexual arrangement wanting to use the term "family"? Allan C. Carlson, writing in *Public Interest*, makes this observation: "If there can be no definition that excludes any form of human cohabitation, then what is a family policy trying to save, or restore, or strengthen, or help? And if all forms of human cohabitation are essentially equal, why have an expensive policy aimed at no particular goal?"

the child-care flap

An example of government intervention of potentially horrendous degree is the rapidly growing field of child day care. The result of massive federal funding for day care will be the advancement of theories of discipline, sexuality, and mental health that are those of the social engineers, not of parents.

Parents are as concerned with what mental and emotional imprint day care makes on their children as with professional qualifications. There is no assurance that, years down the line, day care's influence might not prove negative for some children and their parents. The important question of parent bonding—children's emotional attachment to their parents—has not been assessed by the day-care advocates.

Do parents really want day care for their children, or is this just another case of exuberant social engineering? Of course some parents do. But there is evidence that many do not. When then Senator Walter Mondale introduced his Child and Family Services Act of 1975, which included child care, he received up to 5,000 letters *a day* in protest. A 1975 study from the University of Michigan Institute for Social Research found that only 8 percent of 5,000 families used professionally run child-care centers when they had the opportunity. Most preferred to enlist the help of family members. Suzanne H. Woolsey, in her report, "Pied-Piper Politics and the Child-Care Debate," confirmed that when subsidized child-care programs are available, most eligible parents do not use them. Day-care advocates point with pride to European countries, even Iron Curtain countries, as having the foresight to develop child-care programs, yet Hungary and Czechoslovakia both eliminated day-care programs for young children as a result of independent studies that satisfied government officials that institutional care damaged preschool children. This from countries who *want* state-indoctrinated children.

There is a growing body of evidence that most parents are content with, indeed prefer, informal child-care arrangements they make with relatives, friends, and neighbors to keep their children close to home and give them the kind of care that reflects parents' values.

It is difficult to believe that the so-called day-care emergency, so much a part of the social engineers' agenda for "helping" the family, is real. It is not too paranoid for parents to suspect that what the professional healers are really after is another opportunity to develop children's sense of self before parents have a chance to teach them more traditional ideas, such as respect for parents and duty to family.

If there is such a desire on the part of government to spend the $3,000 to $4,000 per year per child it has been estimated that professional day care would cost, then let government give parents the money in the form of family allowances or direct tax credits or, better yet, control the inflation that demands two incomes for decent living.

The wrangling between taxpayers, Congress, and the federal family experts doesn't concern most working parents I talked with. These parents worried about how they were going to be able to give their children the nurturance, the social, intellectual, emotional, and sexual instruction that only they, as parents, were qualified to give. One Arizona working mother of three children said:

> *There's only so much teaching and emotional interacting I can do after 6 p.m., and there's only so much that my children can pick up from me. We're both tired by that time.*

Most parents thought part of the answer to their child-care problem lay in control of the government spending that caused the inflation making two incomes necessary. Many did not want to see government-financed child-care centers. A working father from Missouri told me:

> *Government can't even get the mail delivered on time. Child care is far too important a matter to leave to bureaucrats and their regulations.*

A California mother of three added:

> *I think the federal government is on an anti-family track. We get a tax break if we turn our kids over to someone else to raise, not if we raise our own.*
>
> *For starters, the income tax deduction for children should be doubled to be realistic about what it costs to raise children today.*

The cost of raising a child through college is rapidly approaching $100,000. Contrast this expense of $4,500 per year (for 22 years) with the income-tax savings of $250 or so on a $1,000 exemption.

After many years of debate, the controversy over government-supported day care is still raging. Perhaps the principal reason for the lack of resolution is that day care has been cast as a political issue for feminists and as a save-the-family issue for the social engineers in government. It is neither. The question of who can best supervise the rearing of children—government or parent-led families—is the real issue to be addressed.

the chaos in family services

Most federal family services are aimed at children and are delivered at the state and local level. Confused at the federal government level, program administration becomes chaotic when filtered downward. A 1980 report on California's multibillion-dollar-a-year system of services to children (including education) issued by the Office of Statewide Health Planning and Development called the system a "miscalculated, misconceived, misguided, miserable mess." The indictment went on to propose radical restructuring of children's services, the largest industry in the state, employing more people and costing more money than any other service. Massive spending alone ($11.8 billion in 1979) has not improved the lot of needy California children. The report cited particularly the inability of the system "to change or eliminate" services that don't do the job once they are established. It might appear the California Office of Statewide Health Planning and Development was on the right track at last. But with typical bureaucratic logic, after a three-year study, their final report recommended the creation of *two* governmental agencies to de-emphasize government involvement in rearing children. In other words, more government to insure less government.

Given the dismal record of state intervention in families through its mental-health healers, the new cries being raised in the 1980s for a cohesive federal family policy and an Office of Families to act as an umbrella for the social engineers give parents little reason to be confident of the future.

The suggestion that a so-called Office for Families be created in the Department of Health and Human Services is one of those periodic efforts to let bureaucracy solve the problems bureaucracy creates. The very idea of an overall federal policy (except one that promotes a hands-off policy) for families is chilling. What kinds of families would be covered, and who would make that determination? What kinds of programs would be implemented, and who would administer them?

Why is an overall policy such a bad idea? Because federal programs either must be so bland they offend no one or so specific that they are divisive and destructive. The federal government is already laced with agencies operating child-abuse programs, drug- and alcohol-abuse programs, welfare programs, and hundreds of others designed to aid families. Yet collectively they surely cannot have proven to be such great successes that the experience would recommend an even greater foray into social intrusion of the family.

In the past quarter-century, government social-service agencies, while providing needed assistance, have often undermined the skills and confidence of families—formerly the primary providers of education, health, and caretaking of young and old alike. Scores of services once considered family duties are now professionalized and provided by outsiders.This is the atmosphere that gave rise to a medicare regulation—among many others—that allows payment to strangers (helping professionals) for care of the elderly but does not offer a cent to families who provide the very same care.

An Office of Families or any other super-family bureaucracy is not what families need; rather, such thinking is a large part of the danger families face. Parents don't need another set of services that, in effect, tells them they are incapable of looking after their own families. Parents need less bureaucratic interference in personal matters that are none of government's concern. The family is the best department of health and human services and is the last stronghold of private freedom in a world where privacy shrinks every day.

I can think of nothing more destabilizing to Mom, Pop, and the kids than Big Daddy Government choosing a model-family structure and enacting unconscious, mindless, and incoherent policies to make it work. It is obvious to some parents that families need their own special-interest group in Washington, D.C., and in the state capitals as well.

the family advocates

In 1979, some family-oriented parents began a revolution of sorts. They opposed policies and attitudes they feared would forever usurp what was left of their parental authority. And, of all things, it was the International Year of the Child (IYC) celebration that helped transform a loosely knit group of parents and organizations into a vocal family lobby to combat the controversial philosophies expounded by supporters of IYC.

The year-long promotion, aimed at improving the lives of children around the world, was a United Nations program that no one would expect to cause controversy. Its aims of opposing worldwide abuse, malnourishment, and undereducation of children were certainly laudable goals. Yet in 1978, the first appropriations bill, for $1.3 million (the United States' share of the IYC budget), was knocked out in the first congressional round and passed only at a much-reduced level the following year. "I am in favor of motherhood, apple pie, and children," said one lawmaker, "but this is ridiculous." There was much muttering on Capitol Hill that the money would provide already well paid people with all-expense-paid weekends at fancy hotels to attend seminars where they would don mantles of self-righteousness and shake their fingers at parents who don't understand their children.

But budget-watchers were not the only ones who raised voices against IYC. In California, when Assemblywoman Maxine Waters tried to get a simple resolution endorsing the Year of the Child and its United Nations' Children's Bill of Rights out of committee, it ran into unexpected flak and she withdrew it. How could this be? Who could object? Apparently several family-oriented organizations could and did. The main objection of these parents was that IYC nowhere mentioned parents or the fact that children were members of families. Protested one mother, a member of the American Family Forum:

> *Our children are not a natural resource belonging to the people, nor do they belong to our government.*

At the heart of the controversy is whether, in terms of government policy, the child will be treated as a part of the family unit or as a separate individual.

Family-advocate groups have been generally categorized as anti-abortion and anti–Equal Rights Amendment, but I found them to be much more than naysayers. An abbreviated statement of their principles submitted to the 1980 (7th Decennial) White House Conference on Families affirmed: (1) We define a family as a group of persons who are related by blood, marriage, or adoption. (This was in opposition to the American Home Economics Association, which urged that the family be described as "a unit of two or more persons who share resources, share responsibilities for decisions, share values and have a commitment to one another over time . . . regardless of blood, legal ties, adoption, or marriage." This definition could very well be called the roommate or POSSLQ—Person of Opposite Sex Sharing Living Quarters, U.S. Census, 1980—concept of family.) (2) We believe that the family is the most important unit of society. (3) We reject public policies or judicial decisions that embody the children's liberation philosophy—that children have rights separate from those of their family and/or parents. (4) We declare parental rights to be primary, unless, by the standards of common law, the parents have been shown to be unfit. We oppose government policies and judicial decisions that permit or promote government-funding "services" of counseling, contraception, and abortion to minors without parental knowledge and consent. (5) We believe that prudent and appropriate action at the state and local levels should be taken to protect the life and safety of any child threatened with child abuse. (6) We feel that parents have the primary right and responsibility to educate their children according to the philosophy of their choice without government interference or financial penalty. (7) We endorse an approach that encourages family, community, and local initiative to support families, not a proliferation of government programs. We reject the unfounded assumption that bureaucrats or "human-services personnel" know better than parents what is best for their families. (8) We expect the communications media to exercise restraints, discretion, and taste in their programming; traditional family values are increasingly attacked, denigrated, twisted, and ridiculed in the media. We also support strong national, state, and local laws that restrict the dissemination of pornographic materials. (9) We believe that the rights of parents to rear their children according to their religious beliefs is fundamental. (10) We support the historic American principle that laws relating to marriage and domestic relations are ex-

status to women in the home. They want to create new kinds of communal-housing environments that could balance the demands of work and home. The feminine mystique of the 1960s, which told women to view themselves outside the context of family, now tells those women without family life that they may be missing something enriching.

The rebirth of the family may seem somewhat ironic to most traditional parents when its midwife is feminism. Nevertheless, the new positions of liberal feminists seem to indicate that a woman's maximum personal fulfillment is not necessarily to be found outside the family after all.

parent revolution can slow big daddyism

Unlike individuals in Sweden, dissatisfied American parents and family advocates can file lawsuits and appeals against government agencies to stop bureaucrats in their tracks. And all parents can bring political pressure to bear and make bureaucracies give an accounting of their actions. In the 1980s parents can insist on bureaucratic accountability to families for every action.

Signs of citizen revolt against the excesses of child-advocacy government are growing. Some states have returned to legal drinking ages of 20 and 21; and New York, for one, has started handing out stiffer sentences to serious juvenile criminals. Of even greater significance was the canceling of Senator Alan Cranston's Child Care Act of 1979 because, as the senator put it, "The mood of . . . the American public in general is very negative toward proposals for new federal programs." Perhaps these and other signs sound a note of optimism for the future of families. After 25 years of unchecked growth, the 1980s could be a time of limits on the power of government and its bureaucracy.

Tightening congressional purse strings will benefit the families of the 1980s. Another equally important check on government will come when parents, not "helping professionals," are the recognized advocates for their own children. This is not to say that our society does not need laws to protect truly abused children; but the reach of child advocacy must be limited, meaning minimal state intrusion into the privacy of family life. When maximum authority rests in the hands of parents, not government, parents' capacity to provide affection, care, education, and protection is enhanced. No state, bureaucracy, or best-intentioned professional child advocate can provide the day-to-day, hour-to-hour supervision and concerned care that a parent can. This means that only parent advocates, not distant social engineers, should have the authority and responsibility to make decisions about the rearing of their children. Family stability requires it; and family stability is the starting point for us and for our society.

CHAPTER 7

big mama education: why parents are angry

Nine out of ten parents I interviewed for this book are dissatisfied with the quality of their children's education. Many of them responded with what can only be described as pent-up rage. An Illinois mother, for instance:

> My 15-year-old girl is a high-school sophomore. Her English is atrocious and her counselor let her drop geometry without consulting me. Her favorite subject, she tells me, is archery.
>
> When I look at her textbooks, they read almost like those she had in elementary school. She hasn't had two hours of homework this entire year; yet she's passing all her classes with Bs. How can you get a B for doing nothing?
>
> Even worse, the school's behavior standards are so bad, I fear she is exposed to really evil things. The graffiti on the walls is so embarrassing, I can't look at it. One time when I went to pick her up at the gym, two young boys followed me, sniggering and talking loudly of female genitals. My daughter told me there have been knife fights between classes. She thinks that's exciting.
>
> The school grounds look like a pigsty. Once I was there right after lunch and every inch of ground was covered with debris. Hundreds of students had just dropped their garbage and walked off.
>
> All of this goes on while the principal assures parents that all is well and our children are making marvelous progress.
>
> Don't tell me to move to a better school district. This is a better school district.

Could these complaints be just another mother's overprotective attitude toward her "baby"? I don't think so. Reading expert Paul Copperman recounts in *The Literacy Hoax* his telling a 1979 senate subcommittee on education that this is the first generation whose basic skills will not exceed, indeed not even approach, those of their parents. "The average high-school student today," declares Copperman, "takes 25 percent less English, 35 percent less world history, 35 percent less government and civics, 30 percent less geography, and 20 percent less science and math than students a generation ago. . . . He is assigned less than half the homework, and his textbooks have been rewritten with a reading level two years lower than the grade he is in."

These lower standards have produced what you would expect. The average eighth-grader today reads only as well as a seventh-grader did in the early 1960s and computes only as well as a sixth-grader of that period. Here's a shocker: A 1978 Gallup poll found that less than half of all high-school students knew the year in which Columbus landed in the New World.

Why do we reap such poor harvests of knowledge? Certainly it isn't for lack of money—Americans spend more educating their children than does the rest of the world. Enrollment in our public schools and colleges has doubled since the early 1950s and the number of teachers and other employees has multiplied three and one-half times, but outlays in inflation-adjusted dollars have *multiplied sixfold* to about $84 billion. In other words, at one end parents are being taxed at higher and higher rates to support at the other end a public-education system that produces increasingly inferior results.

It's no wonder parents are angry at schools. In California and some other states, middle-class taxpayers have put the brakes on unlimited funding of the educational bureaucracy by placing a lid on their property taxes. Hard questions are being asked: How much preschool should a taxpayer be willing to support? What about all the "frill" courses?

Parents I talked with, representing families in every geographical section of the United States, believe that the schools are largely to blame for their children's problems. These unhappy parents see public schools not as an ally in the job of preparing the young for adulthood but as a dangerous force undermining parental authority and family unity.

Primarily, parents express anguish over the lack of discipline and low moral atmosphere in most secondary schools—what one parent called a "moral wasteland." Their next concern is with busing away from neighborhood schools to achieve racial balance, although many parents believe forced busing is dying from lack of support by both black and white parents. Another great worry for parents is the textbooks their children are studying. An Ohio father of two, who joined a parent group protesting the quality of textbooks in his school district, says:

> *There are many references to rock celebrities and movie stars— trivia in a textbook! The history texts, especially, seemed to be stretching to find ways to be relevant to the women's and civil rights movements at the expense of basic information.*
>
> *The level of language for junior high students is about the same as for grade-schoolers.*

It is no wonder that reading-achievement scores are dropping like stones: Textbook publishers say they began simplifying their product in 1970 in response to complaints from the education establishment that a generation of young people raised on television and auto-demolition movies would not read textbooks at their grade level. Why weren't parents consulted before such a decision was made?

Textbooks are only a part of the rampant experimentation parents have seen thrust on the public schools. Most of the experiments have been based on the idea that children should have choices and be able to make decisions about their education based on their own interests. Reflecting the Peter Pan generation's emphasis on the present moment, experimental courses in movies and science fiction have replaced some classes in literature and, in some schools, pupils study parapsychology instead of science.

Educational standards declining in the name of relevance and progress can only mean that some of the members of this generation will never be exposed to their intellectual heritage in the public schools.

Parents want most of all to know that their children are competent in their subjects. And they want this competence tested as the child progresses from grade to grade. After all, it is not too much to ask What is my child learning? What does she know? What can he do? or even Why isn't he or she doing better?

A Florida mother of three told me:

> *Testing for competency is hardly a ridiculous request. Testing is not a new idea. It's simply another way of determining that a student*

*is qualified in his subjects. I don't trust teachers who give all stu-
dents As and Bs; I don't even trust a diploma. Let me see test scores
and then I'll know whether my child has learned what he needs to
learn.*

Parents have good reason to demand to know whether or not
their children are competent in their studies. For the past ten years,
the media have reported disaster stories about high-school graduates
with average intelligence and grades who couldn't get jobs because
they were illiterate. One such student later sued the San Francisco
Unified School District for a million dollars but lost. According to
Paul Copperman, public-school educators breathed a sigh of relief at
the judicial decision because only 10 to 15 percent of high-school
graduates in the last decade have been able to read beyond the fifth-
grade level. The National Commission on Libraries and Information
Science in a 1979 report puts the figure higher, at 20 percent, but
that is hardly cause for jubilation.

There is a minority of parents who complain that the compulsory
school system is all too powerful. It is so strong that in most districts
parents would be accused of an unpardonable crime if they decided
to teach their children at home. Nonetheless, these parents are especially outspoken. One Indiana woman, mother of three grown sons
and wife of a university professor, told me:

*The best thing I ever did for my boys was to keep them out of the
public schools.*

Another mother, a credentialed teacher, said:

*I decided to teach my youngest daughter at home when I saw her
third-grade papers returned to her marked Excellent although they
contained many misspellings. I corrected them and returned them
to the teacher, who sent me a note with three common words misused. I decided then and there that I didn't want my child taught by
people who, never having learned to read or write themselves, were
now teachers.*

Even if you were eminently qualified to teach your own child,
most states would not allow you to do so. Appropriating the prerogatives of the educational establishment evokes a harsh response from
most school systems. Can a tax-supported bureaucracy deny

parents the right to home-educate their children? Is there freedom to learn only within state regulations? Some parents, intent on holding the anti-family force of education at bay, will be asking these questions—and more—in the 1980s.

One of the toughest questions from parents I surveyed was Why is there no discipline in the classroom? One parent, a 27-year classroom teacher, told me:

> *The biggest problem in schools since 1950 hasn't been integration or busing, but the disappearance of discipline.*

Discipline has not always been such a problem. When I attended public schools in the 1930s and 1940s, my mother's dictum was "If you get into trouble at school, you'll be in trouble at home." I knew that my parents and my teachers worked together and that if I misbehaved, I would be the one held responsible.

Now in talking with parents and teachers, I hear each group blame the other for their problems with children. The child who misbehaves is seldom taken to task. Teachers complain that parents aren't disciplining at home; parents counter by accusing teachers of interfering with their families. Each charges the other with incompetence. Most parents directed complaints about discipline not at administrators or school boards but at classroom teachers.

A Nebraska mother of five speaks her mind:

> *They fear the student; they can't punish. If they can't command respect from children, how can they be effective teachers?*

And this from a father in Ohio:

> *Tenure systems permit some terrible teachers to remain in the classroom forever; or they are made principals, which is a bad joke on parents and kids.*

A thoughtful comment comes from a California mother of four who doesn't think there are many dedicated teachers today:

> *Too many of today's young teachers were encouraged to believe that what felt good was good. Such beginnings don't produce fine teachers. A good educator is imaginative and discourages children from tendencies toward mediocrity, their desire to be average. A good teacher insists on this, whether or not it's fun.*

Teachers who are capable of disciplining find themselves trapped like fish in a net of professional child advocacy. Said one sixth-grade teacher:

> From the liberal education courses I took during the seventies, I got the idea that a teacher should never be negative. We were counseled to ignore disruptive students, that by withdrawing our attention the bad behavior would stop. That didn't work; it only put the bad actors in control. Now I'm swinging back to more old-fashioned discipline. When they misbehave, I put their name on the blackboard. I hadn't done that for years, and I'd forgotten how effective it was. Students don't want their names on the board. It bothers them. I'm going to revive more negative discipline methods, and maybe it won't take me four or five months out of every school year to get all the kids with me and doing the work we have to do.

It's obvious to all parents that the level of learning in a classroom is apt to match the level of discipline. There can be no teaching accomplished when the teacher has lost control—and the basis of control is authority. Paul Copperman explains why the practice of dishonoring authority during the past quarter-century has led to a decline in education: "Natural authority is the essential core of the relationship between adults and children, consisting of a nurturing and training function on the part of the adult, and a learning function on the part of the child," he writes in *The Literacy Hoax*. "The basis of the relationship is the autonomy of the adult, his knowledge and competencies that enable him to survive and function in the world, and the dependence of the child on adults for survival."

Nowhere does Copperman mention a child's freedom to choose not to learn if he or she considers a subject irrelevant, nor does he seem concerned with promoting democracy in the classroom. Copperman talks of *adult authority*, which puts him outside the mainstream of youth-culture philosophy, a philosophy that recognizes no dividing line between the status of youth and adult.

The parents I surveyed aren't unanimous on the best method of achieving classroom discipline. Some are for bringing back corporal punishment; some are against. Others deem school spankings proper only if parents give permission. But all parents agree that discipline in the classroom is essential and that respect for authority and order are necessary before learning can go forward. One California mother believes that the schools sabotage their own discipline. She said:

> *Take the smoking rules, for one thing. My son goes to a school that provides a designated student-smoking area, which in essence condones his smoking. At the same time, he is taught in health studies that smoking is unhealthy. No wonder he doesn't pay attention to authority when it contradicts itself.*

A young attorney told me of the following incident during a Law Career Day at a California high school: "I was in the class waiting for it to begin for 15 minutes while students straggled in tardy. Finally, the teacher told one boy she was marking him late and instructed him to take his seat with the rest of the class. 'You can't make me do nothing, mother,' the boy said, and went to a different part of the room. The teacher was terribly embarrassed. Later she confessed to me it was too much of a hassle to take it to the administration."

There is a Parkinson's Law at work in the classrooms. It states that disrespect expands to the extent it will be tolerated. So does almost every other kind of negative behavior.

Back in the early seventies, I covered a "bizarre" story for an Eastern newspaper: a high-school principal who had banned blue jeans as school attire. I expected to find a doddering mossback but instead met a serious educator in his 30s who said he noticed a definite change in attitude and performance when young people dressed with more care. He described what he called "blue jean behavior," which, he thought, affected everything from students' posture to their grades. This principal's viewpoint—avant-garde at a time when freedom to dress as one chose, especially as a way of expressing one's creative self, had been firmly established in the youth culture's bill of rights—has since been confirmed by parents and educators alike.

Neil Postman, in *Teaching as a Conserving Activity*, says, "If we want school to feel like a special place, we can find no better way to begin than by requiring students to dress in a manner befitting the seriousness of the enterprise and the institutions."

One Oregon mother put it more bluntly:

> *Some girls dress like prostitutes. A history class is no place for cleavage!*

Excessive emphasis has been put on the child's right of self-expression. Much of this self-expression has taken the form of youth displaying the symbols of its own culture—jeans, the T-shirt message. What teachers and parents are seeing today is the negative effect this has had on discipline. Private schools have always known that more formal dress meant more formal behavior. This does not mean suits and high-necked blouses for the 1980s, but it does mean there should be no more Do-It-to-Me-in-the-Grass T-shirts in the halls of public schools.

in defense of the english language

Another way parents see the traditional discipline of schools being weakened is through the de-emphasis of standard English and the toleration of "street talk." A Pennsylvania mother of two with a college degree in English says:

> When I overheard my son using coarse and ungrammatical language with his friends, I was shocked. I shouldn't have been. Other parents tell me their children are speaking the same garbage. English that would have once marked a child as deprived is now preferred among young people—even those from good middle-class families.

Dr. Tony Campolo thinks some of the so-called ghetto language used by the young is an extension of their involvement with the moment and their rejection of the future. "I hear young people say, 'I goes to the store and I buys a loaf of bread and I brings it home and I eats it.' That's more than bad grammar. It's an inability to conceptualize the past or the future. We think in words. When a child thinks only in the present tense, then his whole life is wrapped up in the present and in himself."

But it is the argument for a child's right of self-expression—as much as any other—that has undermined spoken and written English in the schools. The permissive education establishment has stated time and again that a child's expression of feelings is primary and that rules of grammar can inhibit that. Perhaps this explains why nearly 80 percent of the University of West Virginia's 1979 freshman journalism majors had to take what used to be called "bonehead English."

English Professor Richard Mitchell, author of *Less Than Words*

Can Say, thinks that basic rules of grammar are important because they work. It's that simple.

Finally, the teaching of English may have suffered because of the emphasis given to bilingual programs supported by federal funds, which totaled $174.8 million in 1981. Cultural background and maintenance of a native tongue used to be the duty of home, church, or community. Now it is paid for by the taxpayer. (If this had been the requirement where I went to school, it would have meant curricula in Italian, Czechoslovakian, Polish, Estonian, Lithuanian, Welsh, Bohemian, German, and Hungarian.)

Perhaps we cannot go back to simpler times, before the social engineers and the education establishment decided that English, the language of the majority, should be treated too often as a second language. But if we can no longer think of English as our first language, we parents can, at least, demand that the language of the street, the movies, the punk-rock records be kept out of the classroom. Furthermore, we should insist that basic English grammar and composition once again be taught and mastered by our children.

In *Teaching as a Conserving Activity,* Postman argues for "rather formal and exemplary language to be used in school. It marks it off as a place of dignity." The language students "wear," just like the clothes they put on, is a sign of the state of discipline in the school.

the fear of using suspension/expulsion

The student mentioned earlier who defied the teacher with "You can't make me do nothing, mother" and the 10-year-old who told one teacher I talked with "You better give me my ball, you fat faggot" would have been suspended on the spot 15 or even ten years ago. Not today. The Supreme Court's decision forcing schools to conduct due-process hearings before they can suspend a student, along with the danger of legal suits against schoolteachers and administrators for damages, has pulled the teeth out of the ultimate discipline schools can impose. Organizations such as the Children's Defense Fund believe that disruptive students are denied an education if they are suspended. This myopic view plainly hampers serious students, who are the ones denied when they must suffer through chaotic classes. The rights of the minority triumph and disorder expands in proportion to the tolerance for it—Parkinson's Law in action once more.

The permissive practice of accommodating the school to every child instead of the child to the school, no matter how bad the student's behavior, has a negative effect on "good" children. Why should they respect rules that can be broken without consequence? Students become alienated from an institution that allows misbehavior without punishment. Copperman writes in *The Literacy Hoax:* "The fact that seems to slip by many educators in these confrontations—expulsions and suspensions—with students is that the students do not really want to win. They want and need adults to exercise authority by imposing limits and holding firm to demands. Their constant testing is really a search for adults strong enough to allow them to be children, which is evidenced by the fact that the only teachers they respect are the ones they cannot manipulate."

one reason for school vandalism

Taxpayers replace about $600 million in stolen or vandalized school property annually. Many reasons have been put forward to explain this staggering evidence that schoolchildren are tearing up their schools. One is that many schools, especially urban ones, have grown so large and impersonal that teachers don't even know their students; therefore it becomes easy to vandalize property and disappear into an anonymous student population. But I believe—and many parents I interviewed believe—that there is a strong relationship between the laxness in enforcing school rules and the disrespect for school property that is the other name for school vandalism. A mother of three in South Carolina told me:

> *Inconsistent discipline in the classroom breeds the same kind of disrespect for teachers and the school as inconsistent discipline in the home does for parents and the home. If punishment for rule-breaking was sure and swift, there would be less vandalism. My neighbor's 10-year-old son broke into a kindergarten room with several other boys and ripped it up—pried the sinks off the wall! He was sent to the children's facility for one night and let go. A few days later I heard him bragging and calling his teachers "nerds."*

If, once school vandals are caught, school administrators are persuaded to file charges and turn the offenders over to juvenile authorities, the courts are so attentive to children's rights that what follows often amounts to protection of violent students from school officials. This is a perversion of due process. Our courts must punish bad behavior; punishment is the major weapon civilization has against the savage. If this tenet were applied across the board to the small number of hard-core miscreants who cause most of the trouble, there would be less school vandalism, fewer intimidated teachers and students, and less time lost from the learning process.

Whenever necessary, strong security measures should be used *without hesitation* to reduce violence and property loss in schools and to protect children from each other and from themselves. This Illinois father would agree:

> *On my daughter's first day of seventh grade, she was assaulted in the hallway and knocked to the floor—only a guard kept her from being kicked and robbed. It doesn't bother me at all that there are special police in schools. I'd vote for more of them and a closed-circuit television-surveillance system to boot.*

a disgrace: peter pan's graduation ceremony

Not too long ago, graduation from high school was considered a watershed in a young person's life. The ceremony marked the end of childhood and the beginning of adulthood; it was a serious, if not a solemn, occasion, a time for looking toward the future and giving recognition to the parents, teachers, and institutions that had brought one thus far. It was particularly a moment when scholarship was rewarded. This was true in 1949 when I graduated from high school; it was still true in 1965 when I attended the graduation exercises of a nephew. There was much nervous giggling, with graduates searching for parents in the crowd and parents trying to pick out their children among the class dressed in sedate black caps and gowns. The board of education and faculty sat on the dais and shook hands with each graduate. Flashbulbs popped from every part of the auditorium as proud mamas and papas took instant pictures and hugged and congratulated the new graduates.

Fifteen years passed before I was to attend another high-school graduation ceremony. I wasn't prepared for the culture shock.

The president of the senior class began to speak. He was recounting the class history, most of it innuendo about things they had gotten away with. The graduates chanted "Yeah! Yeah!" and gave the clenched-fist salute to punctuate his remarks. Behind the speaker on the platform, the president of the student body jumped up and began to lead the cheers, finally throwing his cap in the air. Soon all the students began throwing their caps in the air; some of them stripped off their gowns and threw them in the air. They were out of control, screaming and yelling even through the benediction.

As the students walked two by two across center stage to receive their diplomas, one of the faculty called out their names over a microphone. As one boy went by, he reached out and grabbed the mike, yelling, "Yeah, I made it!" Soon they were all grabbing the mike and giving rousing cheers for themselves.

I looked at the adults on the stage—the principal, the counselors, and teachers—searching for surprise, embarrassment, or anger. There was none.

Later I asked the principal, while standing on the stage in the midst of garbage and gowns, if he didn't think a bit more decorum would have made the ceremony more meaningful for the students and the more than 2,000 parents and friends gathered in the auditorium. Oh, no, he assured me, graduation ceremonies should be freer and express the feelings of the kids. Besides, this class had always had a lot of spirit.

Still unconvinced, I discussed the event later that evening with a teacher who told me that the graduation this year was an "improvement" over those of the past few years. She also mentioned that a nearby high school had had to discontinue the formal graduation and mail students their diplomas after a *riot* had broken out in mid-ceremony.

Although this experience surely doesn't represent all high-school graduations today, parents tell me that graduation itself may have lost much of its former meaning. One father of three in a parent talkshop said:

It's not hard to graduate from high school these days. You do nothing and graduate. I remember when it took effort and I was proud of myself.

It may be that the old verity "You get out what you put in" is still operational, but Professor Ralph W. Larkin, in his book *Suburban Youth in Cultural Crisis*, says he thinks the problem is more visceral: "Kids hate school much more now than they did. . . . And I mean the word 'hate' and underline it."

child advocacy in the schools

Perhaps the greatest concern voiced by parents is the apparent difference between the cultural values of the home and the school. This concern is addressed by Edward Wynne in an article in *National Elementary Principal:* "The structure of the modern school . . . tends to drive students toward extreme individualism, excessive and unstable peer-centeredness, and hedonism. . . . Such behavior is obviously inconsistent with the values of most parents."

Child-liberationist crusaders have interfered as diligently in education as they have in parenting. Their concept of a democratic "let's be equals" relationship between teacher and student has wreaked as much havoc in schools as it has in homes. Copperman calls the misapplication of the democratic ideal the single most destructive force in the education of America's youth. Parents complain that teachers, especially young ones, do not understand that children need an authority instead of a buddy who dresses and speaks like them and who allows them to make decisions about learning (or not learning) that could affect the rest of their lives.

The philosophy of the human-potential movement is evident in the learning-should-be-fun trap into which many progressive teachers have fallen. Reducing mandatory school work loads while putting fun and play into school, they claim, will make the students feel happy and loved. Dispense with all those boring drills on grammar, spelling, and theorems and get right to the fun so students can use imagination and creativity to express their "selves." Fun has become such a priority in the classroom that teachers spend more and more of their time thinking up ways of supplying it.

"The contemporary orientation," observes French educator Jacques Ellul, "is that the child must learn without pain, that it must have agreeable, seductive work, that it must not even notice that it is working, and that in class the teacher must be really a sort of game leader, a permissive leader with whom there is no conflict."

It is not surprising that hard work in the classroom has come under attack. We live in a society where psychologists have labeled industriousness the disease of "workaholism" and have prescribed large doses of forced fun as its cure.

The idea of rote learning and drills brings forth groans and criticism from those who maintain that children should not be exposed to dreary facts but should be left, like little buds, to flower in their own time, to use their natural curiosity to teach themselves. It's true that children are naturally curious—any parent knows that. But how can children know what might interest them unless they are exposed to a wide range of ideas and facts?

Reno Dawson, a sixth-grade California teacher with 25 years of teaching experience in three states, feels guilty, she says, because she swung with the permissive-education pendulum. "It was our training during these last two decades," she says about her generation of teachers, "that children should have this lovely life where they didn't have much work or responsibility, where they had fun and were free spirits.

"It used to be that young children expected to do their schoolwork. Today they can't understand that school, like their parents' jobs, is their *work*. The first thing they say is, 'This is no fun; I don't like it,' and they close their books and draw back. The message I get from kids is that they have a *right* to have fun—make it fun, or they won't do it."

Today, this teacher has reevaluated her teaching style and made a drastic change:

> The first thing I tell my class in September is, "School is not fun; school is work. Now, if you have fun, great—but that's accidental. I'm not here to see you have fun; I'm here to see you learn." Believe me, they're shocked at such an idea.
>
> Another thing I've rediscovered is the importance of facts. We teachers were told that the important thing was to teach children to think. Facts weren't important. Memorizing wasn't important. Instead, we gave them very creative problems that they were interested in. I'd say, "Children, what's your greatest interest today?" Then from that, I'd develop learning centers and teaching aids. I tried them all—all kinds of thinking activities. But I finally came back to the understanding that kids don't think if they don't have any facts to think with. I had to go back again, make a complete turn-

around. I still teach children to think, but before I do, I teach them a vast number of facts.

I've put lots of memory work back in the curriculum. Guess what I found out? Facts help children become more creative.

Parents know that the learning-is-fun notion can be a trap, as an Ohio mother reports:

> *We wanted our son to complete trigonometry, but his counselor told him to go ahead and drop out if it was too hard—no offer of outside help or "don't be a quitter" advice. It was done before we knew it, and now our son finds his career choices limited.*

the human-potential philosophy in education

If feelings and the search for the holy grail of self are the be-alls of life, according to human-potential theory, then it follows that structure and discipline in the classroom are repressive. The closer schools can cuddle up to the democratic classroom, where grades and tests don't limit self-exploration, goes the thinking, the better.

I myself was fascinated by this philosophy and with A. S. Neill's *Summerhill: A Radical Experiment in Child Rearing*, which promoted the ultimate in educational freedom. I was so much taken that in 1971 I begged an assistant superintendent in my school district to transfer my daughter from her more traditional school to a new open school. I had written a series of articles extolling the open classroom, schools-without-walls, and many other experiments, and I was thoroughly convinced that sitting in one of a row of desks would stunt my child's creative capacity forever. When the administration refused to allow her to cross a school-district boundary, I was incensed. Now I believe that the structure my daughter was exposed to in school provided a vital countervailing force to the freedom she was allowed at home. Thank God, in this case, that the school system was indifferent to parental wishes—although for the wrong reasons: The superintendent agreed with me that open schools were better, but he just couldn't bring himself to amend a rule that required all students living on one side of the street to attend School A and all students on the other side to attend School B.

Postman, in *Teaching as a Conserving Activity*, says he doubts the validity of education that includes transcendental meditation, est (Erhard Seminars Training), or any "therapy"—even so-called rap sessions. "It is," he says, "at least an open question as to whether they do more harm than good . . . there is no therapy of which I am aware . . . that does not have a particular philosophic bias with which the students, their parents, or their religion might disagree."

Many parents I talked with had had unhappy experiences with school psychologists or counselors handing out "emotional therapy." A New Mexico mother adds this insight:

> *I told my son to steer clear of the rap centers at school. Too many counselors get their kicks from playing God. The kids use it as a place to get out of class and goof off.*

A mother of three in Wisconsin was upset about the educational advice given her by a school psychologist:

> *On the recommendation of a school psychologist, we held our son back a year when he was 10. I wish we had let him go ahead. We felt he needed more difficult work, not easier work, but I didn't want to go against the expert. As a result, he completely lost interest in learning. So much for such advice compared with a mother's old-fashioned sense of what is right for her own kid.*

Offering unsound advice is not the only way in which school psychologists pose a threat. Too many "experts" during the last two decades have used the schoolroom as their laboratory and our children as guinea pigs to prove their wildest flights of fancy. Stanford's Robert D. Hess reports in an unpublished paper that the results of even minor interventions based on research theories may alter other patterns of behavior not the target of the experiment. Hess points out: "Changes in one area can trigger unexpected changes in other areas. Thus a relatively simple attempt to apply research findings to interaction in a classroom may have unpredictable outcomes."

Sex education, hiding behind such euphemisms as "life skills" and "family living," is another human-potential experiment in education that is billed as enrichment. During the 1970s, this movement helped create a *new* sex education that had some startling results, which I explore in chapter 14.

schools without failure—grade inflation and automatic promotion

Tests show that skills and standards are down, yet grades are up; repeating a grade is now almost unheard-of. Copperman calls this practice of grade inflation and automatic promotion from grade to grade a hoax perpetrated by the educational establishment on students and parents alike. One Ohio mother and her son were tricked by this hoax:

> *Our son was a B student in a school system considered excellent. Yet when he got to college, he had to take remedial English in order to qualify for their freshman program. He feels his college prep courses in high school were worthless, and as tax-paying parents we feel cheated out of the quality education we were told he was getting.*

How can parents help their children get the education their tax dollars are paying for? Perhaps homework is part of the answer. Many parents notice that, unlike in their own school days, homework is now nonexistent or may consist of watching a television program and writing a paragraph about how it makes one feel. Other parents tell of teachers who throw away homework or never grade it, thus undercutting the importance of doing it in the first place.

And although there are teachers who require meaningful homework, their efforts can be undone by parents who have been "psychologized" out of insisting homework be completed. This mother of three, for example:

> *Several years ago, I attended a school lecture on how parents could best help with their children's homework. The advice was not to become directly involved, that homework was the child's responsibility. I was to provide a desk and chair, light and pencils, but no direction or criticism. I was particularly advised not to get angry about bad grades, but to support my child's hurt feelings.*
>
> *So I didn't set any rules, and I didn't tell my daughter how to do anything. Now she's in high school and sits in front of the television—when she isn't on the phone—with her books open in front of her, telling me how hard she's studying.*

The idealistic theory behind this laissez-faire advice to parents in the 1970s was the power of compassion, just as it was behind the no-fail schools. Remove the stigma of failure, proclaimed the progressive educators, and children will flower. And all the flower children will cross-pollinate each other by their success and pursue learning more eagerly forever after.

It is obvious to most parents that failure has not been obliterated with a stroke of the theorist's pen. It has merely changed its name to automatic social promotion. Schools without failure, says Michigan State Professor Robert L. Ebel, are themselves failures for three reasons: "In the first place," he writes in the educational magazine *Phi Delta Kappan*, "success has no meaning or value in the absence of the possibility and indeed the occasional experience of failure. . . . In the second place, failures in learning cannot be abolished. Despite the best efforts of the best teacher, some pupils are likely at some time to make unsatisfactory progress in learning. . . . In the third place, there is educational value in the experience of failure. It can teach. It can motivate."

No parent wants to see a loved child held back a grade, but it is just possible that social promotion and grade inflation constitute a worse failure for a child if he or she learns that there is no incentive to work. Behind the no-failure theories of the experts lurks the school-should-be-fun idea, which equates fun with easily achieved goals. These experts would obviously not agree with classical scholar Edith Hamilton: "It is not hard work which is dreary; it is superficial work. That is always boring in the long run, and it has always seemed strange to me that in our endless discussions about education so little stress is ever laid on the pleasure of becoming an educated person, the enormous interest it adds to life."

higher education—what are you paying for?

Parents also are upset about the permissive atmosphere in colleges. Many of the parents I interviewed had children attending college. A New Mexico mother tells about a visit to her daughter's campus:

> *My husband and I were disturbed about the coed-dorm situation. Our daughter told us she often has to leave her room until two o'clock in the morning while her roommate "entertains" a boyfriend.*

*The college president explains that coed dorms provide young peo-
ple with opportunities to get to know each other in a more natural
setting. Hogwash! We're paying good money for a room our daughter
doesn't have equal use of, not to mention the administrative con-
doning of promiscuous sex.*

A Massachusetts father who used his retirement fund to pay his children's college expenses was more upset about college courses he considered little better than children's games.

Parents are not the only ones questioning whether such education is "higher." According to one college instructor, colleges are
boosting their flagging enrollments by turning the first-year curriculum into a playpen of self-exploration.

What are parents paying for? Freshman English students at the
University of California at Berkeley recently studied *Playboy* to decide if that magazine has liberated America from its puritanical sexual tradition. At another California college, students were given
credits for courses in intermediate and advanced frisbee-throwing!
But it's not just California craziness that afflicts colleges: The same
child-centered, rather than excellence-centered, philosophy—the
same lust for relevance and social fads—infects the entire spectrum
of education in the United States.

During the 1960s and 1970s many colleges dropped mandatory
courses in basic areas of social science, natural science, and the humanities, pumping wind into their catalogs with courses of such
dubious academic value as Soap Opera and Backpacking, the kind
of classes one observer called "quackery in the classroom." Even
Harvard University's course catalog has doubled since 1960 and now
describes 2,600 courses.

Grade inflation is a problem of higher education as well as lower.
At Harvard, 85 percent of the 1977 class graduated with honors,
compared with only 39 percent of the class of 1957 (the better-
educated generation). Thus, these young people reach graduate
schools after they've been handed along through high school *and*
college.

Colleges and universities have failed to maintain superior academic standards, just as elementary and secondary schools have. In
some cases, student committees have the power to make their own
rules, institute nonliterate puffery courses, and change a low grade

to a higher one—yet another example of misguided democracy in action. Perhaps that is why some parents are now questioning the financial sacrifice they have traditionally been willing to make to provide their children with college educations.

Just as certain as multiplication tables, the parent revolution will ask two formerly unaskable questions: As a parent, do I *owe* my child a college education? As a taxpayer, do I owe every child who wants one a college education?

It is unarguable that society as a whole benefits from a pool of talented, educated young people and that with knowledge we become in essence more fully human. Parents in the past have always been willing to pay to gain these benefits for their own children, and also to give the same chance to other deserving children. That we even question these assumptions today shows how alienated from education parents have become.

These, then, are the signs of parent revolution against Big Mama Education. Parents want more order and discipline in the schools; a halt to the use of classrooms for human-potential experimentation; higher intellectual standards; adequate testing for competency; and the involvement of parents in every aspect of the education process.

It is clear what most parents want from the public schools and its teachers. It is also clear what parents don't want. Many would agree with this statement by Postman in *Teaching as a Conserving Activity:* "Teachers are not competent to serve as priests, psychologists, therapists, political reformers, social workers, sex advisors, or parents." After such a statement it is only fair to hear what teachers have to say to parents.

CHAPTER 8

what classroom teachers want parents to know

The first thing that struck me about teachers, who composed 14 percent of my sampling, was that their views were so similar to those of the parents I talked with. In other words, the problems for which parents blamed teachers were the same as those for which teachers blamed parents.

Just as with parents, classroom discipline was number one on the list of teacher complaints. Some teachers, in fact, went so far as to say that the children today's parents sent to school were so badly behaved they were unteachable! What brought about such a harsh evaluation of the young?

Here's a report from one classroom teacher, Serena Niensted, who teaches in the suburbs of a large midwestern city. She came back to the classroom in the late 1970s after 11 years as a consultant. What she found was that children had changed during the seventies. "My best-laid lesson plans," she said, "were easily sabotaged. My pupils could not endure organized, cooperative, and purposeful activity. They wanted an emotional disturbance, a conflict, an acting-out center of attraction."

This teacher said that negative student behavior—which included bullying, refusing to work or to help slower students, playing victim, and procrastinating—was not unusual in her past classrooms; she had always had such students.

What makes it intolerable today is that the culprits included almost every student in the class. Why was there no corps of cooperative students to set a class standard? The misbehaving was the same, but what happened after my intervention was not! Formerly, students expected the teacher would handle the misbehaviors. Now it is popular for the misbehaving

125

students to defy the teacher. The misbehaving child refuses to accept correction, punishment, or guidance—even to accept any group decision on classroom rules or controls.

Any classroom discussion of problem behavior quickly veered from the pupil to the teacher's fairness and the individual pupil's rights. The teacher was always a minority of one.

Mrs. Niensted, a mother of three, decided on a course of action. She would correct each misbehavior in the classroom. If that was followed by disobedience, the child would go to the principal's office. Disrespect, she decided, was so serious it would require a parental conference.

She developed a behavior checklist that she used to indicate how each child had behaved in class. Every child took the list, which showed his or her behavior as commendable, disruptive, or inappropriate, home at night for his parents to sign. A list not returned the next morning brought a loss of recess. The class improved. But suddenly, the teacher began to get parental criticism—a lot of it.

"I had expected positive reactions to my plan," she said. "Criticisms of the plan surprised me. Parents' comments included: 'Isn't loss of recess too harsh a punishment for not getting the paper signed?' Equally surprising but much more enlightening was the large number of parents who in one way or another excused their child's misbehavior."

Mrs. Niensted asked herself, Did all parents excuse and defend their children's misbehavior? Her answer, harsh as it may seem to loving parents, is: Yes, far too many did. "By word and by action," she said, "parents are saying to their children 'You're the boss.' It is no wonder that when they come to school they expect the same acceptance of their self-centered desires."

But she also had charges to level at the experimentation going on in the school system. "While I had been out of the classroom," Mrs. Niensted said, "the school district had been moving to open classrooms, team-teaching, individual progression, individualization of instructions. All of my pupils expected a teacher to offer a smorgasbord of education from which each could pick his own menu. It mattered not that in the scramble no one was well fed."

Not until she made classroom discipline her first priority was she able to get to the business of teaching children. Discipline—for this teacher and for many others I talked with—has become the most basic of all the basics taught.

All of the classroom teachers who were also parents agreed that they could achieve no significant change in a student's behavior without parental support. The problem, as they saw it, is that parents today are not effective disciplinarians. "They confuse loving and caring," said one Virginia teacher, "with protecting their children from the consequences of their acts."

Another teacher put it this way: "Parents cannot stand to hurt their children in any way. The thing that brings a parent into my classroom the fastest is when I deprive his child of a party or fun event because the child has not completed his work. This is usually the parent I've tried to get to support my discipline, but who does not seem to know how. This is the parent who comes to school screaming and yelling to have his kid removed from my room. Why? Not so this child will get a better education. *But so the child won't miss out on anything.* The parent can't make the child study, yet still can't bear for him to miss any fun."

This same teacher, the mother of a 14-year-old boy, explained how she handled her own child's misbehavior at school.

> Bobby started to have trouble in the fifth grade. During a faculty meeting his teacher told me, "His behavior is just out of line. He's too talkative and doesn't get his work done."
>
> The next day I took Bobby into his classroom and had a conference with his teacher. He sat with me while I said, "Mrs. Bryant, I send Bobby to school to behave himself and to learn, and from now on we're going to insure that happens. His Little League team is outside practicing. Playing baseball is the love of his life. I told him that he will sit here while we talk, and whether or not he goes out there will be decided at the end of this conference.
>
> "If it is all right with you, Mrs. Bryant, each Friday Bobby will write this note: 'I have behaved all week as a student should in school. I have studied and learned and done my work.' As long as you sign the note, he continues to play Little League; if you do not sign it, he turns in his uniform. This puts no responsibility on you; it is on Bobby."

For 15 weeks until the end of the school year, Bobby brought home the prescribed notes. In addition, the teacher always added her comment about his improved behavior and schoolwork. Bobby never forgot one week because he knew I meant what I said. But the amazing thing is that Bobby, who had never particularly liked school, started to love school. Even four years later the teacher he likes best is Mrs. Bryant. He says she's the best teacher he ever had, and he still respects her to this day.

This mother/teacher knew what some parents have been socialized to forget —discipline *is* love. She created a genuine partnership with her son's teacher and thus enhanced her child's growth. Here is an example of a parent and an educator developing strategies for dealing with a behavior problem before a child becomes a failure. Without such cooperation, parent-school encounters are all too frequently little more than public-relations efforts.

Why won't some parents be equally firm with their children, teachers asked? The same mother/teacher had this answer: "I've told parents what worked for me, but of the dozens of parents I've consulted about their child's behavior problems, only one was able to follow through, and she was so desperate she told me she'd do anything. Even a school psychologist whose son was misbehaving said he couldn't deprive his son of Little League because that's where the boy was successful. My son was successful on the baseball diamond too; but I decided learning was more important."

Teacher morale is incredibly low for reasons other than lack of parent support. Teachers talked about burnout because their best efforts are undermined by reams of extra paperwork; courses mandated by law that are added to the curriculum but never subtracted; incompetent, out-of-touch administrators; the lack of ordinary school supplies; and bad press. They talked of long preparations that went into each teaching day—preparations they hoped would hold the interest of media-saturated, overindulged students. Not all went so far as to belly dance on top of their desks, as did one Los Angeles teacher, but they all said they spent hours thinking up lessons for students who didn't seem to care.

One parent talkshop I conducted in 1980 was composed of teachers, all mothers and fathers of school-age children. Professionally they had logged hundreds of years of classroom teaching, mostly in middle-class, suburban schools. As teachers, they were worried about what they called the write-off kid. Parents who have heard "each child is unique and will get individual attention" speeches from principals and administrators during back-to-school nights will be interested in these behind-the-scenes stories.

"For the past eight years," one teacher began, "the advice I've been getting from educational psychologists and principals in my district is: 'If your students don't want to do the work, make a deal with them. Tell them they can do anything they please in the back of the classroom, as long as they don't disturb you and the other kids.' "

Another called this the "don't push them" technique. She said: "One psychologist told us to quit wasting our time on the losers. Forget the slow learners and concentrate on the others."

"That's right," chimed in a third, "but when you tell a kid that, you're really telling him 'You're not important; stay back there and play with your clay; no work is required of you.' "

Another teacher in the group said she refuses to write off any student: "Every child in my class is expected to do what he can do, as well as behave and not disturb others. I expect even the slower learners to work up to their best level, and they are responsible for that.

"If I were a parent," she continued, "and I knew a psychologist had decreed: 'That child will never go far anyway, so just pass him on,' I'd sue that psychologist."

At this point a teacher of educable mentally retarded children spoke up: "None of my students has an IQ over 70, but I expect them to learn what they can. Consequently, many of them are doing better than kids who have much higher IQs. We aren't writing off our handicapped students, but we are writing off average kids who could learn if we expected it of them. Does that make sense?"

How did the write-off kid come into being? The consensus of these teachers was that school administrators and psychologists couldn't face a record of children failing in *their* schools. "Pass them on" was the answer. There is also an elitist sentiment at work, the teachers agreed, when slower students are pacified with play to give brighter students more time and attention.

What happens to write-off kids? Chances are they will end their education in a write-off school. In California, the educational pacesetter, each district has what is called a continuation high school for students who cannot cope either intellectually or emotionally with regular high school. One teacher said, somewhat sarcastically: "I had a boy whose car became so important to him that his counselor suggested he transfer to continuation school so that he could work on it all the time and get credit."

In the school district in which these teachers taught, school psychologists received funding for a high school for students who couldn't even make it through continuation high school. "It was their idea of a school-without-walls," explained one member of the group, "but there's no education going on there. Drugs are heavy, and many of the girls are pregnant. They sit in a circle, hold hands, and talk about their problems. The teachers aren't teaching; they're friends. The kids get high-school credit for just showing up."

permissive administrators—the emperor's new clothes revisited

The teachers I interviewed in the all-teacher talkshop were completely frustrated with their administrators. Complaints came fast and were furious. According to one teacher: "They fail to back up good teachers who insist on discipline and who disagree with their philosophies. They either transfer us to another school, saying 'You'll be happier in that atmosphere,' or make it so hard for us that we quit."

The problem, said another teacher, was that the administrators were self-deluding:

> They are all standing around patting each other on the back and they don't even know that they aren't accomplishing anything. They spend most of their time running around doing human-relations programs. For example, look at how they blew up a minor incident into a major program they could play with. Three years ago, we had a small racial problem in one of the high schools. But instead of punishing offenders, the administrators decided that the problem was with everyone—students and teachers alike. They hired outside experts and started an in-service education program for the teachers in the district. The students are sent home for one day while we get together. A discussion leader asks such

questions as Why do you think there are racial differences? and How do you feel about it?

They are nothing but all-day gab sessions and a complete waste of time. This program has been going on for three years, and I've not heard one teacher say there was anything positive about it.

However, our superintendent and the outside consultant they hired for a large sum of money have flown all over the United States explaining our successful human-relations program to other school districts.

At the same time all this is going on, they have hired assistant superintendents and educational psychologists for everything but curriculum. All the emphasis in our district is on rinkydink programs that the administration falls in love with and not on classroom needs.

These teachers—most of whom gave other teachers high marks for wanting to do a good job in spite of lack of administrative support and misplaced emphasis—agreed that every principal and district administrator should be required to teach in a classroom at least part of the time. When they don't, the teachers said, they lose contact with the realities of educating children; like the Emperor and his new clothes, they stand around naked and think they are beautifully dressed.

Explaining the web of educational financing would require another book; but where the money is *not* going concerned my group of classroom teachers and will concern parents as well. "No attention is paid to educating the *average* child," said one teacher, and this brought a chain reaction of nods from colleagues.

"This year," said another, "our school board spent the whole year studying the overall program. One evening they discussed nurses, the next psychologists, an evening on a career opportunity program, another on the educationally handicapped program; but not one hour did they spend evaluating the regular classroom program. They said they wanted to find out what was happening in the schools, but all they ever talked about was jazzy programs."

"We have four high schools in my district," added another teacher. "In two of them students are expected to do average work; it's the other two which get all the attention, the new programs, the special money. In this district kids are rewarded for not doing or being unable to do average work, and the average child is never mentioned—never mentioned."

educationally handicapped: the social engineer's gold mine?

In every area of modern life where teachers, parents, and children come into contact with the social engineers, the experts' tendency toward creating new and exotic specialties and promoting increased job opportunities for themselves is evident. This tendency in education has resulted in rigging the system against excellence and achievement.

No thoughtful, compassionate parent or teacher doubts that it is right and reasonable for schools to spend adequate money to help slow learners and the handicapped. However, something is "grossly askew," notes columnist James J. Kilpatrick, when North Carolina spends $740 per pupil on the handicapped and $40 per pupil on the gifted or talented pupil. I don't mean to imply that the gifted are ignored, but rather that funds allotted them are small change.

In 1975, the Education for All Handicapped Children Act was passed by Congress, which established the rights of the handicapped to education and offered funding to any state that provided such education. Handicapped children were defined as those who required some form of special education and perhaps some related services, such as transportation or speech therapy. These children first had to be judged to be mentally retarded, physically or emotional handicapped, or having specific learning disabilities. This sounds like a just law, if a bit open-ended, but let's see what has happened to it in the hands of the social engineers and the education establishment.

The Bureau of Education for the Handicapped (BEH) has become the source of $800 million in grants each year for the education of the handicapped. It enjoys the enthusiastic support of Congress, especially since it says 12 percent of America's school-age children need special education. BEH experts told Congress while it was considering the education bill for handicapped children that there were *millions* of undiscovered, untreated handicapped children in the schools.

But the biggest problem since the bill's passage hasn't been stretching the money appropriated—it's been finding that many handicapped children. The average number of handicapped reported by the states is only 7 percent of the total school-age population, not 12 percent, and some states have even reported figures as low as 5 percent. Now numbers like these might jeopardize increased appropriations, giving some congressional budget-cutter an excuse to reduce BEH's paycheck. What was the answer? Operation Childfind. BEH, convinced that local educators just weren't looking hard enough for the handicapped, cranked out memos to state-education bureaucrats expressing disappointment with the numbers of handicapped children the states were producing. Next, news stories were launched in the media urging parents of the handicapped to assert their "rights." Unfortunately for BEH, the "shortage" of handicapped schoolchildren persists.

What did my group of teachers have to say about education for the handicapped? There was no argument that the special-ed classes for the retarded and the physically handicapped were necessary. But there was no unanimity on the subject of educationally handicapped, or EH, children. An EH child is classified as one of normal intelligence who is doing work two years below grade level and who may have learning problems such as reversing or jumping vision, poor hearing, or writing problems. Other EH students have emotional disabilities such as hyperactivity and inattention. These students can definitely benefit from good EH programs. They are not the problem.

"Out of the 12 students in any EH class," said one teacher emphatically, "it is my opinion that maybe two have genuine learning problems and the other ten have behavior problems. They're the kids who have been written off and allowed to get two years behind."

It is ironic that the education experts who encourage teachers to write off children in the first place later provide costly catch-up programs for these same children. "A district doesn't get extra money to be firm with kids or to label them behavior problems," observed a male teacher.

According to this group, teachers do not want their own children in EH classes. Said one:

> I know a junior-high teacher who thinks EH kids are goof-offs. Whenever he is firm with them in his classroom, they

complain to the EH coordinator, who excuses them from his class. This teacher sees these kids as just not wanting to work and thinking they don't have to. You can imagine how upset he was when a teacher told him his own little girl's behavior was so bad she would have to go to EH. "Would you give her one more day?" he asked the teacher.

The next morning when he brought his daughter to her classroom, he told her that if her behavior wasn't perfect he'd spank her, even though he didn't believe in spanking. After school the teacher told him her behavior wasn't perfect but that it had improved and she could come back one more day.

The next morning he took her to class and again insisted that her behavior had to be perfect. He's a gentle man, but he did mean business. He said, "I don't think EH is the answer for most kids; I think making them behave is the answer."

Not all in my teachers' group agreed with such methods. "You can't threaten a kid into learning," one said. But all agreed they might be tempted to try something similar if the child going to EH were their own.

Why? Because few EH children ever make it back into the mainstream of education, say the teachers I talked with. "They're gone," said one of the group. "These are the kids we don't save. I'm afraid we're putting a lot of money into programs for children who have discipline problems, calling them handicapped, when all they are is overindulged."

We need more parents in the schools, agreed the teachers. "Parents could make a real difference," says sixth-grade teacher Reno Dawson. "If parents took turns on the playground and heard the foul and vulgar language their kids use, things might begin to change."

Things must begin to change. Parents need to get personally involved in their children's schooling, to be visible in every aspect of education. The decline of education is not irremediable. Parents *can* make a difference.

CHAPTER 9

the parent revolution goes to school

Having worked their "magic" on the family, the social engineers turned to the schools in the 1960s, finding them an ideal testing ground for their entire package of nostrums. Neil Postman notes in his *Teaching as a Conserving Activity* that "the student population was viewed as through a Rousseauian glass, unrealistically. Typically a school was imagined to be a place of obtuse, malignant adults who were dedicated to oppressing pure-hearted, liberty-seeking, instinctively humane children. With such cartoon-imagery as this it is no wonder so little was accomplished."

understanding the let's-all-hate-teachers syndrome

Talking with teachers about their work, as well as conferring with them as fellow parents, I found that I had a residue of ill feeling toward their profession. How could this be? My sister and brother both teach, my mother taught in a one-room country school, and my grandfather taught mathematics at a military academy in the 1880s. Schoolteachers have had a beneficial influence on and in my life. As a mother, my contacts with my daughter's teachers have been mostly pleasant. Why, then, did I feel this lurking prejudice against the entire profession, the same feeling I heard other parents articulate? What is happening to erode teacher status in our society?

The real villain is neither parent nor teacher—it is the submarine of social engineering. Parents and teachers, in the same lifeboat, have been torpedoed by the permissive child advocates of the Peter Pan age.

Lessened respect for teachers is related to the same youth-culture changes that belittled parents. In the case of teachers, the process was given a boost by such best-selling books of the 1960s as John

Holt's *How Children Fail,* Jonathan Kozol's *Death at an Early Age,* and Herbert Kohl's *36 Children.* These and other books, berating all authorities including parents, police, and employers, created an image of the classroom teacher as inept at best and a tyrant at worst. Sound familiar? Change the word "teacher" to "parent"; the same propaganda worked to undermine both. The education experts portrayed youngsters as victims of teacher failings and exonerated them of the responsibility for learning. Parents didn't even have to read these books to begin to believe that all teachers were not to be trusted—the idea percolated into every home through television interviews and newspaper stories.

The social engineers, supported by media hype, succeeded within a few years in breaking up the traditional collaboration of parents and teachers. Divide and conquer, if not the motive, was the result. Parents were fed stories about teachers who were unqualified, sadistic, money-hungry, and unwilling to help little John or Jane reach the peak of self-expression and creativity. Meanwhile, teachers were told that parents were apathetic, alcoholic, no longer active as parents, and trying to dump all their problems on the schools. The result: The adults who mean the most to children and who, in many ways, share the same "lifeboat," were set at each other's throats.

There are bad teachers, and the criticism that *some* young teachers are purveyors of anti-family youth culture has merit. There are bad parents, and the charge that *some* parents expect the schools to parent as well as teach is also true. But the majority of teachers and parents are caring and well qualified. In the parent-led counterculture of the 1980s, let teachers and parents join forces—teachers to support parental prerogatives and parents to support the teachers' authority.

For years we have lived with interference in the education process by social engineers. Now it is time to restore mutual respect between parents and teachers, bring order to the classroom, and teach children to use their own language properly and their own reasoning powers. All this—not to mention imparting knowledge of mathematics, history, and literature—might seem like trying to put the toothpaste back in the tube. But I am convinced that it is possible to install this reasonable platform. Of all the anti-family forces parents face today, the education establishment is the one with which we can deal most directly. It is in the schools that we can have our greatest impact. Parents in the 1980s will knock on the schoolhouse door and stick a foot inside before the door can be slammed. Even though it sounds like a slogan for the annual PTA membership drive, parent participation is a viable answer to parent dissatisfaction with the schools their children attend. But not many parents can manage this traveling-salesman chutzpah without first getting rid of all notions of inferiority skillfully planted by education's professionals.

government and the schools

Parents will be faced with these crucial questions in the 1980s: Is the public school a delivery system for social change, or is its function the teaching of basic skills? What skills should be taught to the approximately 45 million students in more than 90,000 schools at an annual cost to taxpayers of more than $84 billion?

Most of the parents I heard from believe that the primary purpose of schools is to teach children what they need to know to function in the world—the basic skills of reading, writing, and computing. But these parents think today's schools are not teaching skills but are meddling in the areas of sex; drugs; and racial, social, and psychological counseling.

Parents have the educational bureaucracy and its coterie of child advocates to thank for much of this situation. Under cover of enlightened ideologies and self-righteous social progress, these elements have used the schools to feather their own professional nests. Unfortunately, they have the power to move Congress far beyond what one would think possible, considering their relatively small numbers. Claiming to speak for parents as well as for every minority group in this country, their latest federal-funding successes (at this writing) have authorized federal money to cope with just about every social, racial, ethnic, and intellectual problem in existence. The 1978 omnibus education bill authorized federal money for poor students; gifted and talented children; bilingual education; adult education; energy, environmental, consumer, and biomedical enrichment curricula; school guidance and testing programs; schools under desegregation orders; after-hours use of school buildings; educational equity for women; ethnic heritage programs; Indochinese children; and so forth. Evidently the serious doubts of the 1950s about whether the federal government belongs in education at all have long been resolved. Congress acts more like a giant county school board than the federal legislature, dealing with questions that should never get beyond the local level of parent-influenced, elected school boards.

A basic controversy arises between New Traditional parents on one side and the educational establishment, funded by the federal and state governments, on the other: Whose values shall be taught in the public schools—those of the parents in the community or those of the professionals?

To Paul Haubner, an inquiry specialist for the National Education Association (the powerful 1.8-million-member teacher's association/ union), there is no question about the right answer. Speaking in a curriculum workshop, Haubner said he thought there could be no room at the local level for parental preferences about the kind of values they want taught to their children. "The key here is the search for truth," he said. "Our goals are incompatible with theirs [parents]. . . . They want to tell you what the truth is and not search for it. We must challenge values. The schools have to have controversy."

Few parents would agree that the values of the experts should supersede their own. Neither does Dr. Onalee McGraw, education consultant with the Heritage Foundation, who says in *Family Protection Report,* "Educators currently simply do not respect the values of the community. They think they can autonomously decide what is good for children. But they can't; parents have that right."

Parents should be aware that the federal educational bureaucracy has wrested most of the power from local government and parents. Massive federal funding of education has led to government intrusion into local curricula. The whole pattern of federal funding has been to extend control, which limits the freedom of parents to educate their children as they see fit. Local education is choking on red tape and regulations, not only from federal but also from state intrusion. In California, state regulations fill four volumes; they even control the number of fruit trees permitted on school grounds.

Despite widespread talk about reinstating local autonomy, the trail to Washington is heavily traveled by the professionals in the educational establishment seeking funds. The only solution for parents who want to regain control of their children's education is to restore the capacity for local response to local problems. My research has convinced me that parents will regain power only when they keep school-funding monies in their own hands.

the department of education versus parents

"When a bureaucracy is ineffective," says Paul Johnson in his *Enemies of Society*, "its frustrated response is invariably to seek more authority and expand its bureaucracy."

Rounding up more than 150 federal agencies and programs that had been operating in six different cabinet-level departments, the Department of Education was formed in 1980 with a start-up crew of 17,000 and a budget of $14.2 billion. Shirley Hufstedler, a former judge and the first secretary of the department, while paying the required obeisance to local control, also stated that the department would focus on the needs of "the deprived, the handicapped, and the disadvantaged." It is clear that instilling social, not primary, skills remains the goal of the new department. Once again, the federal government has sent the arsonist to put out the fire.

Installing a voracious professional bureaucracy and feeding it extensive funds will almost inevitably heighten federal intervention in local education. Rather than simplify, it is sure to complicate the miasma of "mediocracy" now passing for federal education programs.

"Most federal programs don't work," said one classroom teacher I talked with. "Right now we have a right-to-read program going on that a number of teachers are paid an extra $1,200 a year to attend. Most of them use the time to catch up on their crocheting.

"One worthwhile piece of information came out of the whole year's program. The reading teachers learned a simple system to help poor readers get more facts out of nonfiction reading—but that could have been taught in two hours."

The Center Joint School District in North Highlands, California, set a precedent in 1973 by pulling out of two government-funded programs (one federal, one state). Eighteen months later student test scores had *risen* in reading, mathematics, and language. Other bonuses—this time for teachers—were less paperwork, fewer government regulations, and fewer outside evaluators "dropping in" to impose their ideas.

Charles Frye, a California public-school teacher, says this of a cabinet-level Department of Education: "It will produce a veritable bonanza for the establishment, a potentially limitless source of jobs, funds, and authority. On the evidence, it would almost certainly tend to institutionalize the erosion of standards and calcify the inanities of the last ten to 20 years." Few parents would argue against a national education policy evolved through public debate and study. But that is not the case when powerful bureaucracies mandate change and dictate to local school districts.

how parents react

Parents are their children's first and most natural teachers. Every professional teacher I talked with assured me that it is impossible to teach children without the support of the children's parents.

I asked parents in my survey whether their experiences with their own children's schools had been positive or negative. Their answers were mixed: 40 percent said their experiences had been negative; 30 percent said they had been positive (30 percent of this number had children in private schools); and 30 percent said that they had had both negative and positive encounters. Many of the negative responses reflected feelings of being shut out of the educational process.

One of the ways in which parents feel cut off from decision-making is in teacher selection. Not only do parents in most school districts have nothing to say about who teaches their children; they also find it nearly impossible to get rid of bad teachers. Tenure laws, which after a certain number of teaching years virtually guarantee jobs forever, make it difficult to fire a teacher. And the legal responsibility for assessing teacher competence usually rests entirely with the school administrator, who may be understandably reluctant to admit a mistake in hiring. A Kansas mother of five told me this story:

> My youngest daughter had a fourth-grade teacher who was unbelievably insensitive. She made remarks such as "You must have been dropped on your head when you were a baby," or "Do your parents feed you right?" My girl was mortified and upset almost every day. We had one conference after another with that teacher until one day she sent home a note, saying our daughter was masturbating in class and should be taken to a psychiatrist! I was

shocked. I went to the classroom and discovered that the floor under my daughter's chair was uneven, causing the chair to wobble back and forth. This teacher hadn't even bothered to check before making such an accusation.

I went to the principal and got a transfer for my daughter and suggested that the teacher should be fired. You know what he said? "It's true this teacher is a little eccentric, but it would be too much trouble and cost too much money to try to get her fired"!

Stories like this get around a community. There need only be a very few such instances to completely spoil an already strained parent-teacher relationship.

Teachers in my talkshop group told me they don't want such people teaching any more than parents do, but they have just as much trouble getting rid of them.

Parents in three school districts, one in Utah and two in California, came up with a way to weed out unsatisfactory teachers. Under the plan, parents who question the competence of their child's teacher can request a Review of Services. The district administration then appoints a learning specialist to investigate. If the allegations are verified, the teacher is given additional training in his or her problem area and then is reevaluated. If at that time the teacher has not met the standard, resignation, early retirement, or termination follows. Since the same process applies to administrators, parents in these school districts have a heightened sense of participation. It should be pointed out that less than 4 percent of these districts' teaching staffs are reviewed in any one year.

A similar system in every district could go a long way toward improving school staffs and eliminating parents' frustration.

the voucher system and return to fundamental schools

The dissatisfaction with public education runs very deep among most parents. A New Jersey mother of three, a former teacher, summarized the feelings of many parents:

Billions of dollars are being poured into this country's educational system every year, but educated kids are not pouring out. Parents, who pay for it all, are being ripped off, and kids who won't get another chance at an education are being cheated, too.

The only way out of this mess is for parents to put the money back into their own hands; because once the bureaucrats get hold of it, parents have no control over how it is spent.

What this parent advocates is the voucher system. According to economist Milton Friedman, who first proposed vouchers in the 1950s, this plan would bring the philosophy of the marketplace to education. The government would provide parents of every school-age child with a certificate, or voucher, good for one school year of education. The parents would then use the voucher to enroll their child in a school of their choice, public or private. However, if the parents should become dissatisfied with a particular school, they would have the right to transfer their child to another. Simply stated, the traditional allotment of public tax money to schools would be replaced by handing the same money directly to parents to buy whatever kind of education they wanted for their children, including private and religious schools. Parents who want their children to have special opportunities in music, science, or athletics would be able to enroll them in schools that emphasized those subjects. Parents who wanted their children to have a strictly disciplined three-R's program would have as many rights as parents who wanted their children to have unstructured self-exploratory programs.

What could be more logical? Given falling test scores, rising illiteracy, top-heavy administrations, busing, and educational experimentation, is it so farfetched for parents to say, "Okay, if the government can't educate my kid for $3,000 a year, give me the $3,000 and I'll find someone who can"?

But giving parents a choice always throws the educational bureaucracy into a tizzy. Their decision-making power threatened, they fight every voucher plan with wild rhetoric. California state schools chief, Wilson Riles, declared during one such "family choice" drive that it would pave the way for state financial support of schools run by "cults" such as "the Ku Klux Klan, Nazis, or the Moonies."

While concerns over legitimate minority interests are sincere, the basis for such fears is usually the idea that parents really don't know what is good for their children and professionals do. The educational bureaucracy is not about to give up its power to parents.

Two California law professors, John Coons and Stephen Sugarman, in their book on the voucher system, *Education by Choice,* say: "The combination of compulsory school attendance, the public school administrative structure, and the taxing apparatus displaces the normal parental choice standard and substitutes a presumption that . . . the state must dominate the prime hours of the average child's day."

What voucher plans try to do, according to Coons and Sugarman, "is build a new system of public education that is attractive to the middle class, which ultimately must pay for it." Under such a system, the schools would no longer be controlled by federal or state educational bureaucrats and legislators but by parents, who would become the center of power in education. The educational establishment either would have to respond to parents' demands as education consumers or go out of business.

traditional schools

Earlier in this century, Justice Oliver Wendell Holmes wrote: "At this time we need education in the obvious, more than investigation of the obscure." Holmes was right then and what he said is just as true today.

In my home state of California, 13 percent of all school-age children are enrolled in private—for the most part traditional—schools because parents want their children educated "in the obvious," now called "basics." These schools have waiting lists of not just wealthy parents, but of working-class parents as well. In fact, 59.4 percent of parents sending children to nonpublic schools nationwide have incomes of less than $20,000. These parents know that students in such schools score about two grade levels above the national average and that the schools accomplish this with a smaller teaching payroll and fewer frills. Basic schools, traditional schools, or fundamental schools—whatever you call them—emphasize reading, writing, math, science, and regular homework. They also have strict discipline, which includes no smoking or free dress code on campus.

One of the most miraculous of the small, traditional private schools sprouted in a shabby, all-black, poverty-level neighborhood in Chicago. Nearly two hundred children crowd into the school of teacher Marva Collins (the waiting list contains hundreds more). These ghetto youngsters learn Shakespeare and Dante, drill in multiplication tables, write daily essays, and memorize a poem every week—all without federal funds and with nary an administrator in sight. They are not gifted children. Many of them, according to Collins, were seeing psychologists or were in special learning centers when they came to her. These same children who now tackle Aristotle and Nietzsche would probably have wound up in classes for the educationally handicapped had they remained in public schools.

At private St. James Academy, also in Chicago, inner-city children, many of them public-school dropouts, are given a course in basic discipline as well as basic academics. Students wear blue-and-gray uniforms and stand when answering questions and whenever an adult enters the room. Tardiness is fined. Graduation requirements are rigorous: Students must maintain a 3.5, or A, average and be accepted by three colleges. These standards of excellence insure that 97 percent go on to college.

With such shining examples, parents cannot be blamed for turning to the private sector or for seeking a voucher plan to put their children into schools that reflect their family educational values.

in the 1980s parents should be seen and heard

A teacher strike is a crisis for a family, and 59 percent of parents I surveyed feel strongly that there should be no such thing. But parents realize that strikes have increasingly become a teacher weapon. In 1960, there were only three strikes in the entire nation. By 1980 the average was 122 walkouts annually. If strikes are inevitable, many parents believe that *they* too should be represented during arbitration. A father from Washington, D.C., says:

> *The teacher's union represents the faculty and the school board represents the administration; but parents and children get lost in the shuffle.*

Among parents surveyed, 12 percent said that they should not be on arbitration committees because "that's what we pay administrators for." Some of these parents were also strong union people. Almost a third of the parents had no opinion about parental involvement, many of them voicing the belief that they were unqualified to judge teacher disputes. However, the majority of parents thought parent representatives should sit in on teacher–school-board negotiations, not merely as observers, but as participants with the clout of a vote. Parents could act as a strike-breaking third party in bogged-down meetings.

When parents have a voice in strike negotiations, other fantastic things might happen, says Louis Fein, founder of the Palo Alto (California) Learners Association. "Take such things as teacher evaluation, tenure, or student discipline," he says. "The teachers' unions are so strong, and the [school] boards so eager to reach some sort of settlement, that these things, which might be of major interest to parents, get pushed aside in favor of such matters as pay and working conditions."

New Traditional parents must be ready for more direct involvement in the decisions that make a difference to their children's education. Recently activist parents crossed picket lines at a "struck" school in Honolulu to teach classes themselves.

Another area in which parents of the 1980s will be seen and heard will be the selection of textbooks. The parents I surveyed voted nine to one in favor of parent representation on committees that select textbooks. One Ohio mother of two, with a master's degree, gave a thoughtful answer:

> *Which parents should be on the committee? English majors like myself, or conservative high-school graduates who become irate when the curriculum committee selects "immoral" books—like something by Norman Mailer, for instance? If both types of parents were included, it would give fair representation. Parents would have to be selected as carefully as a jury.*

Other parents embraced the idea of parent input unequivocally. This from a Georgia mother of four, a former teacher:

> *Yes, yes, yes! Part of the problem with education today is the course of study presented by anemic textbooks. I had better textbooks in Iowa a jillion years ago!*

An Idaho father concurred:

> *Parents need to be included. We shouldn't leave such a heavy responsibility to an agency too easily influenced by free gifts from publishing companies. I'm not advocating censorship, but parents look at textbooks from a different perspective, which the schools need to consider.*

Book-burners! Censors! These old scare cries are nearly always raised when parents want an equal vote with education's professionals. Yet something must be wrong with textbooks when more than 200 formal and informal organizations of concerned parents rise up in one decade to question the content of textbooks, as they did in the seventies. The literati, as H. L. Mencken called them, have brought it on themselves, and nowhere was this point made more clearly than in Kanawha County, West Virginia, in 1974.

A "passel of over-educated doctors of philosophy," in the words of columnist James J. Kilpatrick, sought to impose what the parents considered ultraprogressive texts on a Bible-believing rural community. The parents rebelled. "Nothing in the name of academic freedom," commented Kilpatrick, "requires that taxpayers forever yield to the supposed superiority of professional educators."

Mothers and fathers of this West Virginia school district pulled their children from public schools and bitterly protested the teaching of values that were totally opposite to those they taught their children at home. Parents charged that their children were being taught so-called situational ethics, a doctrine that says there are circumstances when it is "right" to steal, kill, or have premarital sex. One parent, a critic of textbooks, called this "advocating psychological warfare against parents."

There are new and different textbooks in Kanawha County's public schools today. The new books were chosen from 6,000 screened by textbook committees made up of teachers and parents.

The list of communities where concerned parents are questioning the quality of textbooks began growing at the end of the 1970s. "The primary cause of widespread citizen disenchantment with school policies," says Dr. Onalee McGraw, "is the education establishment's insistence that the main purpose of education is social engineering at the expense of development of basic skills and the intellect." She sees a loss of local control, replaced by a state and federal takeover of the public-school system and by groups of politics-playing professional educators with "pseudo–social science nostrums."

Every public-school district needs to establish a parent-review policy before textbooks are adopted. Committees should be weighted in favor of parents and teachers, not in favor of professional administrators and others far from day-to-day contact with children.

your child's education—the rights you have and need

You have rights as a parent: to see instructional materials funded by tax monies; to visit your child's classroom; to call a conference with the teacher; to request that your child be excused from certain school activities to which you object; to look at all your child's school records; and to speak at public meetings of your local school board. Some of these rights are restricted in certain states, while additional rights, most concerning appeal procedures, are granted by other states, but basically this is the lot. (Citizens in Education, 410 Wilde Lake Village Green, Columbia, MD 21044, has printed a Parent Rights Card that lists them all.)

Parents need to lobby for parent participation in the basics of school operation. Parents should be included on committees for curriculum-planning, teacher- and administrator-hiring, textbooks, and strikes, and on any other committees that relate to the education of their children. The schools should bring parents right into the classroom to share their skills and experiences. Education will be more effective when parents are directly involved in school activities with their children, and the earlier they become active the better. The presence of parents in the classroom, starting with elementary and continuing in secondary schools, could help with the adolescent's separation from the world of adults. And above all, parents need to hold out their hands to good teachers, reforging a broken link in the chain of authority that children desperately need in a confused society.

We parents are powerful because we pay for schools. We have allowed the professionals to run things because we *trusted* them. Now we must take the reins into our own hands.

As members of the new parent counterculture of the 1980s, we must fight to regain local control of public schools and resist further government encroachment. As parents, we must unite against the desire of social engineers to promote permissive values in our schools. The family and schools have been conceived of for more than 20 years as two separate educational systems, linked only by the child who moved between them. In the 1980s, they must become *one* system, learning from and respecting each other. Most important, this united system must foster in children the idea that they come to school to learn, to behave, and to do their work.

Family-oriented parent groups—PTAs, too, if they are willing to shed their image as cookie-sellers and administration go-alongs— must become involved in evaluations of parent-school relations and help determine how individual schools can improve communication and establish real, working partnerships with parents.

The future must provide more consensus, not more diversity, in education. As Donald Thomas, superintendent of Salt Lake City schools, says: "Creating more diversity among schools in an already diverse society could only lead to greater confusion and conflict." Consensus, on the other hand, would ease the strain on many American families and help speed the transition to the New Traditional Family.

legal entry—television intruders in the parent-child relationship

Television dominates many American homes. Parents and children sit in front of the set (or sets) much as families once gathered around the fireplace for warmth. Yet this new family center results in little warmth and almost no family interaction, even in homes where traditional values are esteemed.

Survey statistics in this chapter do not begin to convey the intensity of parents' feelings that there is something malevolent in the way television, with its repudiation of middle-class values, has invaded our homes. We cannot help but see how this youth-oriented entertainment medium has increased the deep preoccupation of our children with themselves, since youth today takes its image of itself from itself—an anti-Pygmalion effect. "The media give substance to and thus intensify narcissistic dreams of fame and glory," says Christopher Lasch in *The Culture of Narcissism.*

Mass communication, like big government, big education, and big social services, is incapable of being neutral. When the youth culture is the dominant influence, as it is today, parents and traditional values are bound to be ill served. Any number of learned studies have asked the question, Is television a mirror of society or the inventor of society? One would hope that it does not mirror reality. A study of 58 hours of prime-time television, cited in 1980 by Michael Robinson, a Washington professor, found five rapes, seven homosexual acts, 28 acts of prostitution, 41 instances of intercourse between unmarried people, and six instances of intercourse between married couples. (Unmarried sex was about seven times as popular with television writers and producers as married sex.)

What have been the side effects of this kind of communication in middle-class homes? How have the technological innovations that thrilled us so when we watched our first Ed Sullivan show come between parent and child?

Parents in my talkshops and surveys believe that television has presented their children with views of life that they think about and, in some cases, try to imitate. How children speak to each other and their parents, whom they admire, how they behave, what values they hold, their human sensitivity—parents think that all these things have been negatively influenced by the medium.

how television undermines parental authority

It has been said that most parents welcomed television as a built-in baby-sitter. But there is more to the story. Parents have been told, and have believed for a generation, that modern society is based on information and that the future belongs to those young people who are getting up-to-date facts. That is one reason parents have said a reluctant yes to television, despite its cultural impact on families.

But by the 1980s television had managed to provoke something close to a rebellion among the parents I interviewed. Many described the ways in which they were trying to control this technology and not play second fiddle to it in their own homes. Methods ranged from putting the set under lock and key to not having broken sets repaired. These parents expressed a fighting-the-good-fight philosophy, like modern-day St. Georges slaying evil dragons.

It is not surprising that parents react heatedly to the very mention of television when one considers that from age 5 to 18 the average American child views between 15,000 and 18,000 hours of television. The chunk of time taken from family life is enormous. And the result of all this watching is not children soaking up more useful information, but passive youth absorbing more love-thyself messages. Another result can be put in terms of what these children are *not* doing: They are not reading, helping about the home, working with Mom and Dad, or practicing the piano; they are not listening to *real* adult conversation or assimilating the values of their families and their ancestors. Instead, they are getting an overdose of permissive, child-liberation viewpoints.

Television writer Ben Stein claims in his book *The View from Sunset Boulevard* that each night television audiences are exposed to near-lethal doses of permissiveness from a small band of fewer than 400 Hollywood writers and producers who exercise an enormous influence over prime-time programming. Kathleen Nolan, president of the Screen Actors' Guild, says: "The heads of the networks are parasites and tasteless mercenaries. They've trashed up the airwaves almost beyond repair."

During the late 1970s and into the 1980s, a succession of sitcoms and made-for-TV movies promoted a glossy, anything-goes attitude toward premarital sex, homosexuality, and even incest, all in the name of encouraging democratic tolerance. This move toward wide-open social values may have been envisioned as bringing realism to the small screen, but it has caused deep divisions in American homes. As media-soaked youth have moved leftward in social matters, parents, seeing the discouraging results of permissive child-rearing, have begun a shift to the right.

For years such anti-violence groups as the Boston-based Action for Children's Television and the National Congress of Parents and Teachers have blasted away at Saturday-morning television shows that portray gratuitous mayhem and sell with a pervasive commercialism sweets that batter young bodies with sugar overloads. But minimal attention has been given to the moronic light in which parents and families have been depicted, conveying a frightfully unbalanced picture of the American home.

Dozens of doctoral dissertations every year argue whether or not television is powerful enough to make a change in the way parents and children in the 1980s interact. Most parents I talked with tend to believe that, of the four anti-family forces I explore in this book, television has created the most mischief.

A Wisconsin working mother gave me this thoughtful reply to a question about the power of television in her family:

> When my kids compare me to the Brady mother, who sits around talking about her children's mundane problems while the maid does the work, then I know I'm coming off second-best. It's unreal when TV parents are always focused on their children and not on paying the bills and making leftovers stretch another meal—at least part of the time.
>
> Of course television is powerful. If TV has no impact, then why do politicians spend millions on it?

how parents are patronized on television

I asked parents in my survey an open-ended question: How are parents portrayed on TV? Ninety-three percent had negative answers; 2 percent said they weren't portrayed at all; only 1 percent felt that they were portrayed positively; and 4 percent thought television parents were a mixture of positive and negative. This is not the picture of a satisfied audience. In one parent talkshop, a mother interrupted a discussion of the effect of cartoon programming on children with this thrust:

Parents are the real cartoon characters on television.

In today's television, children know best. They have taken over the role of authority figure from Father and Mother, who, in episode after episode, just can't manage life in the new youth culture without supercilious instruction from their patient but despairing offspring. Grown-ups and parents are always in a dither over sexual questions on which the nearest adolescent enlightens them along with some near-incomprehensible human potentialism. For example: Father— "How can I keep my son at home?" Daughter—"Hold him with open arms."

Adolescents on television, sensing the "incompetence" of their elders, often turn to understanding peers for guidance and when parents try to intervene, treat their ideas with amusement and contempt. To quote again from Stein's *The View from Sunset Boulevard:* "Television shows on prime time are a new folk culture . . . contending with the time-honored wisdom. . . . This new folk culture is relentlessly attacking the old."

Almost every parent critical of television felt there had been an unhealthy erosion of children's ability to emulate parents and that this was perpetuating the child-centered family. Some parents thought television had supplanted parental authority and even the natural affection children feel for parents. Many had heard of the Longwood College (Virginia) study that compared the degrees of attachment children feel for their parents and for television, finding that almost half the preschool children preferred the tube to Daddy. Adolescents rated parents even lower than did preschoolers. Another study showed that three-fourths of the boys and four-fifths of the girls wanted to trade in their parents for more glamorous models.

No corresponding studies are available for the 1950s, but it is beyond belief that children of that period could have preferred Howdy Doody to Father or rated Lucy, no matter how they loved her, over Mother. What has brought about such a change in values? It must have something to do with the way parents are depicted on television. Here are some observations by parents, the first from a father in New Hampshire:

> *I see parents walking around with a drink in their hand, usually rich and attractive, often single, and almost always not as smart as their kids.*
>
> *They don't act like parents at all, they're so permissive and modern.*

A California mother sees more variety in television parent roles but concludes they don't help parents much:

> *I find it just as negative when TV portrays parents as either models of virtue and intelligence, knowledgeable beyond belief, or as abusers and negligent. Both the mollycoddler and the tyrant are unreal. Where is the average parent?*

This from a South Dakota couple with two children:

> *We feel the insidious approval and encouragement of casual sex, drugs, and violence on television is ultimately more harmful to the family than hard-core porn. We can control the movies and the magazines our children see but it's difficult to monitor all the television they view. Most of this indoctrination in garbage is aimed at our adolescents—that's just the time we try to solidify morals and values and the time when our kids think we're square old fuddy-duds who don't know the score.*
>
> *Television has made our job almost impossible.*

television and your child's behavior

What does television do to your children's behavior? This is not an unreasonable question, since you have to live with the results. I was not smart enough to know how corruptive television could be, thinking that all information was a good thing. I now believe that every viewer is to some degree brutalized by watching violence. Young children, especially, are desensitized to parents and family values by watching oversexed, undereducated, drug-oriented, illiterate characters on the screen. There are plenty of reports from individual researchers to the American Medical Association that point to a rise in the level of aggression in youngsters watching "kidvid," from Saturday-morning cartoons to prime-time sitcoms. But how does this translate to behavior in the average American home? An Indiana mother of two answered this way:

> *TV makes my kids very sassy and their conversations are unreal. At first I thought they were simply using their imagination but now I think it's TV's influence.*

A Colorado mother had this to say:

> *They think whatever they see on TV must be okay, including scant clothes, foul language, disrespect to adults, and violence. It makes corruption, evil, and violence an everyday occurrence in our house.*
> *TV introduced them to ideas before they were mature enough to sort through their own feelings about them.*

Ninety-one percent of the parents I surveyed thought television had a negative effect on their children's behavior; 7 percent thought their children unaffected; and 2 percent were not sure. I am not being unfair in presenting only negative parent quotes: *Not one parent out of more than 400 thought television had a positive effect on their children's behavior.*

Neil Postman, in his report on how television affects schoolchildren, says, "There are, even now, observable behaviors in our youth that indicate they are undergoing certain serious psychological changes, at least in part attributable to television." Among the behaviors Postman notes are a shortened attention span and diminished linguistic powers, which include a decline in writing ability. Lack of adequate language, Postman points out, can lead to emotional maladjustment.

television and your child's moral growth

Many parents think television has enormous power to change the moral tone of society. But most of those I talked with felt that television was using this power to replace the home-taught values of

their children with, if not a preference for the vulgar, at least a toleration for the violation of basic rules of decency. Mother-son incest,
the gang rape of an adolescent girl by other girls and unnumbered
other rapes, murders, mindless brutalities, and both extramarital
and premarital couplings are examples of this kind of violation.

The parents were asked: How do you think TV affects your child's
moral growth? Sixty-six percent thought television had a negative
effect; 32 percent thought television had no effect (primarily because
they believed they countered it); and 2 percent thought it had a positive moral effect, most of these parents citing *The Wonderful World
of Disney, Sesame Street, The Waltons,* and *Little House on the Prairie.*

One Nebraska father wrote to me of his adolescent daughter:

> *Her moral values differ from mine and I truly think it's the result
> of seeing divorce, extramarital experiences, and homosexuality
> treated on TV as normal ways of life.*
>
> *I believe that my standards of morality have been sabotaged, even
> though I am constantly teaching correct principles and my daughter
> doesn't even watch television all that much.*

A Wisconsin mother of four thought:

> *Television is bad and getting worse. It exposes our children to
> ideas and concepts before their morals and values have had time to
> formulate or be tested in a slower manner.*
>
> *The government—or somebody—has to control television before
> it gets worse. Television has no conscience.*

Despite screams of McCarthyism, some people have joined together to boycott the unwholesome in television. A group called the
National Federation for Decency (NFD) is aiming its protest where
it counts—at the advertisers. None other than former Federal Communications Commission (FCC) head Nicholas Johnson thinks such
a boycott is a legitimate weapon. "In every other market," he explains, "the consumer can register his views with dollars. If he
buys a product, he makes a vote. If there were an alternative to boy-
cotting sponsors, I would be the first to welcome it. But the networks
offer no recourse but protest. They brought it on themselves with
their intransigence, insularity, and refusal to deal with viewer
complaints."

How effective is this tactic? NFD boycotted Sears, Roebuck and

Company stores in 36 cities before Sears' announcement that they had withdrawn commercials from two programs with a high titillation quotient.

While doing some research for a historical piece, I recently came across two news articles, both from 1906. One detailed the accidental hanging death of an 8-year-old boy while playing cowboys and Indians, and the other told of a boy who was paralyzed after jumping from a cliff in imitation of a hero. The young, of course, have always been fascinated by the celebrities of their age and have emulated them. But the process has become considerably murkier since these pre-TV days. Parents complain of behavior that runs from "He thinks he can break up our furniture just like the Hulk" to "She wants to dress like Charlie's Angels." But imitation may be even more subtle. Television analyst Dr. Arthur Asa Berger speculates that the medium may be changing our basic concept of personality with its super-rich diet of strong, assertive celebrities. "Without realizing it, " he says, "the silent, passive nobodies may be adopting these flashy individuals as role models."

Has television helped give the Peter Pan generation its norms? A Wisconsin mother of three adolescents thinks so:

> *Television is shaping my children to a standard that doesn't exist in the world we know. But I think my kids are growing up today to think that what they see on TV is normal. Last year, it suddenly became fashionable to have actors play homosexuals in series. My junior-high son looked at that and thought, "Maybe I am, too."*

the built-in family separator

While Daughter is in her room watching cartoons or *Star Trek* reruns, Dad is in the living room watching a sports broadcast and Mom is in the bedroom watching a drama. Television sets proliferated in affluent middle-class families to accommodate individual tastes, but soon they served to confirm separateness. In my own home, I gradually became aware that occasionally two of the sets were tuned to the same channel, but this did not serve to bring those members of the family together. Our solitary viewing habits had become entrenched.

Marie Winn, in her landmark book, *The Plug-In Drug*, says:

"Early articles about television were invariably accompanied by a photograph or illustration showing a family cozily sitting together before the television set. . . . The splintering of the multiple-set family was something the early writers could not foresee."

In one of my parent talkshops, a mother warned other parents present:

> *If I had it to do over again, I would never get my children their own sets. I thought I would be alleviating the fighting between the children over what programs to watch. I thought I was giving them a marvelous present but it turned out to be a weapon aimed right at the heart of the family. They can go to their room, shut the door, and escape into a world I am no part of. There is no togetherness when there is more than one TV set in the house.*

Sociologist Urie Bronfenbrenner gives this explanation of how television comes between parents and children: "Like the sorcerer of old, the television set casts its magic spell, freezing speech and action, turning the living into silent statues so long as the enchantment lasts. . . . Turning on the television set can turn off the process that transforms children into people."

Fifty-one percent of the parents I surveyed thought that television had negatively affected their child's attitude toward them; .5 percent thought it had positively affected their attitude; and 48.5 percent thought there had been no effect, although several of these parents said, "But I may be a fool."

why not turn the set off?

Sociologist Henry Malcolm observes that television tends to short-circuit the parents' attempts to civilize the child. Dr. Benjamin Spock adds that watching too much television can also inhibit the development of a child's imagination and that "all that action is too appealing for children to turn off the set by themselves." If that's the problem, then the solution seems to be that parents need only pull the plug. Almost every article or talk-show discussion of recent years ends with the parents being held responsible for abolishing the negative effects of television on their children. Just pull the plug, goes the prevailing wisdom. "There's always the off button," says family counselor Eda LaShan.

Of course supervising television in the home is the parents' responsibility. But I do not believe that parents are thoughtless, selfish creatures who have abandoned their children to the television set any more than I believe that parents need continuous, expert counseling on every aspect of parenthood. And turning the set off is only part of the answer for families. According to Colonel Doner, head of a TV watchdog group called Christian Voice, "You can't turn off TV after the fact. If you see or your children see something offensive on television, you have already been assaulted. It's too late to turn it off then."

Then there's television fallout. You may turn off your set, but if 50 million other sets are on, television is still shaping the world in which you and your children live.

What's the answer? Most parents I talked with nixed the idea of getting rid of home television entirely—they enjoy relaxing with a good television program, too. But they did have definite ideas about program content. Here are some of them, the first from a Utah mother of three who wanted to see fewer movies about the broken family:

> *Too many TV shows make the broken family seem the norm. Personally, I feel it's less harmful to see violence than the subtle insinuation that there really are no families consisting of Mom, Dad and kids or even grandparents who aren't divorced or sleeping around.*

A mother of five from Louisiana wanted to see the parents' side on television:

> *On our TV stations we get announcements, I think from the Mormons, that are well done but slanted toward the child. One showed a child bringing in the groceries and the mother finding fault, or the dad not having time for the son when he asks him questions. Of course, we parents need to be considerate, but how about a few announcements showing children mouthing off or being thoughtless, demanding that parents pick them up or bring them this or that? How about showing Mom wearing a ten-year-old coat because the kids need orthodontia or Dad working with Scouts rather than playing tennis?*
>
> *I have a very complex 16-year-old child, who runs the full gamut from being "the neglected child," "the overprotected child," "the no-body-cares child"—whatever has been shown on television lately. It*

would be refreshing to hear about "the abused parent" or, better yet,"the neglected parent" on television.

A Massachusetts mother of three added this thought, which was typical of many parents:

> *Let's have more family shows that extol solid virtues, that show parents knowing best. Many critics find it insipid, but strong moral lessons taught by TV parents who know best and whose kids are able to see their mistakes have a power not lost on the young viewer. I know sophisticated people look down their television noses at the 1950s, but that was the last time television was a truly positive family activity.*

television and the new traditional family

It has come to this: Parents believe that television has usurped their role as principal moral teacher and that it has caused children's lives to separate from those of parents, even while they live together as a family. When parents perceive this, they often want to turn the set off, black it out, throw it away. That's a normal reaction to danger— but it's not a panacea for a family's problem with television, because television in the 1980s is for this culture something like water for fish—we're so surrounded by it we can't swim out.

Getting rid of television may be a legitimate answer for some families, but not for most. Television provides us, parents and children, with a vital window on the world. The instinct to protect children is nonetheless correct. Parents of family-centered New Traditional families must take control of television's influence in their own homes.

Taking control will often mean saying no—an unpopular thing to do in a society that says yes indiscriminately, not only to television but to all things that feel good at the moment. But there are as many ways to take control as there are determined parents. For example, a single mother told me she had her set rigged with a lock so her children could not watch while she was at work. Other parents had a master switch that turned off the circuits to their living room. All these parents wanted was to insure that children did not watch TV when they were not there to identify family values.

The most successful control of television was among families in which parents selected the programs. Parents *can* select. One Massachusetts mother of three tells how it works in her family:

> *Every Sunday when the television-program guide arrives in the paper, my husband and I sit down and plan the family's viewing for the week. We limit viewing to one hour on weeknights and two hours on Saturday and Sunday and* we *choose the programs. As our children grow older, we will invite them to take turns making choices for the family, but we will have a veto based on our understanding of program content. In our family, parents are the television critics.*

In some families a period of abstinence from television has improved family interaction. Dr. David Clark, dean of the graduate school of communications studies at CBN University in Virginia Beach, Virginia, told the American Family Forum in 1980 that his family practices a one-week television fast every month. "The first week we did this," he says, "strange things happened. We discovered that we didn't use the same tone of voice with the television off. When it's on our voices were much more strident."

A California mother of two told me she had turned the set off for an entire winter when her two children's grades began to slip:

> *At first there was bitterness and recrimination from the children. They hated it. I even wondered if I wasn't being too harsh, especially when I missed something I wanted to see. But gradually at first and then more rapidly, I began to see marvelous changes. Not only did schoolwork improve, but our family life was more creative. We did things together, we talked, we argued and we played—and yet, we all had much more time than we had ever had.*

Not all parents reported success at their attempts to control television. A Nebraska mother of five says:

> *Forget it! We tried family viewing and I tried to raise conversation about a moral issue and got derisive laughter.*

If parents are to control television in the home, there must be a functioning family, which means parents who demand respect and assume authority. In my own case, family viewing helped me to define my own values. There was no way I could watch most prime-time television with my child without agreeing or disagreeing out loud with the values represented there. More often, I discovered that my beliefs could not remain theoretical but had to become specific in terms of everyday living.

defusing the entertainment-media mine field

In the New Traditional Family, the television must be a part of family ritual; it must have the warmth of a fireplace, where parents and children interact with each other. Parents report that some rather simple steps can enhance family television use:

1. There can be no family-centered viewing with parents in control if there is more than one set. New Traditional parents, as they prepare to fight media intruders for the hearts and minds of their children, have to place restrictions on second and third sets in the home or get rid of them.

2. Parents must select or approve the programs to be viewed by the family. Children presently spend twice as much time in front of the television (six hours a day, for a total of 42 hours a week) as they spend in school. It is the main source of their ideas, so in that way all television is educational. Parents must decide what kind of "education" they will allow their children to receive.

3. Parents should structure the television-viewing area so it takes on the aspects of a second family hearth. Seating should be arranged so parents and children can see each other, as well as the screen, to allow maximum interaction even when there is no conversation. Facial expressions are important. An alert parent can discern emotional responses to television material and speak to them.

4. At times, parents may decide that a TV fast or a reduction in viewing is wise. At other times, an especially worthwhile program can bring a relaxation of the rules. Parents are certainly free to watch adult programs whenever they wish. Older children may view programs not allowed younger ones. In far too many homes today, the overdemocratization of the family has forced parents into stunned hours of cartoon-watching and children into viewing programs that are too sophisticated. Television is as good a place as any to return to the sensible idea that maturity has its privileges.

In the hard, day-in, day-out work of trying to teach our children values, parents realize they are going against the grain of the current culture. The only way to rebut anti-family messages coming through television is to sit down together with our children in front of the set. The aim of the New Traditional Family is to build a family-centered family. There is no reason that television should not be included in home life as long as we parents remember that we have a perfect right to say yes and no to what our children watch.

television advertising—education in consumption

Children's author Maurice Sendak once wrote a story about a pampered dog who had her own pillows, comb and brush, a red wool sweater, two windows to look out of, two bowls to eat from, and a loving master. Despite all this, the dog ran away from home, complaining: "I am discontented. I want something I do not have. There must be more to life than having everything!"

Parents reading this story to their children today must find it disturbingly familiar. We give and give, but our children often tell us in so many words that having everything isn't fun anymore. A Nevada mother wrote:

> *We can afford it so we indulge our children's material requests. I purchased an expensive English racing bike for my son, who refuses to ride it because it's the wrong make.*

Other parents I talked with thought that there were disadvantages to the many advantages that middle-class children enjoy today. An engineer father who said he had given his two adolescent boys "everything" told me:

> *They have $100 skateboards and $3,000 cars. They don't have to work the way I did when I was a boy, yet I wouldn't trade my childhood for theirs. They are constantly whining about how rough they have it; how miserable they are; how much more every other kid has compared to them.*

A whopping 98 percent of parents thought television advertising seduced children (and themselves) into a materialistic view of life. Parents said that commercials "make children think everyone has got one" and "make Christmas a nightmare of 'gimmes.' " A Rhode Island mother of two young boys said:

Every commercial brings on an "I wish I had that" or "I want that."

It is not just preschool youngsters who are affected, but also adolescents, according to this mother of three from Oregon:

I resent the commercials that tell my teenagers that they can't enjoy a picnic, boating, or skiing without the "right" designer jeans and shoes.

During their growing-up years, American youngsters with $30 billion in annual discretionary income are bombarded with more than 675,000 full-color commercials. They are, in fact, becoming what social commentator David Riesman once termed "consumer trainees." In television commercials that are present-oriented, individual-centered, and age-hating, adolescents are told that the sponsors' products guarantee happiness. The fraud of Madison Avenue perpetuates the self-delusions of the youth culture since it reinforces the concept that happiness is external, is only a matter of attaining the proper image by drinking a macho beer, driving an expensive automobile, or taking the right vacation.

Advertising encourages an "unappeasable appetite," says Lasch in *The Culture of Narcissism*, "not only for goods but for new experiences and personal fulfillment . . . upholds consumption as the answer to age-old discontents . . . institutionalizes envy and its attendant anxieties."

The psychology of the human-potential movement, with its twin themes of self-commitment and desire-equals-need, is a crucial tool for advertisers in an age when many products are essentially the same. "When two or more brands are generally perceived by a substantial number of consumers to be comparable," says one advertiser of competing colas, "the brand that says the more desirable things about the user will have the greater chance for success."

If I read that quote right, the advertiser is really saying three things about youthful consumers, who spend $300 million on cola a year: (1) Many young people know there's no difference in the products; (2) The triumphant cola will be the one that flatters the young more; and (3) The important thing is not a better product but better advertising.

Advertising flatters the young by giving them a mirror image of their own culture and acknowledging them as full-fledged consumers, independent of parental controls. According to Lasch and others, this has altered the authority of parents in relation to their children. This consumption propaganda raises the anxiety level of parents, who ask, "How can I satisfy their needs when they need so much?"

A California mother of one boy says:

> *As a young child, 3 to 6 years old, my son would constantly call me into the TV room to show me what he wanted. He had a long list of wants. I felt guilty because it required so many "no's" just to get through the day.*

One Ohio mother summed up the feelings of a lot of parents who are constantly badgered for slickly advertised products:

> *I must spend half my day explaining why this cosmetic or that one is no better than a cheaper product. But my daughters think only superhyped cosmetics are the "real thing." They want to buy every expensive shampoo, deodorant, and mouthwash on television. They think every product mentioned will make them beautiful and desirable. In our family it has caused an "inflation" problem. One of my daughters has 12 hairbrushes and her hair still looks terrible.*

A Virginia mother of two said advertising was the number-one villain of television:

> *Advertising reaches far more people than most programs because it is shown over and over. Such repetition promotes the idea that you can buy your way to happiness. Advertising gives my children a superdose of the importance of physical attraction, stereotyped male-female roles, and the idea that sex can be bought with the right mouth lozenge. Products on television seem to solve in 30 seconds the problems that my children will have for a lifetime. What a hoax!*

how can parents counteract harmful television advertising?

The purpose of television advertising is to make money. Teaching children this will help them view advertising more realistically and will be more effective than any government regulation or intervention. So much of advertising claims to offer children better lives, help them develop poise and confidence, and win the attention and admiration of peers. The truth is that modern advertising seeks to create needs, not satisfy them, and to promote new problems, not solve real ones.

In the New Traditional Family, it will be just as important for parents to point out the sell intent of advertising as it is for them to point out the moral content of programming. Parents, far better than some national nanny in Washington, D.C., can teach their children to evaluate product claims and can bring their own consumer experience to bear on brand choices. One mother in a parent talkshop has helped her children develop a healthy skepticism by reproducing selling gimmicks in her kitchen:

> We tried a paper-towel test and found that a soggy, wet towel will not hold a cup of water. My son tried to make margarine talk and the vitamins march around the table. It was all silly but that was the point. Now my kids talk back to the commercials. The other day my 4-year-old daughter was watching a little boy's stomach ask for more cereal and said, "They just want me to buy that cereal, huh, Mom?"

Several groups, including Action for Children's Television and the National Congress of Parents and Teachers, have attacked sugary advertising aimed at increasing the desire of younger children for sweet snacks. As far as I can determine, no group has come out against the candy-coated life-style advocated by many commercials. Everything that the fun-loving young do, from taking instant pictures to using the right toiletries, fits into the happiness-through-consumerism message.

Abstract qualities like self-control and discipline were once seen as marks of character, and children were encouraged to control their appetites. Today, through television advertising, the young are encouraged to satisfy their appetites without delay. Character-building has been traded for self-image.

Parents are fighting a Goliath of slick advertisements for the minds of their children. The marketplace is willing to spend $600 million a year to win, to show children the illusion of a world that can be possessed, enjoyed, and even manipulated at will. Parents will have to spend more—in time and energy—to train children that deferred gratification is often the greater value. A Pennsylvania father of two, a sociologist, told me:

> *The whole culture is indoctrinating our kids by appealing to their impulses—the sexual impulse, the impulse for excitement, the impulse for a good time. Be spontaneous, they are told. But we parents have to counter this cultural influence with what may seem very old-fashioned advice—you work hard, you save your money and then you get what you want.*
>
> *We must do this. We parents represent the last generation who knows that the spontaneous life is a disastrous life.*

A good many parents, more than 100,000 every year, complain to the FCC about television programming and advertising. These complaints are usually passed along to the networks because the FCC is prohibited by the constitution from censorship or prior restraint. That makes the networks powerful indeed, and puts a few top executives in charge of just about everything beamed in to our families.

Product boycott is one of the most direct ways parents can take *action* to let sponsors know they are unhappy. There's nothing subversive about a boycott; it's a cherished American right. I am struck by the double standard the entertainment industry applies to First Amendment freedoms: The networks seem to believe they have an inalienable right to broadcast any material, but groups with differing opinions that choose to use the same free-enterprise system are guilty of censorship.

But you as a culture-countering parent of the 1980s are even more powerful. You can control television instead of letting it control your family. Once aware that television too often reflects and reinforces the culture of the street, you can select and supervise the information you want your children to receive in the home. You can concentrate the family's free time on sports, hobbies, family ritual, or academic and social pursuits—a host of almost forgotten alternatives that will bring parents and children closer together instead of driving them farther apart.

CHAPTER 11

media fallout: movies, junk rock, children's books

Parents have termed the portrayal of middle-class families in television silly and stupid, but the portrayal of families in movies (that eventually reach the small screen) is nothing short of disastrous. Movie parents are variously incestuous (*Chinatown*), repressive (*Interiors*), ethnically neurotic (any Woody Allen film), cloying yet domineering (*Lost and Found*), or neglecting (*Autumn Sonata*).

The back-to-back successes of *Easy Rider* (1969) and *Woodstock* (1970) ushered in the movie mentality that condemned everything traditional in American society, repudiated the desirability of growing up, and romanticized the fierce demand by youth for approval and immediate gratification. This new theology—orchestrated by screaming tires, crashing trucks, and the endless liturgy of the moment, the now, the feeling—dominated films aimed at our children.

Sexual sophistication and eroticization of very young girls were the themes of a succession of R-rated movies during the seventies: *Taxi Driver, Pretty Baby, Little Darlings*. The peers of these barely pubescent actresses were not supposed to be old enough to see them, but they flocked to theaters; in the case of *Little Darlings*, to discover which actress would lose her cinematic virginity first. I can only guess how it affected adolescent boys and girls, but as a parent of a 16-year-old girl sitting in the audience of some of these movies, I kept thinking, "Say it isn't so."

Home life in these films, when depicted at all, was usually a chamber of horrors with parents the ultimate in uncaring, unfeeling ogres. I can think of no more dangerous cultural force against parents and family life than these films.

Also in the 1970s, a strange new breed of film appeared. These films, including *The Exorcist* and *The Omen*, featured evil children with supernatural powers who preyed on parents, portrayed as their

167

hapless victims. Heaven knows what psychiatrists could make of this.

The slick young stars of today are hardly in the same league as those of the pre–Peter Pan era. Who can imagine Donald O'Connor worried about impotence, Jane Powell betting she would bed a boy before Margaret O'Brien, or Andy Hardy, a devil incarnate, plotting the ghoulish demise of his mom and the Judge?

Joan Didion, in her *White Album*, comments on made-for-youth movies that adults are not meant to see. They show the young hating everything moral and decent and tolerating necrophilia, gang rapes, the brutalization of citizens who get in their way, and multiple beatings for anybody who "acts dumb." The point Didion makes is that the young, as pictured in these movies, see themselves as justified in the grossest behavior because they have been "hassled"—beating up an old man who gets in the way then becomes a "right."

"To imagine the audience for whom these sentiments are tailored," she writes, "maybe you need to have sat in a lot of drive-ins yourself, to have gone to school with boys who majored in shop and worked in gas stations and later held them up . . . children whose whole lives are an obscure grudge against a world they think they never made. These children are, increasingly, everywhere, and their style is that of an entire generation."

I asked parents how they determined whether or not their children should see a film. Many said they used the alphabetical rating system (G, PG, R, or X) but most thought the system didn't work very well. Most concerned parents felt the PG rating (Parental Guidance Suggested) was the most ambiguous; one mother told me she thought it should stand for Pretty Gory. However, many parents thought any system was better than none if violence and sex were going to be incorporated into the majority of movies. Does the current rating system work? I asked parents. Seventy-four percent said no. Only 47 percent thought their children observed the rating system, but they weren't sure. "Once they're on wheels," parents said, "you don't know what they're seeing." One Ohio mother had the cynical thought that the rating system was just another ploy to disarm worried parents:

> *It doesn't work the way they say it does. Theater owners don't turn any kid with $4.50 away, and if there is an honest owner, my kids can always find some obliging adult to take them in.*

This Arizona mother of two thought R ratings actually attracted young people to more adult films; she made a funny—but sad—observation:

> *Sure the system works. My girls see every R- and X-rated movie that comes to town.*

But an Oklahoma mother thought ratings were a helpful early warning system:

> *It alerts me to the type of movie it might be; then I can apply some good old censorship.*

In general, parents' criticisms of movies were similar to those they had of television: too often they reflect a taste for violence; they show explicit sex and use raw language; everybody is divorced; everybody lives in New York or Los Angeles and has an interesting, high-paying job; and all the children are trendy and liberated.

Richard D. Heffner, the chairman of the Code and Classification Board of the Motion Picture Association, rightly says it is the role of parents to express their will and control their children, but wrongly absolves the film industry of moral responsibility. The rating solution, says Heffner, is "the best solution I can think of when you come to the question of freedom of the filmmaker and creator and the responsibility of the industry to the public and public interest."

Not many parents are as concerned about the freedom of filmmakers as they are about what passes for family entertainment in the theater. An Idaho father of three concludes:

> *There were only two G-rated movies shown in our town last year, so if I want to take my family to the movies very often we have to include some PG films. That means if my 14-year-old enjoys it, my 6-year-old will have nightmares for a week. Going to the movies is no longer a family activity.*

But a mother of two adolescents, who spoke of the "immorality and general grossness" of films today, struck a sensible note when she said:

> *In reading over my responses to this media survey, I certainly sound like a cross between the inventor of the chastity belt and Carry Nation. I'm not quite that prim. On occasion, I enjoy a risqué film. But I'm not 12 years old.*

In 1968, when the Motion Picture Association of America's rating system began, 41 percent of all films were rated G; by 1980, only 3 percent were. The G-rated film carries the stigma of not being able to attract audiences. Even the Disney Studios admitted to having a character in *The Black Hole* say "damn" to ensure a PG.

During the 1970s, as films became more adult while audiences grew younger, some excused the violence and near pornography of many films because they were portraying a serious slice of life that could provoke profound thoughts. Asked to comment on such films, Academy Award–winning actress Katharine Hepburn said: "Filth is not an intellectual pastime, it's filth."

It may be difficult to prove a connection between youthful aggression and movie violence or between increased teen pregnancies and "sexploitive" films, but are parents to assume these are mere coincidence?

A Minnesota mother of six wouldn't chance it:

> *One day in 1978 I was driving to pick up my children and passed through an area just three blocks from the high school where so-called adult bookstores and X-rated movie houses were operating. I was shocked to see young people entering the theater.*
>
> *The next day I returned with four other parents and we observed boys and girls whom we knew to be under age buying tickets. We filed a complaint with the district attorney and a judge issued a warrant closing the movie house.*
>
> *We lost the trial because the theater owner was able to prove that some of the kids used false identification. At first I was frustrated but now I really think we won a victory. The publicity has made theater owners think twice about checking IDs, and parents are much more aware of the films playing in town.*
>
> *Some people thought I was a real busybody, but I believe I have a right to raise my children in a community free of the influence of pornography. The Supreme Court says I have that right. We parents have to work to make society safe for our children.*

Not all of us can or want to go to the barricades like this parent, but we can assert parental censorship over the films our children see and, insofar as possible, try to make movie-going a family activity once again.

music that creates the savage beast

Parents of every generation born in this century have cried wolf over the way their children expressed their view of reality through music. My grandparents, raised to the strains of Sigmund Romberg, looked askance at ragtime and jazz. My own parents saw lasciviousness in the "jungle beat" of Stan Kenton. But now that the wolf is actually here, no one is listening. In the sheep's clothing of the $4 billion rock industry, a real wolf is devouring a generation of young people.

Routinely, Top-40 songs pay incredibly crude tribute to prostitutes ("Bad Girls"), necrophilia ("Cold Ethyl"), homosexual love ("Glad to Be Gay," "Get Down and Make Love"), sexual gratification ("Wild Love" and hundreds of others), marital infidelity ("Part Time Love"), cruising and boozing ("2-4-6-8 Motorway"), adolescent sex ("Good Girls Don't—But I Do," "Baby Talks Dirty"), and drugs ("Cocaine").

Accompanied by a surging, sexually explicit beat, rock music took a horror-movie turn in the late 1970s. Groups like Alice Cooper, the Sex Pistols, Black Sabbath, and, most notoriously, Kiss—the vampires of rock—screamed songs in the style of "Psycho-Killer" and "Werewolves of London" and pandered to the inexplicable taste of some young stagedoor zombies for on-stage vomiting, spitting, and spurting blood.

There is something about the obsession with the self that makes this horror revival a look at the dark side of the human-potential movement, says Ron Rosenbaum, author of *Rebirth of the Salesman: Tales of the Song & Dance Seventies:* "The assumption of the therapies associated with that movement is that, once freed of internal and external restraints, the self will be free to grow and fulfill itself." The idea that the rock-music ethos is mind-controlling is not just old-fashioned parents crying wolf again.

It's not difficult to see why the young have responded to the brainwashing lyrics and music of idols who have become, literally, a pressure group for a drugged-out, sexed-out life-style. A London magistrate put it mildly when he told Hugh Cornwell, lead singer of the punk rock group The Stranglers: "You have a great influence on the life-style of teenagers and should not cause damage to those who admire you."

But musicians who owe their popularity to the young have not been constrained by youthful hero worship. A long list of rock musicians have self-destructed on drugs—uppers, downers, and everything in between. The picture of drugs as an integral part of the profession that is the most attractive to the young and one of the most rewarding financially is bound to have brainwashing power.

This music also provides the ritual chorus, the superseductive background for boy meets girl. Henry Malcolm, in *Generation of Narcissus*, calls it an erotically oriented cultural force: "The songs which are sung," he says, "are filled with completely explicit erotic meanings, couched in a message for the youngsters to appreciate, while in the dance styles, the male and the female participate in what amounts to ritualized lovemaking. . . . The fact that the old 'bump and grind' movements which used to be characteristic of the gyrations of an erotic dancer or stripper have been adopted by most younger people today points up how physically erotic the dances are."

Malcolm would get no argument from two-thirds of the parents I surveyed, who think that "junk" rock has had a terrible influence on the morals of their children. A mother of three girls said:

> *The worst influence of their young life came from rock music, the musicians who perform it, and the irresponsible creeps who market it.*

An angry Ohio father of four:

> *Only one of my daughters was really into rock music and she was on drugs bad—that music was just part of it.*

A mother of six from Louisiana even blamed rock music for traffic accidents:

> *Try driving in a 35-mile-an-hour zone with a rock group screaming through four speakers. The kids can't do it. No wonder so many young people smash themselves to bits on the highways.*

In their obeisance to the great god Communicate, some parents have tried to establish family intimacy based on listening to rock music together. A California mother of one boy described something more akin to martyrdom than communication:

We sat with him and listened to each new album. Although we heard rock music ad nauseam, we did not criticize in a derogatory manner. We respected his right to enjoy "rotten music." I'll never forget the day my husband and I sat for almost three hours listening to one album!

But the worst of it was when we finally realized that what we were doing had nothing to do with real communication. It was all one way.

And from an Indiana mother:

I'm not a snob. I like all kinds of music, including rock. Young people will always have their own music: I know I did. My problem with it is when the message is pro-drugs, pro-sex, anti-family and anti-America. My family is in enough trouble without messages like those.

Seventy-five percent of the parents I polled said they had made an effort to listen to rock lyrics, often with shocking consequences. Parents said they were "sick" to think that their children heard this "trash" for hours on end and that most of them seemed to accept it as ordinary, everyday reality. An Idaho father of nine has made a personal crusade of copying the lyrics of current hit songs and passing them out to parents at meetings. He told me that 71 percent of the popular records he heard in 1979 contained sexual innuendo aimed at youth. (Ironically, public-service ads on rock-music stations, sandwiched between "let's get it on" records, often advertise prenatal clinics for expectant teenage mothers.)

I go to parents' groups and urge every mother and father to turn on the radio and listen, really listen, to the words of the songs their children are hearing. Then I tell them to write to the radio station and tell the manager exactly what they think. If parents don't complain, there will never be an end to it.

Many parents I talked with noted, as I had, that too much rock music, rather than being a forum for interaction, is an almost insurmountable barrier between parents and their children today. "It prohibits conversation; it blocks out attempts to communicate," they told me, confessing that their children used their music as an adolescent security blanket that helped them to wall themselves off from the rest of the family. Parents saw this as a sign that their children had further seceded from family life to hear the messages they preferred full-time. A sorrowful mother, troubled by her 14-year-old daughter, put it this way in a parent talkshop:

She climbs into rock music and pulls it over her head.

When the self becomes the goal of existence, such music is the ultimate way to pay attention to one's self. Parents perceive reality in different terms, so often our children can play their music right in front of us and we cannot decode its message (that is one reason, I believe, that 33 percent of parents thought children unaffected by rock music). But parents must decode it to counter its influence in the home.

The youth-music industry is an incredibly powerful institution and so much the fashion that many parents are embarrassed to challenge even the worst of it. We have been manipulated into believing that it is an art form, both musically and poetically. Remembering our own parents' cries of "Wolf!" we have feared to appear foolish. We have assured ourselves that at worst it is banal, not dangerous. Such thinking is cold comfort. Given the opinions of the majority of parents I interviewed, I don't believe there is any question that the message of much of the music our children listen to daily is the total destruction of a moral code thousands of years old.

Parents have every right and responsibility to listen, really listen, to the messages their children get from music and to censor them when they are in conflict with family values. Most parents exercise control of the volume of stereos in the home; surely the battle for our children's minds is at least as important as the battle for their hearing.

children's books—look what slid down the rabbit hole

Parents found children's books the least objectionable of all the media influences. When I asked them what they thought of the social-awareness themes in books, 48.5 percent thought these were positive, while an only slightly larger group, 51.5 percent, thought they were negative.

Many parents believed reading so beneficial for their children that they encouraged it without too many reservations. Other parents were as concerned with the possibility of censorship as they were with moral problems raised by controversial, downbeat children's books about such social themes as divorce, homosexuality, incest, drugs, interracial marriage, adolescent sex, suicide, and alcoholism.

What may be unknown to parents is that this emphasis on social problems is not happenstance, as Children's Book Council Director John Donovan confirms: "The great effort right now is to integrate books with American society. A great many books are being published for social rather than literary reasons. Books with a social message dominate the scene . . . books on every conceivable ism—books that make a point or teach a lesson."

As a writer I am protective of First Amendment rights of free speech, but I do not think that we parents can suspend individual judgment in the name of democracy, even though the book-burner epithet may sometimes be thrown at us.

Many parents do agree that there is a need for the so-called problem novel for young people. One mother said:

Such a book might help a child make peace with himself or bring a problem out into the open so that parents could deal with it.

But few parents who support the problem novel are talking about the "will she or won't she" books that deal with the "problem" of teenage virginity in such explicit scenes that the fact that she "doesn't" is hardly more than a technicality. Other books apply the popular human-potential movement theme of "discover your feelings" to a wide range of what were once considered adult dilemmas. These and other social-awareness books tend to support the youth-culture status quo, which all too often runs counter to family moral teachings.

Problem novels have proved to be highly profitable in children's book publishing, which netted $185 million in 1979. School libraries stock them, teachers assign them, and even reluctant young readers read them. And isn't that the idea—getting kids to read?

Although about half the parents I talked to said yes to problem novels, to protesting parents these books look less like literature and more like primers for crude street language and sexual precociousness. Parents hate to be called censors or, even worse, Nazis, so few will lodge a formal protest with librarians or school boards. A Pennsylvania mother who did told me her experience:

> *The school librarian made me feel like I was incredibly backward. She said, "Kids are exposed to all kinds of language and life-styles in newspapers and on television. They live in the real world." But that was just my idea. My kids are exposed to bad language, drugs, and rotten behavior all the time. Surely when they pick up a book, they should be able to read works of art, the classic tales. There should be one place left in this world where they can enjoy enchantment.*

It is not just the proverbial overprotective parent on the political right who wants to monitor children's reading. Attacks also come from the political left and from minority groups, who succeeded in having *Mary Poppins* removed from the children's shelves of the San Francisco public library because of its offensive treatment of minorities. *Tom Sawyer,* too, was removed from other libraries for similar reasons.

Children's books, especially those aimed at the teenage market, are sophisticated and flashy in theme and design. But how do they treat the parent-child relationship? In far too many of the ones I reviewed, parents have replaced the wicked stepmother of folklore. Parents are too often portrayed as insensitive and downright abusive, and there is an enormous amount of hostility expressed by youth toward adults. The happy ending comes when the young person throws off the adult yoke and becomes, in terms of the human-potential movement, his or her "own person."

The trade term for books that present both problem and solution is bibliotherapy. It seems unlikely that the same therapy would work for every child, just as the same medicine would not; indeed, it could make some sicker. A California mother of two girls worried that too many books for young people painted an unnecessarily grim picture of the world. She said:

> *I think a steady diet of the lower realms of reality gives children an unbalanced and scary view of the world. I don't want my daughters haunted by drugs, drinking, divorce, and despair.*

No one expects young people to read mild little stories of friendship between animals forever. But the usefulness of relentlessly grim books filled with stereotyped realism and shallow solutions involving "learning more about me" is equally questionable.

Almost half the parents I talked to thought problem books for young people could be a good thing if parents were there to answer questions and point out areas of conflict with family standards. These parents, who remembered a time when the rites of passage involved a harmless first lipstick or first date, were grateful that contemporary problem novels gave them a starting point in family discussion.

A step in the right direction is the Children's Book Council's parent activities committee, as long as it represents the spectrum of views, including the traditional. But the most important step for the family will be parents exercising their right to supervise their child's reading so that it teaches, encourages, and dramatizes the dignity and basic worth of family life.

In the late 1960s, social prophet Marshall McLuhan wrote: "Just as we now try to control atom-bomb fallout so we will one day try to control media fallout." For many parents that day has come. The influence and youth-culture bias of some television, advertising, films, junk rock, and children's books constantly amplify the effects of the outside forces against the family. The entertainment media transform the destructive ideas of what is essentially an "adversary culture" (to use sociologist Daniel Bell's term) into acceptable images and parade them before our children dozens of times daily. The awful fact is that families are being methodically preyed upon.

When we parents complain, the purveyors of these destructive images crawl behind the skirts of the First Amendment and suggest that we don't have to watch or listen if we don't want to. Similar logic comes from drug pushers who say, "If I don't sell it, someone else will." Can you imagine the outrage if the water coming into our homes were laced with poisons and the utility company suggested it would be our own fault if we drank it and got sick?

We certainly don't want federal bureaucratic control of the media. But we *are* demanding self-control of the media. In the meantime, we parents must assert our traditional rights—those of selection and rejection based on our individual family values—so that our homes become not conduits for an image-huckstering, showbizzy, valueless culture, but havens from it.

PART THREE

FAMILIES RENEWED

founding the new traditional family

take-charge discipline

Parents today face an enormous challenge: getting our derailed families back on track. We can accomplish this by reoccupying our rightful places as heads of our own households. But first we must reject as false the warning that our actions are a negative influence in our children's lives. Before we can take control again, we must overcome these feelings of self-doubt and recognize how tremendously positive our contributions to our children are; in short, we must reactivate our good parenting instincts. The result will be the New Traditional Family—a family that operates on a balance of love and discipline.

I asked parents of grown or nearly grown children what they'd change if they had child-rearing to do over again. Increased discipline was the most frequent response. "I'd insist my teenagers accept more responsibility for their actions" and "I'd hang on tighter, longer, and be tougher" were typical answers. A number of parents, looking back, rejected the guilt they had felt: "I wouldn't worry as much about all the 'what ifs' in parenting"; "I agree with Art Buchwald that there are more disappointed parents than disappointed children." A father of five in Missouri summed up the feelings of many parents:

> *For years I've been asking myself, Where did I fail? And my kids, especially my oldest boy, have been laying a guilt trip on me, telling me it's my fault they're hooked on dope and can't hold down a job.*
>
> *Just this past year, I've been able to get out from under all that guilt. I'm sick of taking the blame for their messed-up lives. I look around me and I see lots of young people who didn't have what they had, whose father didn't work two jobs to send them to college— I see these kids making it.*

In the family-centered New Traditional Family, a system of love and discipline in the hands of take-charge parents can help eliminate false guilt and allow parents to say once again, "I don't know if this is right or not, but this is the way we're going to do it."

recognizing the pitfalls of parenting in the psychological age

Although the following points have been addressed generally in earlier chapters, it is important for us to confront them specifically in the context of take-charge discipline.

The first trap that has been set for parents is the communication trap. Bringing interplay into the parent-child relationship, we are assured, will increase understanding between the generations. "But there's such a thing as too much communication," many experienced parents tell me. The sad reality, as more than one parent has learned, is that "understanding" misbehavior often leads to setting too few limits. The French have an expression for it: *Tout comprendre c'est tout pardonner,* "To understand all is to excuse all." If we parents understand that a particular misbehavior is the result of this or that set of psychological circumstances, how can we hold our children responsible for their acts?

Despite research to the contrary, parents are listening to children. Parents want to be fair with their children, to hear their side. But the current emphasis on parents listening to children, while little or nothing is said about children listening to parents, has caused a kind of paralysis of discipline in some homes. Such parents are starting to ask, Are we "understanding" ourselves into immobility? The solution does not lie with standards of conduct so flexible that any emotional upset absolves a child of responsibility for behavior. Children learn from parents who set firm standards of behavior and then expect their children to follow them—not just when it's convenient and easy, but when it's difficult as well.

Another trap that blocks discipline is the professionalization of parenting. The love affair with experts that permeates this psychology-oriented age produces an environment in which parental impotence thrives. Parents tell me that when they began doubting their own problem-solving skills and sidestepped discipline, mothers, in particular, were afflicted with perfectionism. As one wrote, "I tried to iron the wrinkles out of everything." Both fathers and mothers longed for "the right to be wrong sometimes." It was as if they had actually lost the right to be humanly imperfect.

As parents we should be parents and not professionals. Our children are really our apprentices, learning from our mistakes as well as our strengths. What do we teach them if we convert their misbehavior into our own ineptness?

The shadow-parent trap is another pitfall. It's not surprising that loving parents don't like to discipline their children. I doubt that they ever did. But they like disciplining children even less in a period when traditional parenting duties such as discipline have come to mean "bad" parenting.

The notion that parental love must protect our children from emotional pain has supplanted in too many of us the traditional idea that love has to be accompanied by parental leadership. The conjunction of love and discipline is what will give our children the ability to accept the responsibilities of adulthood. Says Christopher Lasch in *Haven in a Heartless World*, "Without struggling with the ambivalent emotions aroused by the union of love and discipline in his parents, the child never masters his inner rage or his fear of authority. It is for that reason that children need parents, not professional nurses and counselors."

unspoiling psychologically spoiled children

Parents today are not encouraged by the how-to-parent experts to expect good behavior and good work. Rather, they are advised to "relate" in a "meaningful" way. Since few parents understand what this gobbledygook means, many loving parents end up permitting bad behavior because they have abandoned the take-charge attitude necessary to discourage it. "Relating" is translated by many parents to mean talking-listening-understanding. Dr. C. R. Partridge, a California child psychologist and a friend of parents, points out that this kind of relationship makes the child all the more comfortable with misbehavior and puts him in control of the family. Dr. Partridge believes that such a child's anxiety should be *increased*, or he runs the risk of remaining an emotional and social infant for life.

I'm convinced that many of the problems today's parents have with discipline began with the idea of the family as a democratic unit. This ridiculous philosophy, which has seeped into our consciousness from everywhere during the last 25 years, advises parents to eliminate the vestiges of their authority, to let their children grow without parental interference or instruction. Don't force children to do anything, the message implies. The result is that children begin to believe they are their own bosses, and parents—educated, caring parents—begin to believe they might be right.

So too many of us relinquished our right to expect much of our children, worrying that they would become overachievers or suffer emotional collapse under our "unwholesome" pressure. The results are in. This is the first generation of youth that will not achieve anything like what their parents have—in education, in job advancement, or in living standards. Of course, there is a raft of reasons for this, economic and demographic, but surely one of the primary ones is the false freedom of too few parental expectations. Lasch, in *The Culture of Narcissism*, points out: "When elders make no demands on the young, they make it almost impossible for the young to grow up."

getting tougher

"Permissiveness has not just been a failure; it's been a disaster!" says James Dobson, a psychologist whose book *Dare to Discipline* puts him firmly on the side of parents in the family combat zone. He goes on to give an excellent definition of child-rearing permissiveness: "The absence of effective parental authority, resulting in the lack of boundaries for the child. This word [permissiveness] represents childish disrespect, defiance, and the general confusion that occurs in the absence of adult leadership."

Instead of treating his spoiled patients conventionally with large dollops of support and image-building, Partridge takes a different approach. "Parents and teachers must also understand," he says, "that *augmentation of anxiety* is central to the treatment of these children" (my emphasis). In other words, he advises getting tough.

Along with suggesting behavioral techniques for teachers, Partridge recommends that parents withdraw regular privileges and "goodies" with a "we mean business" attitude. He warns against professional help (if parents think it necessary) of the usual kind. "Children who are already too comfortable and confident are not helped by professionals who hang on their every word and who counsel parents and teachers to remove pressures from them. . . . Generally someone who operates with a *strong measure of old-fashioned common sense* will be the most helpful." (Again, my emphasis.)

A message both revolutionary and liberating lies just beneath the surface of Partridge's words. *Stress can strengthen our children.* "Ironing out all the wrinkles" for them and protecting them from the frustrations of their own mistakes can deprive us of the very children we want to raise. Since so many families have been absolutely devastated by living with a Peter Pan child, this is a message of pure hope.

Don't mistake me. Children have human rights to loving care and protection from abuse and social rights to sufficient education to make their way in a highly technological society. *They also have an absolute right to adequate parental discipline to teach them how to eventually control their own lives.* The origin of the word "discipline" is, after all, the Latin *disciplina,* meaning "teaching."

Getting tough is not a reintroduction of nasty, repressive old authoritarianism. The dissolution of parental authority in these last decades carries with it no new freedom for our children; rather, it means a new form of tyranny by the youth culture over our children and us.

how parents discipline today

It appears that the "rod" is spared by parents I interviewed. Less than half (42 percent) spank their children. Of these, 45 percent use physical punishment only occasionally. Parents who spank do not belong to any one age group, profession, or philosophy. The only discernible pattern I found is that the larger the family, the more likely parents were to use spanking as a discipline. Most of these parents indicated that they also used nonphysical discipline along with spanking.

The controversy about spanking that has raged in recent years was very much on the minds of the parents I talked with. Many justified at length their use or rejection of corporal punishment. Generally, parents who spank thought physical punishment, as long as it was not brutal and was delivered in response to behavior a child knew to be unacceptable, was an important tool parents require to civilize a child. Parents who don't spank usually cited such reasons as the "sacredness" of the human body and their belief that violence teaches a child to be violent.

As a child, I was spanked. As a parent, I do not spank, having made a conscious decision that I am personally uncomfortable with this mode of discipline. However, my sister spanks and feels no such qualms.

I do not believe that corporal punishment is harmful in itself. The same can be said for the absence of physical discipline. The total picture of parent control is what counts. The cause of major problems is the failure to require children to obey the rules or suffer the consequences, whatever they may be.

The disciplinary measures reported by the nonspanking majority of parents in the 402 families I contacted can be loosely gathered under the heading "removal of privileges." These included, in the order of frequency reported, taking away something they wanted, sending them to their room, and restricting or grounding them. Other disciplinary measures parents used frequently were assigning extra chores, giving small fines, or letting children suffer the consequences of their acts, such as making a child walk to school if he misses his ride. More than one-fourth of parents said they tried "explaining, talking, reasoning, and understanding" instead of punishment. Only 5 percent listed such old-fashioned punishments as "standing in the corner," "writing 'I must not . . . ' " "washing the mouth out with soap."

Often parents wrote of specific, logical disciplines they had found successful. This mother of three, living in Virginia, said:

> *I caught my young son playing with matches one day. For the next two weeks his job was to empty all wastebaskets and burn the papers. Whenever a match was needed, he was chosen to light it. He was soon very tired of match striking.*

This Ohio mother notes that "humor helps":

> *When my kids get on a crying jag for no good reason, I tell them to go to the special "crying corner" and there they can cry as long as they want.*
>
> *Or I might grab a potted plant, rush over and stick it under the child's chin, saying: "Wait a minute, don't waste any of those tears!" The kids look at me like I am crazy, but the crying usually turns into giggles.*

A Georgia mother told me that it was hard to really discipline a child in middle-class families today:

> *Punishment means sending a child to a room that contains a radio, color TV and stereo record player.*

A savvy Oregon mother took a poll of her children to find out what her most effective discipline was:

> When I discussed this question with my kids, they said grounding was the most ineffective discipline and did no good at all, which leads me to believe that it was the most effective and did the most good.

five take-charge parenting attitudes

For a variety of reasons, we parents feel unsure. We wonder how far we ought to go to get our children to do things they don't want to do. There's no single prescription that will magically insure that all children at every age will go to bed on time, come to meals promptly, wear clothes appropriate to the occasion, help around the house, and keep their rooms neat. Child-rearing formulas for manipulating children's compliance might work with some children but create power struggles with other children.

However, there are *attitudes* New Traditional parents can have about their own authority that will allow them to discipline in their own way in their own homes. The first is that adopted by the mother who saw a "monster developing" and threw away her how-to-parent books: She has since stopped equating her worth as a mother with her boy's emotional response to her discipline. This was her way of dismantling the Love-Machine Mother:

> At first I kept thinking, "If I'm a good parent, my child will always feel good," and this was my downfall. When he'd cry and complain, I'd give in, cancel the discipline, and feel like a miserable failure.
>
> Finally, I realized that I was teaching my son that acting unhappy was a way to get what he wanted. I made a list of five progressively harder penalties for bad behavior—from 1, no television for a night, to 5, grounding for a week. Now, most of the time he chooses to behave rather than lose his privileges. But on occasion, when he carries on about it, the rule is that we go straight to penalty 5. I don't reward him for feeling bad anymore, and we both feel better for it.

A second attitude New Traditional parents need to cultivate is the sense that discipline *is* freedom for our children. What began as a movement to release children from the restraints of authoritarianism by giving them more freedom of choice has spawned anarchy in many homes. Far too many families today have become a mirror for permissive, child-knows-best theories. A mother of four adolescents says:

> *"Trusting their judgment" is just a code phrase for letting them do what they want. But they're too immature to exercise good judgment. When they make a mess of things, I have to pick up the pieces.*

It has always been assumed that there is no pleasure involved in being disciplined, but the opposite is true. When firm discipline based on family standards has a place in our relations with our children, they are more free than children with no constraints.

Look around and compare children who are controlled with those who are not. It is the undisciplined rather than the disciplined who are being punished by failure in school, in their relationships, and in the job market. One father of two put it this way:

> *I make sure my children hear the word "no" often enough so that it won't come as a shock when they leave home.*

This father knows that the world doesn't say to our children "You're terrific, no matter what." The world outside our homes has standards, tasks, and tests.

The third attitude New Traditional parents need to acquire is that parents are the leaders in their families. Rearing your children is *your* business. *You* are the expert. As an expert, you have the *right to be different.* You don't have to succumb to every new child-rearing mode, nor do you have to respond to anyone's criticism. Ultimately the most effective parenting techniques for you are methods with which you feel comfortable. These techniques will most likely come out of your own experience and judgment.

A fourth attitude necessary to New Traditional parents is that your firm discipline will not forever damage your child's psyche. Recent psychological research confirms this. Dr. Diana Baumrind of the University of California at Berkeley has studied how various types of parental control affect children. She found that the most assertive, self-reliant, and self-controlled children had parents who were "controlling, demanding, communicative, and loving." These parents were as apt to use corporal punishment for bad behavior as they were to grant rewards for good behavior; in other words, they favored negative and positive reinforcement. In the same study, children with the least self-reliance had parents who were loving but noncontrolling and nondemanding.

From a review of other research on punishment, Baumrind concluded that punishment is most effective when it is swift, consistent, and inescapable, and when it is accompanied by an explanation of what behavior parents want. It is good to hear contemporary confirmation of ideas that have been around for eons under the label of old-fashioned horse sense.

A fifth attitude that will help New Traditional parents feel comfortable with their own way of disciplining runs counter to the media's depiction of them as passive and supportive. It is the realization that being a parent today means being an activist parent. I talked with parents in all stages of parenting, from a mother and father helping a 30-year-old son find his way back from heavy drug use to those dealing with daily storms of rebellion. A Louisiana mother of two told me:

> *Today parents are supposed to be reasonable in their discipline. It's important to listen and care about my children's point of view. But I think understanding them ought to be followed by their understanding me. Instead, I get a whole range of accusations like "You don't trust me," "You're old-fashioned," "It's not fair," "Everybody's going."*
>
> *After all the "whys?" and "why-nots?" I finally shout: "Because I said so." Sometimes they argue that's not a good reason. But whether they know it or not, it's the best reason of all. That's when I put my knowledge and experience to work for their own protection. I love them, but I'm in charge.*

Parents in charge of the family send this clear message to their offspring: Mom and Dad are providing the safety you children need while you mature. Such a message shows children that you care about them; at the same time, it communicates that they are a part of the family, not the center of it.

Parents in charge in the family-centered family can impart that sense of "we-ness" that makes a family special and gives children roots. My mother sent me a constant series of messages when I was a child, all beginning with "we." "We don't eat with our elbows on the table," she said. "We don't call people names." "We never stare in public." I, on the other hand, wanted my daughter to know her own uniqueness, and she grew up without a sense of the family "we." I think children's uniqueness can only be enhanced by giving them a feeling for who "we the family" are.

disciplining with take-charge love— for the new traditional family

Every parent has read and reread the admonition Discipline with love. The term has become an immobilizing cliché. What do I mean by take-charge love? Simply this: It will be necessary for me to love my child with a firmness that encourages me to act with his or her future in mind. It may be easier, for the moment, to look the other way, but in the long run it will be harder for my child, for me, and for the family.

In my own child-rearing experience, I found it difficult, as do many other parents, to administer love and discipline together. It seemed to me that one cancelled the other. I now believe that my laissez-faire, take-it-easy-on-the-child standard was no standard at all. New Traditional parents should apply these goal-oriented yardsticks to discipline: Does it maintain order? Does it develop my child's immediate sense of responsibility? And does it build future character? These are tough standards and require take-charge love to make them work.

The good life every parent wants for their children requires self-discipline. None of us is comfortable when out of control. Today, with anti-family forces battering the front door, it takes love plus discipline, tied to parental standards, to help our children toward the time when they can discipline themselves in an undisciplined world.

Paradoxically, although many children rail against limits to their behavior, they are "crying for parents to take control." One parent I interviewed, a child psychologist, talked about an adolescent patient who protested, "Why doesn't my mother ever say, 'You can't go there' instead of 'It's your decision'? It makes me feel frightened and alone. If she really loved me she wouldn't let me always do what I want."

When parents give children direction, when we set standards of behavior, of work, and of a sense of duty to family, our children take this as a sign that we care about them and that they belong to something bigger than themselves. I think there is a positive *craving* in the young for tradition, form, orderliness—an intensive *desire* to be protected from their culturally inspired "me-ness." Most young people aren't conscious of these needs, and certainly many parents I talked with haven't read the signs in their own children. One California mother of three *has:*

> *My children seek discipline from me, even though they may be angry when I enforce it.*

Everywhere parents are beginning to awake from the spell cast by a psychological age to become—once again—parents with freedom to act as they see fit in their own homes. Parents in my talkshops longed to become more action-oriented. One had this to say:

> *I'm going to give my kids the gift of accountability; I'm going to say, "You are accountable to me for what you do."*

Another action-oriented move on the part of parents I talked to is to stop worrying so much about their children's mental health. Child psychologist Dr. Kevin A. Leman of Arizona agrees in an article in *Frontier:* "Don't ever be afraid to pull the rug out and let the little buzzards tumble. Their psyches are not indelible. We do not have to treat kids with white kid gloves. Children need practice at failure . . . the right to fall on their faces so they can pick themselves up." Partridge also urges parents not to fear harming the developing psyches of today's young people. On the contrary, he says, these children probably have egos like rocks!

New Traditional parents must learn to trust their age-old instincts once again. Children, as parents intuitively know, are considerably less fragile than professionals fear. And yet this parental instinct has been submerged in a hail of what's-best-for-the-child theories.

There is nothing inherently emotionally unhealthy about the existence of parental authority in the family. In fact, we have seen a growing number of our children, when denied discipline at home, seek it elsewhere. The strong influence of a number of outlandish cult leaders gives testimony to that fact. Take-charge discipline, based on a standard of family values, will put authority back where it belongs—with parents.

assertive discipline, or "if you do that again . . ."

A psychologist friend who teaches assertiveness-training at a local college told me a curious thing about her classes. Most of the women students, she said, were there not to learn how to be more assertive with their husbands or their bosses, but to learn how to say no to their children.

It's not surprising that parents, especially Love-Machine Mothers, suffer anxiety, guilt, and feelings of ignorance about discipline. These feelings are effectively manipulated by their children to get what they want.

Many parents feel that somewhere along the road of permissiveness they lost the right to arbitrarily impose their wishes. They taught their children that they didn't have to please parents, that they should meet their own needs. When all the "shoulds" have been removed, both children and parents regard parental authority as invalid. Such parents feel powerless because they are convinced that their opinions don't count.

Assertive discipline is no more or less than firm limits—the "shoulds" of life—expressed in a positive manner. To be assertive is to know what you want to say, and say it or to know what you want to do, and do it. Parents have a perfect right to establish family structure and routines that provide a comfortable living environment for *all* the family. When they realize this, they can be assertive without going to extremes.

New Traditional parents need to be especially on guard against two all-pervasive child-rearing nostrums of the past quarter-century. The first says that to get your child to behave in a desired way, you should reward good behavior and ignore bad behavior. The second says that if your child is misbehaving, you should encourage him or her to express negative feelings. Both these permissive disciplinary reforms have failed miserably. They tend to make parents endlessly question their discipline. A mother of three in Wisconsin typified such parents:

I constantly asked myself, Was I too hard on them? What are their needs? and Do they have emotional problems? The more I questioned, the more I felt guilty, anxious, and frustrated. I didn't think I could do anything right.

Things were pretty bad before I saw that I was letting them take advantage of my feelings. As a result, they didn't have any respect for me and I didn't have any self-respect.

Assertive discipline grows out of parental self-respect. You care too much about yourself to let your children take advantage of you. Conversely, you care too much about your children to allow them to misbehave without responding in a firm way. In general, parental assertiveness merely means identifying bad behavior with an uncomplicated "I don't like that" and good behavior with "I like that." We have to persist, saying it over and over, using a firm tone of voice and looking the child right in the eye.

When I first tried being more assertive, I was amazed at how often I prefaced discipline with the words "I'm sorry." Unconsciously, I'd say, "I'm sorry, dear, I want you to stay home tonight" or "I'm sorry, but you can't have a new Trans Am." My "sorrow" opened the door to manipulation until I learned to say exactly what I wanted: "I want you to stop stalling and get to your homework."

Parents who best practice assertive discipline tell their children in advance just what the consequences of bad behavior will be. Knowing that *something very definite* will happen is a powerful force for changing behavior. These parents aren't caught in the twin traps of too much or too little punishment during moments of anger or confusion. In other words, such parents are not as apt to overlook misbehavior because they are so upset they can't think, nor are they as likely to sentence their children to life in their rooms because they're so mad.

The assertive parents in my sampling were better able to say no without feeling guilty and, more important, to stick to their guns against childish demands for "equality." Parents who don't feel guilty and who feel a perfect right to discipline don't often give way to complicated negotiations based on bargaining with the child for his or her rights. Dr. Dan Kiley, author of *Keeping Kids Out of Trouble*, gives support to parents as disciplinarians. "Don't try to be democratic," he says. "When you say no or use another form of discipline you must maintain a supervisor/subordinate relationship with the child. You can't expect to maintain a democratic, equal relationship when teaching children right from wrong."

responsibilities should equal privileges

In many homes, parents tell me, the rise in their standard of living has meant a reduction in the work they expect their children to perform for the family good. Consequently, children often think that their role in life is to take what parents so freely give without giving anything in return.

Most of us start giving our little children small jobs, but too often their duties don't keep up with their ages. When they most need the experience of contributing to the work of the family, we let them off the hook, thinking that fun and socializing are more important. They are not. Most older parents, looking back, see this attitude as a mistake. A Vermont father wrote:

> *My kids were free boarders and rather unpleasant ones at that. They treated their home like a hotel and their mother and me like servants who should always be ready to drop everything and wait on them.*
>
> *I was too easy on them, thinking they'd only be kids once. Now it looks like they'll be kids all their lives.*

Assigning duties and holding our children to them is one of the trickiest jobs we have to perform as parents. Rather than becoming involved in daily power struggles, we have to become really firm. If we find ways to give our children a sense of usefulness and to make them feel they are a part of family work, then they are likely to believe they are valuable, contributing family members.

the parents-in-charge new traditional family

It's only natural that we parents, who love our children, would like to live with them without conflict—to have options that don't provoke emotional upheaval. We would like to think that there is a magic way for our children to grow up without experiencing pain and discomfort.

Discipline, even the take-charge kind, brings conflict, but in the end it causes less conflict than does no discipline at all. Parents who take charge take a constructive step for the whole family. Permissive child-rearing is based on the premise that children are more important than parents; indeed, that children *are* the family. The New Traditional Family with parents in charge is based on the premise that the family unit is as important as any of its parts.

There is no "recipe" for every child-rearing problem, nor is there a quick answer to every confrontation of will; but I pass along the following specific steps of take-charge discipline, with their goals, from parents who put them into action:

1. Meet defiance immediately. Invoke stringent punishment for all such misbehavior. Respect for parents (and other adult authorities) is *the* most critical factor in child-rearing. Without this, nothing works. The goal is to establish parental leadership in the family.

2. Start at a very early age to reprimand bad behavior—some parents recommend spanking—when family rules have been broken. Such discipline helps children learn the difference between right and wrong. The goal is to correct the behavior before it becomes a habit or a right.

3. Give children responsibilities (jobs) that increase with age or maturity. Require them to complete their tasks before recreation begins. The goal is to show children they are needed by the family and that the family has the first claim on their time and energy.

4. Be firm. No means no. When older, children can present their "case" to help parents understand their reasons for disobedience; however, they must know that understanding does not automatically imply that parents will say yes to their wishes. The goal is to maintain parental control.

5. Treat older children differently from younger ones, commensurate with their ages and behavior. The goal is to stress maturity and earned privileges.

6. Give children what they need but not everything they want. The goal is to help establish a sense of reality, which is the ability to differentiate between need and desire.

7. Monitor television, radio, films, and books according to family standards and the child's age and maturity. The goal is to teach selectivity and clarify values.

8. Insist on knowing who your children's friends are, where your children are going, and the approximate time of their return. The goals here are multiple: to relieve unnecessary worry on your part;

to help control peer pressure; and to teach accountability and common courtesy.

9. Show your anger when serious infractions occur. It is important to demonstrate to a child that his or her misbehavior can *change* you. The goal is to teach accountability.

10. Insist that children face up to their mistakes at home, at school, and socially—even if this requires emotionally painful confrontation with parents or other adults. The goal is to teach honesty, self-possession, and courage.

11. Make your own well-being and that of the family just as important as the child's. The goal is to teach perspective.

Admittedly, these are high standards of disciplinary excellence. But parents tell me that when they compromise on behavior by failing to lead, the entire family is compromised. Taking charge does not mean being rigid and never-bending; taking charge means being predictable and consistent in defending family standards. Being fair has nothing to do with take-charge discipline. As columnist John Rosemond writes: "Fair exists only in baseball. Trying to be 'fair' will drive you bonkers. Children don't even want you to be fair. To them, 'fair' usually means, 'Me first.' "

The belief in the child as an individual separate from the family and the total denial of the state of adulthood have dominated our culture and our child-rearing for too long. We see the wreckage of these illusions in children out of control. We also see the importance of parent-led families rejected. A former governor of New Hampshire, Meldrim Thomson, says there is an "urgent need for the home to once again become the center of responsibility. Our parents of today must take back the initiative of directing their children in the way they should go and in fostering healthy, creative interests, moral values, and a proper set of priorities based upon the [Judeo-] Christian ethic."

Success in the 1980s for the New Traditional Family may not be judged by how much a family has in material things, but by how often parents and children have come to accept the same standards. Success will mean family success—what *we* have done together.

CHAPTER 13

this we believe: parents' right to teach morals and manners

Morals, manners, and age-old social institutions have come crashing down in less than two decades. The counterculturists, with their social-engineer and media go-alongs, preach moral autonomy—the idea that every experience should be permitted—and that indifference to traditional values is the supreme value of all. Our children are brainwashed by their own peers—the members of their subculture—who contend that once their moral liberation is complete, their lives will be free and full. But the bottom line of the new morality is not a new moral meaningfulness, but a new moral emptiness. The work ethic dies; drugs are sold in junior-high locker rooms; 14-year-olds mug grandmothers in the park; athletes cheat; the collective toes of youth tap to high decibel, orgasmic music; pornographic magazines are sold next to the Pepsi in neighborhood supermarkets; and young marriages terminate at a whim.

No one is sure what the long-term effects of the loss of innocence or the shrinking of childhood will be, but some experts are worried. "There are enormous pressures on children and adolescents now," says Dr. Peter B. Neubauer, director of the Child Development Center in New York City. "We are running behind in our understanding of what's going on—but there's no question that something major is happening."

The virtues basic to the renewal of family strength have become clichés in an amoral culture. Love between a husband and wife; family moral standards; the value of effort, risk, and application—all these, once supported, now receive little public praise. In fact, these values are often held up to ridicule. Nonetheless, I trust these clichés, which have come to us through wisdom and suffering to produce happy, moral citizens, more than I would all the complex, professional interpretations of "value systems."

The basic truths of universal morality are not complex. But along with so much else, our society tends to make them appear difficult or even psychological "problems." In a world dedicated to Making It and Getting Mine, associating happiness with virtue is an idea whose time has come again.

The perils of immorality have engaged the thinkers of every time, from Socrates to Thomas Aquinas to William James. But during this psychological age, the seven deadly sins have come to represent the path to liberation for the human spirit. Pride, covetousness, lust, anger, gluttony, envy, and sloth are touted as normal, and abstaining from them is deemed inhibiting or, worse yet, guilt-producing.

I don't mean to imply that all American youth and youth-serving professionals are immoral. However, the lack of moral limits plagues us, both as individuals and as families, with anxiety, depression, and inner emptiness—the very things the new morality is supposed to cure. Although 96 percent of parents I talked with view the entire society as undergoing a steep moral decline, many of these same parents thought that a renewed and strengthened family could make a big difference with children and with society. An Idaho mother of six argues that the family is still a powerful force in moral training of the young:

> It's up to parents to teach children values. The church and the school can help, as they always have, but moral training has to start and end in the family.
>
> Everywhere I see a hunger for trash, so my husband and I think it is our duty to teach our children what is genuine. We teach them to distinguish between self-interest and selfishness. We stress being truthful and kind; all the old ethics that worked so well for so long. We also emphasize that talk is cheap and that action is the magic word.

Parents *are* a child's primary morals teachers, but since the social engineers view most parents as inept, they have decided that today's values must be clarified by professionals, particularly in the schools.

teaching morals in the classroom

Values clarification, courses of prepackaged moral instruction, can lead to the teaching of situational ethics in the classroom. Such teaching emphasizes the building of self-esteem and denies the idea that right and wrong are fixed standards. According to the theory of situational ethics, actions can be justified by their circumstances, morals are relative, and there are no right answers to moral questions.

I see this as a barely disguised version of "the ends justify the means," but some professional educators believe the study of situational ethics provides a new arena in which to pit "expertism" against parental prerogative. *Newsweek* magazine estimated that more than 300,000 classroom teachers have attended workshops for this kind of study and that 6,000 school systems have offered such values programs. While Scholastic Aptitude Test scores fall and academic course content is diluted, teachers are asked to integrate moral "feeling" games into business, art, history, literature, and other subjects. These games pose such discussion questions as, Should I go to bed with my boyfriend?

Many parents are opposed to these techniques, which, in effect, make the teacher a therapist—or at least a moral mediator. A Washington father told me:

> *I think this is an invasion of my family's privacy as well as my son's. Some of the kids are very aggressive and they soon take over the discussion. Their viewpoint prevails.*

"The movement appeals," says Edwin Delattre, director of the National Humanities Center, "to the American preoccupation with easy technical solutions."

Educator Onalee McGraw of the Heritage Foundation asks: "Who decides which values are the best values?" Certainly not parents. If such guidance is needed at all, "values" should be an identifiable elective instead of being slipped into regular academic courses. In this way, both parents and children would have an opportunity to evaluate the programs for what they are.

Values clarification is one more way in which the social engineers keep busy redefining the family in terms of today's morality and attitudes. Chipping away at this great institution is bound to deteriorate its good standing. Why not redefine today's morality in terms of what is best for the traditional family? In our rush to rid ourselves of the constraint of old moral rules, we forget why we developed these rules in the first place—to shield the family.

To prepare children adequately for a future that presents problems in the realms of science, international relations, and natural resources, we parents must teach them that there are non-negotiable truths on which to base their conduct. The solution to the problem of world survival will not be found solely in the increase of intellectual ideas; we must also realize our full potential to be better people. The danger is not, as the psychologizers would have us believe, that we will return to mindless puritan rigidity, but that the people entrusted with choices about our nation's destinies may be guided by an immoral intellect.

The importance of the New Traditional Family to the building of a moral country cannot be overstated. It has been said that there can be no public virtue without private morality, which logically begins in the home. Morality in the community and the nation cannot be decreed by experts in government or schools. It must be nurtured by parents with what Clare Boothe Luce has called "their *interior* devotion to the principles of the universal morality."

do parents have the "right" to teach their moral code to their children?

Sixty-three percent of the parents I asked this question answered, "Yes, of course." Some even thought it was a silly query. But, amazingly, a significant 37 percent did not think they had any right to pass along their own moral code to their children. Many, like a Pennsylvania mother of two, were confused:

> *It's hard to know what to teach my children because I hardly know what to think myself. What is right? Presidents lie, celebrities boast about their live-in lovers—everything's out in the open.*

Some parents had been confronted by hardened youth-culture attitudes. A Nebraska mother says:

> *My daughter laughed at me. Told me my morals were out of date*

and that I had no right to try to tell her what was right or wrong,
since I'd been born before covered wagons.

These attitudes seeping under the family's front door have precipitated a "belief crisis" among parents. Their values are in turmoil.
They ask, Should we remain morally neutral and allow our children
to make up their own minds? Should we rely on our good example
to teach standards to our children? Do we have the right to make
moral judgments about others in front of our children? In other
words, says Henry Malcolm in *Generation of Narcissus,* today's parents "are caught up in a value conflict that is without recorded par-
allel. They do not know what values to teach their children."

The question of teaching children ethics and morals came up in
all my parent talkshops. Many parents assumed that their children
would learn by their unselfish example. One mother was not so sure:

When I sacrificed, my children became takers. My unselfishness
made them selfish. Moral behavior isn't caught like colds; it's taught
by saying "This is right," and "This is wrong."

Some parents were confused about what to teach because their
children skillfully exploited their lack of knowledge about what was
common practice. A father of two adolescents said:

I feel constantly out of step and off guard because my kids can
always point to friends who are doing what they can't do. Sometimes
I don't know what I believe anymore.

Sadly, some parents have given up. A Nebraska mother of four
wrote:

I am afraid to say what I believe lest I offend them. If they find
out I really believe in something, they go out of their way to make
me feel like a fool.

But many parents, fortunately, aren't buying what one father
calls the "junk-food morality" of some of our younger generation.
One mother said:

If I don't give them my values, they'll pick up trash from the street.

The social engineers who blame parents for the immorality of society will scream with pain when parents—whom they see as hopelessly authoritarian and out of date—assert their rights as morals teachers and begin to denounce values clarification.

the moral generation gap

Many parents are concerned about the generation gap between their morals and those of their children. A 1980 Boston poll confirms that they have good reason for worry. Pollster Irwin Harrison, in a survey conducted for the *Boston Globe*, found that 18- to 29-year-olds answered ethical questions quite differently than did 40- to 55-year-olds. The younger generation was much more willing to step in front of another person in line, to drive through a stop sign, to refrain from informing a salesperson that he or she had undercharged, to take extra lunch time if the boss was out, and to cheat on an expense account.

The poll seemed to indicate that members of the younger generation were much more apt to bend the rules in their favor than were their parents. Commenting on the survey results, Paul London, professor of sociology at Tulane University, said, "The young . . . presume to be entitled to have things their own way. They have been prone to see the world in terms of their own psychological needs. They are less concerned with the minor rules of living."

Other commentators on this poll thought parents were at fault for not doing the job of teaching their children ethics and morality. Nothing was said about the culture's crescendo of feel-good advice to our children, almost drowning out parental voices.

Since the cultural upheavals of the 1960s, there has been a taboo against preaching the concepts of right and wrong. The result: a kind of no-fault morality. From everywhere parents hear the message that truth and morality are subjective and therefore unteachable. The ultimate expression of this philosophy is in the human-potential movement, which promotes the equality of feelings with morality. "If it feels good," goes the rallying cry, "it is good."

Among all the concerns of parents, the fear of inflicting guilt on their children seems to be the one that brings on the most anxiety. Yet, some parents are beginning to ask themselves, Isn't shame over wrongdoing a way humans modify antisocial behavior? And isn't shame the sense of having let somebody down that we wanted to please? "Guilt," as author Willard Gaylin writes in his book *Feelings,* "is a guardian of our goodness."

The mistaken idea that all guilt is mental sickness has left too many young people without the ability to condemn their own or others' bad behavior. They are bereft of a useful emotion, one that signals loudly when they fail to live up to the best that is in them. Without a sense of guilt, our children will likely substitute anger against others—especially parents—for their predicaments. The elimination of a sense of guilt and a sense of right and wrong in our children probably hampers their ability to survive, since survival requires the ability to see one's mistakes and correct them.

The new morality has left young consciences of the last two decades vastly underdeveloped. It has replaced the philosophical and religious dictum of self-denial with the new psychological religion of self-love and instant gratification. This new moral standard is most harmful to traditional family values when it throws off the "chains" of virginity, chastity, and fidelity, a trend that has been celebrated in countless recent books, movies, and songs as the ultimate in fulfillment and freedom. Along with the "right" to sexual activity at any time and with anyone came the "right to privacy," swinging a sword through laws on abortion, pornography, and homosexuality.

History warns us that societies fail when a high premium is not put on public and private morality, when societies fail to raise up moral men and women as their heroes.

the hero business, new-morality style

If public opinion is the ultimate arbiter of conduct, public-opinion makers in government, the professions, and particularly in the media must be held accountable by parents for the value-free, hero-less lifestyle they encourage our children to adopt.

When *Senior Scholastic* magazine took a poll in 1979, asking 21,000 teenagers to list their heroes, 75 percent answered "No one." British journalist Henry Fairlie writes: "If we no longer have any heroes, it may not be because no one is fit to be a hero, but because we are not fit to recognize one."

When I was a child, pictures of George Washington crossing the

Delaware and of the statue of Abraham Lincoln in the Lincoln Memorial hung on classroom walls. Stories of bravery and sacrifice became familiar to me. I knew the men at the Alamo had died for their beliefs rather than give ground. I heard the call of Paul Revere and knew that he rode out of loyalty to his cause. How many today would risk that ride, knowing they stood to lose everything? Where might we be if Revere had been "doing his own thing" in his silver shoppe and wasn't "into" liberty? "If I have never been fascinated in childhood by my heroes and the wonders of life," says Josiah Royce in *The Philosophy of Loyalty,* "it is harder to fascinate me later with the call of duty."

One of the welcome tasks of New Traditional parents will be to take up this challenge dropped by our current culture. We can teach our children about heroes and adventures that call them to a commitment that is more than just "coping" or "making it." Heroes are more than people who are very good at guitar-playing or at combing their hair in a style that sweeps the country. These are shabby heroes for the twentieth century. Our children need to know what *deserves* to be idolized and emulated. We should tell them stories, true stories, about heroes who possess the qualities we think men and women should possess.

working our way out of values conflicts

"You can't lay your puritan hang-ups on me" has become a theme of the Peter Pan generation. This rallying cry has caused untold problems for some parents who have been persuaded, for their children's psychological good, to surrender the right to teach them a family moral code. In too many American homes this acquiescence has blossomed into a full-blown hang-up phobia.

Although one brave father of eight told me, "The trouble with kids today is that they have too few hang-ups," most other parents tell me, "I can't ask my children to follow the moral code my parents passed to me." It will take uncommon courage for parents to change this attitude. But it can be done.

Permissive society tells parents that we should accept people on their own terms. The rhetoric of individual freedom is fed to parents and children like pabulum to starving babies. Personal moral growth, parents are warned, is achieved through teaching our children decision-making skills. To do this successfully and to prevent mentally unhealthy hang-ups, parents are urged to be as morally flexible as putty, as up to date as tonight's television sitcom.

I asked parents in my talkshops and surveys: Do you believe your children are capable of making independent value judgments? Eighty percent said no. The reasons most often given were (1) capitulation to peer and other social pressures; (2) an inability to make the connection between a choice and its negative result; and (3) a lack of maturity and experience.

I had my own phobia about causing hang-ups when it came to moral instruction. What had happened to me in those years since my daughter was born? Age, I suppose. Then there were assassinations, Vietnam, corruption in high office—disillusionment. The old traditional morality hadn't worked, I thought, blaming the code instead of its violators—a favorite moral defense of the 1970s.

But now I question the doctrine I once thought liberating, the doctrine that values are entirely personal, each person's values having the same value as anyone else's. I have reclaimed the right to make moral judgments about behavior, both public and private. Although I would defend an individual's right to behave according to standards to which I don't subscribe, I reserve the right to teach my child, "In this family, *we believe* that is wrong."

In a day when there are so few limits on personal values, it's not surprising that there is little scholarly research on the subject of parental transmission of family values. However, a recent study by Loyola University sociologists Lauren Langman and Richard Block makes good sense and is supportive of the aims of New Traditional parents. Langman and Block found the following: (1) Young people brought up in authoritarian families tend to see less of a gap between their values and parental values than those raised in families holding permissive values; on the negative side, these liberal youth hold even more permissive new-morality values than their parents; (2) Parents who are viewed by their children as warm and self-assured have children who are in closer agreement with their values; (3) Regardless of social class, a high degree of family interaction (young people participating with parents in conversation and other activities) is significantly associated with more conservative values.

If you wish your children to grow up holding many of your own traditional values, self-assured parenting in a family-centered family—the New Traditional Family—offers the best chance for success.

Of course, good parents must have firm standards of their own. That so many parents I hear from want to swing the pendulum back, to teach again the old civilized restraints, is cause for cheering. The most important step for parents is to understand and clarify their own values so that they can teach them, since a parent cannot logically cope with that which he or she cannot define.

The great child psychologist Erik Erikson said it more than 30 years ago in *Childhood and Society:* "A child cannot develop a strong as well as adaptable and working conscience . . . without being guided by adults with a reasonably convincing consensus of ethical values." I think that reintroducing absolutes in moral teaching is the answer for families in the 1980s. If there are no constants in morality, there are no constants in human relationships. What could be better for our children than certainty?

this we believe—the traditional basic virtues

Parents whom I identify as New Traditional parents seem to agree with the dictionary definition of morals as a set of principles of right action followed by the majority of people over a long period of time. They reject the new-morality concept that traditional morals are out of fashion; that every man, woman, and child is morally unique; that what is wrong behavior for one could be right behavior for another.

These parents believe there is a universal morality, a basic, unchanging code of virtues that they want their children to observe. It is not a long list, but it is an important one:

1. *Honesty.* "Unless we can trust our kids to be truthful, even when it hurts," they say, "the family doesn't function."

2. *Justice and fair play.* "Following the idea of the golden rule," declares one father, "is the only thing that separates us from animals."

3. *Duty and loyalty.* Allegiance to others in the family, at school, and at work is a moral precept parents want their children to acquire, but one they see rarely practiced in our society.

4. *Moral responsibility.* "I teach my kids that it takes courage to admit moral mistakes," parents tell me. Parents were particularly

unhappy about young people who took the Freudian cop-out of blaming their weaknesses on what their parents (particularly their mothers) did or didn't do for them in childhood.

5. *Compassion.* Kindness is an essential attribute listed by almost all parents. Said one mother: "I believe the only cardinal sin is to be unkind."

Hardly any parent, of whatever child-rearing persuasion, could disagree with this tight little list. The disagreement comes when teaching morally right behavior begins. Where should parents start? And how?

Obviously, your 4-year-old is not going to understand the morality of honesty, justice, duty, self-responsibility, and compassion in just the same way your adolescent does. From studying numerous research reports and talking with a large group of parents about the development of morality in children, I have come to this conclusion: Parents who stand up for their beliefs and are not bystanders—in other words, parents who tell their children how they feel about their behavior and what they expect from them—were most likely to be happy with their children's moral standards.

"It makes me very sad to see you do that"; "I don't like to be with you when you act this way"; or "I don't want you to do that again, I want you to do this instead"—such statements seem to have a greater impact than does ignoring bad behavior or distracting the child with a toy. "The more altruistic children," concluded one commonsensical study from the National Institute of Mental Health, "were those whose mothers used effectively arousing explanations in handling the child's transgressions . . . the more neutrally-toned messages were not effective."

Most of us obey moral rules when we are very young to avoid punishment; when we are older, to avoid the disapproval of others; then, with a developed conscience, to avoid self-condemnation; and finally, to confirm a belief in the sacredness of human value—the mark of the truly moral person. Bringing their children to this last level is the goal of most parents as they actively guide their children's moral thought and behavior through their stages of growth.

Belief in the importance of New Traditional "we believe" messages to children was expressed by most parents. Parents, they contend, must not only have specific ways of guiding children's moral development, but they must also represent the conviction that there is a deeper meaning to what they are saying. This deeper meaning, for many adults, is religious belief based on the Ten Commandments, the oldest moral injunctions of Western civilization. Nonreligious parents have their own "commandments" with strikingly similar goals. Notice how uncomplicated and straightforward these parents are. One mother of three reports she teaches her children:

> *Live a straight life. Be decent and kind and considerate to other people. Keep your promises. Don't sleep around, and keep your sex life to yourself.*

An Indiana father of two narrows down his moral code to keeping his word and reputation:

> *I tell my sons that the thing they'll be most proud of at my age is that they've honored their word. There have been women who looked good to me and I had chances with them, but I never followed up. Discovery would have ruined my good reputation with my wife, my children, and my friends. No momentary pleasure is worth sacrificing your good standing.*

A Pennsylvania teacher/father of two girls explains to his children the true meaning of commitment:

> *The other day I attended the wedding ceremony of a couple of my students in which they promised to stay with each other as long as they both loved each other.*
>
> *What a difference between this pledge and " 'Til death do us part"! To me, the old way says, "Damn it, we're going to make this thing work one way or another, or we're going to die doing it." I tell my children, "That's commitment!"*

One wonders what today's young literature students make of George Eliot's *Middlemarch*, in which the lovers, Dorothea and Ladislaw, practice such restraint that readers are absolutely ravenous, after 600 pages, for the one trembling kiss that seals their love. The romantic possibilities of love delayed or even denied must escape a generation brought up on instant gratification. Here's how a New Traditional parent of three counters such a social attitude in her home:

I'm for bringing a lot of phrases back into style. I sprinkle my child-rearing with lots of words like "No," "Wait awhile," "Think it over," "Skip it for now," "Have it later," and "Save for it."

The problem that arises is how to accomplish the passing of family moral tradition to the younger generation. It's not enough just to make the information available to the young; we parents want our children to adopt our values and carry them on to their children. How do we do this?

Many parents recognize that moral training is never-ending, starting when the child is very young and continuing until the day he or she leaves the family as an adult. Most parents espouse this repetition theory: "You keep your standards high and you never stop telling them what you expect." Parents also think that "watching out for peer pressure" is a very large part of moral training. Some say: "I try to be fair, but I don't fall for the 'everybody's doing it' line."

A California mother of three adolescents told a parent talkshop that her continuous moral teaching had protected her children from the worst of peer pressure:

In the end, I think, teens tend to gravitate toward peers who share the values parents teach. It doesn't always show up right away, and I had some scary moments, especially with my older boy; but eventually all of them took on our family character. Moral training does pay off if we hang in there.

A few brave parents, in this age, expect their children to follow family moral standards—if for no other reason than to please them. One Illinois mother writes:

I don't hesitate to tell my kids: "Listen, I want you to make Mommy proud of you." Why not? Otherwise, it's all give and no take.

It's not just the large moral issues that command a parent's attention, but the everyday expression of consideration for others once called good manners. There is a depressing, even shocking, quality in the public behavior of some of our young, condoned by a compulsively aggressive culture. Only parents can counter this influence by providing moral rules of conduct and even, if necessary, some inhibition.

minding manners

If possible, manners are held in less regard than morals. A 77-year-old arthritic grandmother stands in the bus while seats are filled with elbowing, punching, raucous, thoughtless adolescents. Youths on bicycles, skateboards, or roller skates dare you to use their sidewalks; homes near schools, once prime property, are daily trashed with junk-food wrappers; and gangs of incredibly arrogant teens turn some public games into the sporting equivalent of the London blitz.

Back in the 1960s manners were declared to be at worst sexist and at best laughably quaint—leftovers from a hopelessly repressed Victorian parlor. The new manners are predicated on the logic of "firstness"—who gets to the door first, who's first on the elevator. Out went stuffy old rituals, traceable to the age of chivalry, and in came the manners needed by the liberated, with-it generation. This new etiquette is not concerned with deference owed to sex or age. Rather it addresses such vital questions as norms for coed dorms, how to invite the divorced to the same party, and how to introduce your daughter's live-in date. Answering these perplexing questions hardly provides inspiration for parents trying to teach their young basic manners.

Along with the anti-traditional onslaught of feminism, the stance of anti-establishmentism administered the coup de grace for old-fashioned courtesy. Many young people began to view manners as capitulating to the establishment. Saying ma'am and sir was toadying to authority.

In the 1980s authority figures everywhere are faced with offensiveness, but nowhere more visibly than in some major sports. Certain athletic stars exhibit gross crudity in front of television cameras, and their actions are tolerated by judges and fans.

Everywhere ugly habits are socially tolerated in the name of mentally healthy letting-it-all-hang-out. The private sexual behavior of celebrities is discussed openly on morning television. Everybody, including presidents, is referred to by first name. Decorum is an idea that slipped through the cracks of the 1970s.

The implications of the idea that good manners are old-fashioned and artificial were not lost on well-meaning parents during the last 25 years. Considering the popular concepts that education should be fun and that children learn by parental example, it's not difficult to see how demanding courtesy from children might be seen as inhibiting young, creative minds.

When my daughter was 15, I discovered that, although a basically thoughtful girl, she lacked instruction in the social graces. I was lecturing on a cruise ship, accompanied by my family, and was fortunate to be seated at dinner with three of the most graciously mannered elderly ladies I had ever met. My daughter's manners in this society left something to be desired. Although my husband and I have reasonably good manners (I was raised south of the Mason-Dixon line, where more elaborate politeness was stressed), I had not coached my own child in these niceties. I feared to suppress her potential to express her feelings and thought I'd destroy her youthful and charming spontaneity. Like so many other parents, I thought she would follow my example without formal instruction. But being a model is only half the answer to teaching children. Active instruction is the other, even more motivating, half.

Like discipline and moral standards, politeness can be taught to children at every age. Even a 3-year-old can learn to say please and thank you and to eat with a fork instead of fingers. I'm in favor of more formal manners training as children grow older, as are many parents. When I asked my fellow parents what they considered important to teach, the most frequent response was "writing thank-you notes." Surprisingly, this old-fashioned example of formal consideration for others took precedence even over proper table manners.

An Ohio mother of four explains how she taught her children manners:

> *My boys loved to be center stage; and they weren't above pushing, shoving, and interrupting to get their way. Sometimes it was an uphill battle; but I taught them to mind their p's and q's; to say sir and ma'am; to be cordial to guests; and to eat artichokes properly.*
>
> *I know they thought it was silly at the time; but now they are more socially confident and poised. They generally know what to do with themselves in public, and that makes them happier kids.*

Teaching civilized habits by example is sometimes more difficult. A divorced California mother of two told me:

> *I practice good etiquette. I was raised that way. I thought my manners would rub off on my kids; but they didn't pay any attention.*

Finally, I realized that if my son and I started through a doorway at the same time, I was the one who gave ground every time.

The youth-dominated society's understanding of what constitutes good manners changed during the 1960s and 1970s. Being civil, considerate, and polite to all meant being square. To counter this cultural fashion, which essentially promotes self-centeredness, New Traditional parents need to be ready to teach the timeless rituals of courtesy as part of their overall moral training. Consideration for others is a symbol of the moral person.

As usual, the forces behind alternative life-styles have it all wrong. They think that by resisting tradition they become more individually human. It does not occur to them that the elderly grandmother hanging with gnarled fingers to a bus strap might not agree.

foul-mouthing

One of the most disgusting manifestations of the freedom of expression is the offhand way ugly, vulgar words having to do with sexual or excretory functions trip lightly off so many tongues. Although I know youngsters of good family who do this, my mother's admonition, "Nice people don't," tends to stay with me.

It's painful to hear young people sprinkle obscenities throughout even the most ordinary conversations. Even more offensive than the words themselves is the unthinkable casualness of most vulgarity. I recently heard three adolescent girls seated in the next booth at an ice-cream parlor nonchalantly employing the coarsest possible language. They weren't angry or hurt or excited. I don't think they realized how vulgar they were.

I'm aware that coarse language is thought to mean freedom from oppressive moral strictures and that for women, public vulgarity supposedly demonstrates the equality of the sexes. It does neither. Obscenity was invented to convey excessive anger, and it still does. It is just one more facet of our less than civil culture that caring parents must counter at home with their own children.

a moral and happy life for our children

Many New Traditional parents, often without knowing it, are now in direct conflict with psychological advice-givers, whose profession is built on the desirability of need gratification. In the past two decades, moral instruction by parents has been declared taboo; instead, we have been encouraged to help our children develop their own value systems. New Traditional parents are returning to the idea of teaching the ethic that self-control gives children (and everybody) the greatest satisfaction in life. Self-control, these parents are saying, is more important than self-expression.

It is true that a parent who fights the new morality may suffer sneers and accusations of being out of step, but one who does not fight almost certainly will suffer. And, suffer or not, the parent who fights back retains dignity and self-respect. Your first concern is your family and teaching your beliefs to your children.

As a parent, I believe in the primacy of parental right. I am not humbled by all the "right to do my own thing" talk that pervades society, telling me at every turn that my rights are secondary to the moral dictates of the youth culture. I look upon it as my social and parental duty to resist.

If the new morality is to be curbed, only the intended victim—the family—can do it. Parents in charge of children clamoring for "growth," "consciousness," and "experiences" must see that such total preoccupation with emotional well-being leads down a hundred dead ends. We need to be utterly straight with our young: If you don't grow here as part of the family, you will dodge true moral commitment forever.

New Traditional parents will have to take into their own hands the responsibility for forming a moral society. No one says it is going to be easy, but it will at long last alleviate the enormous pain wrought by the new morality, a pain that is tearing so many families apart. The family stands as the only unit capable of putting forward the case for a code of ethics that can be carried out the front door to the outside world.

CHAPTER 14

the "wrongs" about children's sexual rights

How dare the child-expert/media conglomerate blame parents for a sexually permissive society! The scenario—as played on countless television talk shows and in articles and books—is that parents, inhibited about sex themselves, fail to educate their children. Thus parents are really responsible for the 250,000 teenage gonorrhea cases, 1 million pregnancies, and 400,000 adolescent abortions every year. Here and there voices question the negative influences of a pleasure-bent, no-wait culture that advocates adult rights for children, but these voices are buried in a hail of rhetoric about "owning your own body." The battle cry of the sexual revolution is: "What one does with one's own body is the business of only the person involved."

Briefly putting aside the moral and emotional aspects of 1 million pregnant daughters, the fact remains that somebody has to pay for what all those self-owned bodies are doing. In this case, you the taxpayer do, and the bill comes to $8.3 billion a year or nearly $100 billion (adjusting for inflation) for the 1980s, according to the Population Resource Center. Fifteen-year-old mothers cannot support themselves, let alone their babies. They drop out of high school and often go on welfare. Seventy percent of our huge national welfare tax burden is for dependent children.

But the hidden cost of out-of-wedlock adolescent pregnancy is not the money but the broken hearts of parents. The mother of a Wisconsin 16-year-old told me:

> How could I know my daughter was having sex in her bedroom after school while I was at work? By the time I found out, she was four months pregnant and it was too late. I sat with her through hours of hard labor that I would gladly have gone through for her. The last thing she said before they took her to the delivery room was "Mommy, please don't hate me." She looked like a baby herself.

Her father and I stand by her, but we are sick at heart. Her life is full of hard choices she's scarcely old enough to make. She tries to be a good mother, but in other ways, she seems to want to be our little girl more than ever. Our family will never be the same.

Another result of the sexual revolution is its impact on the health of our children. Medical evidence draws a direct link between early sexual activity and cervical cancer; birth-control pills have more than 100 serious side effects; and younger mothers, as well as their ·infants, face higher health risks. The double sexual standard so much deplored in these liberated times would seem to have a practical purpose—protecting the lives of young girls.

Gonorrhea and syphilis are equal-opportunity diseases; boys as well as girls contract them. Added to the standard forms of VD is the relatively new herpes simplex II, a genital virus that now infects 5 million Americans, with 500,000 new victims every year. Besides blisterlike sores and emotional trauma, this herpes can cause serious birth defects, including blindness. There is no cure. Owning your own body, in the sexual-revolution sense, has never been more risky.

These vitally important facts about the danger of early sexual behavior are screened by those who insist that children be granted all the sexual rights of adults. All consenting forms of sex are good, say the theorists; the only sexual problems they can envision arise from guilt and repressions.

This philosophy is reinforced throughout our society by tax-supported social services and family-planning agencies. In one community report (filled with such noisome psycho-speak terms as outreach, awareness, and nonfragmented counseling), teens who were not pregnant were identified as *pre-pregnant*. In the child-welfare world, it seems that every young girl is grist for the mill of premarital child-bearing.

American family life is under attack by a sexual revolution that considers marriage dispensable and sexual restraint by young people an empty, or even psychologically unhealthy, concept. No agency can undo the influence of a dozen new life-styles, nor can education create a more traditional sexual norm. Moreover, the helping professions have little desire to distance themselves from a set of sexual ethics that provides them with well-paid employment.

It is up to parents—New Traditional parents—to evolve and promote family sexual values that will reemerge as guides for the culture. Many of us already realize this; but far too many earnest parents, constantly assaulted by permissive propaganda, try to understand their children's "right" to sexual freedom and end up as the scapegoats for what's going terribly wrong with our young.

parent sexual attitudes

Many of the parents I talked with, especially the ones I've identified as New Traditional parents, had one overriding attitude toward sex and their children. A mother of three teenagers typifies these parents:

> *I've read reams of material that emphasizes teaching children the values of sexual responsibility, awareness, and caring; but all the literature omits something important that I believe in—that the best birth control for adolescents is abstinence.*

And this word from an Ohio father:

> *Everywhere I hear that sex is so natural it's like eating and sleeping—just another bodily function. If that's the case, any adolescent should practice it. But that's not all there is to sex—there are also human relationships. These take understanding and sensitivity, which are part of growing up. Teenagers haven't lived long enough to develop these abilities; most of them just want to satisfy their glands.*
>
> *I tried to teach my son these things, but he thought he knew it all. He dropped out of college to marry his pregnant girl friend. Now, instead of studying pre-law, he's digging postholes.*

Others I met had been model "liberated" parents. A California mother, for example:

> *When my daughter became sexually active, I took her to family planning, and we discussed alternative methods of birth control. Later I paid for an abortion, follow-up psychological counseling, and more birth-control procedures.*
>
> *I saw to it that she had all the help in the world, but she never had a feeling of responsibility for her activities. My daughter had all the rights; I had all the worries. I won't play that game with my youngest, and I've told her so.*

Other parents told me how they tried to be impossibly modern—

listening in a nonjudgmental, supportive way to tales of their children's sexual adventures. One mother said:

> *It's a very difficult situation for a mother. You don't want to shut off communication; you're even half-flattered they want to confide in you, but it hurts like hell.*

Few parents feel relaxed about their children's sex lives. Of the parents interviewed, 93 percent thought their children's sexual awareness was running well ahead of their ability to cope with the consequences of sexual behavior. Most of these parents speak out in defense of sexual conventions not much honored in contemporary life. Sixty-three percent of the parents I surveyed teach their children that premarital sex or living together is wrong. Not surprisingly, the parents of daughters are the most vociferous, many mothers commenting, "It's always the girl who gets hurt." Ninety-eight percent of parents think extramarital sex is wrong and pass this belief on to their children. One mother calls open marriage "part of today's craziness," and another says it simply gives its adherents an "excuse to satisfy their sexual whims." One father, who was happily married for 26 years, proudly adds that "limiting your sexual relations to just one woman creates an unbreakable bond."

Today the rules forbidding premarital and extramarital sex are often breached, but in no way does this diminish the importance of passing along clearly established guidelines to our children. These guidelines represent the values and the conclusions that we parents have reached through living. When parents are able to set down their own sexual guidelines, they can better provide a balance against the negative pressures coming from outside the home. A California father of eight told a parent talkshop that he and his wife had to sit down and decide where they stood when their children came of dating age:

> *We asked ourselves questions like, What if she's at a party, and someone turns out the light and some heavy petting starts? My wife and I felt if our children are totally inexperienced, it's not good enough just to give them generalized "don'ts." We tried to imagine real situations they might encounter and give them a way out.*
>
> *For example, if there are drugs or alcohol at a party, we've told our kids to call us and we'll pick them up.*

Any number of parents emphasized in talkshops and interviews that it was not enough to set standards for at-home behavior. A California mother of two said:

> *I try not to give them the idea that what I don't know won't hurt me. I stress that their father and I expect them to behave away from home as they behave at home. I'm not so naive that I believe they always do what we expect, but it's not because we gave them permission by saying, "You can do that with your friends, but not around here."*

sex education—who should teach your child?

There is a rampant mania in our society for taking children's education out of the hands of parents. The sad results of this trend, especially in the area of sex education, are obvious: rising rates of pregnancy, VD, and abortion.

Who knows the child's need for information—when and where—better than parents? Above all, who can impart this information and connect it logically with family moral standards? Parents, or course. They are far more capable sex educators than all the prepackaged courses now so popular with professional educators and family planning groups.

Most experts agree; but, they add, parents do *not* educate their children about sex, so we have to take over the job. (With their usual diligence, they have increased their numbers to handle the task: The American Association of Sex Educators, Counselors and Therapists grew from a charter membership of 250 sex educators in 1967 to an organization of 43,000 in 1976.) This familiar cry has reverberated throughout the ranks of the child-rearing professions. When professionals mention parents who do not educate their children about sexuality, they tend to mean that some parents are not giving specific information about contraceptives. The passing on of parental sexual standards and beliefs to children doesn't count for much with experts in the mechanics of "feel good about yourself" sex.

In my survey of 402 families, 96 percent of parents said they did give their children verbal sexual instruction, either in the form of answering questions or of acceptable literature. Even the more formal "sex talk" is still in use by some parents. Fifty-six percent of all parents said they also give specific contraceptive information. Most of them (89 percent) report using such occasions to impart moral training, but only about half believe that their children benefited. The other half believe their children thought parents were out of date. Many of this group still think parents should set a family standard, no matter how these standards are received.

Almost all parents emphatically disagree with the idea that their children have any innate right to sexual activity. The parental consensus, even among self-styled sixties rebels now entering their 30s, is that "sex is not children's entertainment" and "the glandular whims of adolescents don't count for as much as the ability to assume the consequences of the sex act." And few parents saw teenagers as capable of accepting this responsibility. A Missouri parent wrote:

> *My 16-year-old niece is due to have her baby this month. My brother-in-law will have to raise the child on a mailman's salary.*

In my survey and others, a great majority of parents favor sex education for their children. But parents part company with the experts on the question of who delivers the education. This viewpoint, from a mother in North Dakota, where the state requires sex education in the schools, was representative:

> *Sex education involves spiritual values that cannot and, indeed, should not be taught by teachers. I don't feel teachers are trained or even comfortable with teaching sex to youngsters. How, then, is this an improvement over what parents try to do?*

Some teachers are the first to admit they may have problems with sex education. "I had no choice," a California grade-school teacher told me. "The principal mandated that all intermediate teachers had to teach sex education. I was told to indicate that *every* question the kids might ask was all right. But I became really uncomfortable when some of the more 'mature' fifth-grade girls asked me about the actual mechanics of sexual intercourse. I got the clear idea that they were interested in this information because they wanted to get started."

This teacher refused to teach the class the following year and was "punished" by being required to sit in while another instructor handled the subject. "The administration missed my point," says the teacher, who had more than 25 years of classroom experience.

> I objected to the lack of limits in the program itself, but they insisted I was just being a prude.

I believe that the very best way to teach sex in the schools is with parents—not just with their permission, but in their presence. All the films and material should be presented evenings or on weekends, when parents can come to school. I wouldn't let a child attend who wasn't accompanied by a parent.

The best possible program would be one where teachers were there to act as a resource for discussion between parents and their children.

The Roman Catholic schools of St. Paul and Minneapolis agree with this teacher: Parents take the same courses as their children and even do homework in common.

But the problem of sex education in the schools is not only one of teacher sensibility or even parent participation. The problem is *how* the subject is being taught—whether we are talking about true education with facts and all sides represented or whether we are really talking about indoctrination into the beliefs of the sexual revolution. There is a clear difference. And there is much evidence that is not reassuring for New Traditional parents.

One curriculum guide for elementary schools includes a section that purports to help youngsters "develop an understanding of homosexuality." The section covers such subjects as the vocabulary and social fads of homosexuals, and psychological theories about homosexuality, as well as including films and role-playing—all followed by a test on the topic.

Another model curriculum guide contains an exercise for first-graders called "the bathroom tour." In this bit of inspired voyeurism, both boys and girls are taught the names and operation of the male and female genitals.

In one California high-school class, mixed groups of four to six students were told to draw female and male reproductive organs and genitals in detail and then discuss how they felt about drawing sex organs. The "group experience" is stressed in the teacher's guide because it can build "trust and sharing."

In Richmond, Virginia, a sex-education program at the Open High School created a role-reversal game called "The Trade-off." The boys visited a Planned Parenthood clinic for a "pelvic exam," during which they placed their feet in the stirrups while girls walked in and out of the room.

The high-school sex-education guide for Ferndale, California, suggests that boy-girl couples collaborate on worksheets on which they define "foreplay," "erection," "ejaculation," and similar terms. The guide also proposes an interesting variation on "How I Spent My Summer Vacation"; the topic in this case is whether students are satisfied with the size of their sex organs.

The point of all this is not to illustrate silly sex-education teaching methods. Rather, it is to show how far instruction has strayed from the biology of human development—the kind of sexual instruction that most parents support—and has marched in the direction of self-awareness and acceptance of one's own sexuality.

It will probably come as no surprise to New Traditional parents that it isn't biologists who are now in the forefront of the movement toward expanded sex education in the schools, but psychologists and family-planning social workers, funded by upward of 20 federal agencies dealing with teenage sexuality. Could this coalition be another attempt to mold young minds toward the new morality? If so, it puts many parents on a collision course with sex education. The subject matter of the new sex education goes to the very heart of most family moral values.

By no means do all psychologists agree that sex training in the school is a great good. Psychologist Dr. Rhoda L. Lorand says: "Twenty-five years ago, I and many other child analysts might have enthusiastically endorsed school sex education . . . because we believed at that time that emphasis on sexual knowledge could do no harm, only good. We have since learned that it is harmful to force sexual preoccupation on children of the elementary school grades. . . . Forcing of sexual preoccupation on the elementary school child is very likely to result in sexual difficulties in adulthood, and it can lead to disturbed behavior in childhood." Dr. John Meeks, director of Child and Adolescent Services at the Psychiatric Institute of Washington, calls mandatory school sex education "unwarranted and potentially destructive." And Dr. Thomas Szasz, a psychiatrist who is a critic of his own profession, goes so far as to view sex education as unnecessary since it treats a nonexistent condition: sexual ignorance. But these voices are whispering against the wind unless funds for these programs are cut. In this, as in all public programs, the number of professional experts on sex education has continued to expand to meet the funds allocated.

Leaving aside, for a moment, the questions of whether these school programs are moral or beneficial, there is another fundamentally objectionable element inherent in the new sex education: Family privacy is endangered. Ever since sex education turned away from biological information and stumbled toward "consciousness-raising," educators have encouraged teacher-student exploration of feelings about family. Marriage, divorce, the birth of new siblings, physical abuse, alcoholic parents, and sexual molestation are a few matters about which often very young children are prodded into exposing the most private and personal information. Leading the discussions are teachers or nurses who, almost without exception, do not have the training to deal with their emotional results.

In a slightly different vein, the question must be asked: Will sensitive tests and questionnaires be routinely given in tax-funded sex-education courses and fed into a government computer system? It is naive to think that, eventually, some sort of data bank will *not* be established, if for no other reason than to justify the cost of sex education.

Such a conclusion is not an empty scare tactic on my part. The Federal Department of Health has funded a study to identify and evaluate "exemplary" sex-education programs throughout the country. One evaluation tool developed for use with junior-high and high-school students is a confidential questionnaire, designed to measure changes in behavior after a sex-education course.

does sex education lead to more responsible behavior?

The whole rationale behind the sale of sex education to parents was that adequate information would lead to responsible behavior. I have no quarrel with this conventional wisdom as it applies to the academic subjects of anatomy and physiology, but I doubt that the atmosphere of chalkboards, desks, and rooms full of giggling youngsters is the place to develop positive healthy attitudes toward sex. I further question the use of the classroom as the place to "get in touch with one's sexuality." Removing sex instruction from biology and transporting it into the never-never land of human-potential psychology has brought no corresponding decrease in the incidence of teenage pregnancies, venereal disease, or other precocious sexual adventurism. Indeed, in Sweden, where sex education is compulsory, the number of illegitimate births doubled between 1966 and 1975, according to the 1975 *United Nations Demographic Yearbook.*

Even some of sex education's proponents, such as Paul V. Crosbie, don't make claims one way or the other. "No one knows," says Crosbie, professor of sociology at California's Humboldt State University, in *The Public Interest,* "whether sex education is helpful or harmful or simply benign."

If, as the professor says, no one knows, and pleasure-bent adolescents already live in a culture that provides few roadblocks to "discovering your sexuality," then the question logically follows: Why have expensive, family-intrusive, controversial, sex-education programs in the first place? The answer seems to lie, at least in part, in the influence of a sexual conglomerate—the public- and social-health establishment, the psychosexual movement, and Planned Parenthood—backed by an annual $200 million federal Title X subsidy to control population through family planning.

The primary aim of this conglomerate is to free sex from procreation and to defuse the "population bomb," a bomb that, by the way, may no longer be ticking since we have already dropped below the national goal of zero population growth. It seems to me that emphasizing the problems of overpopulation to youngsters from first grade on is, in a larger sense, anti-family. After all, if less is better, the ideal would be none at all!

who took the parents out of planned parenthood?

To be fair, Planned Parenthood, and its many dedicated members, sees itself as a vital health-service organization doing the kind of thankless work for sexually active young people that parents and society have shirked. Since 1968, Planned Parenthood has pushed for universal sex education in schools; provided trained instructors when schoolteachers weren't up to the task or available; established birth-control clinics; and helped do away with age requirements, as well as parental consent, for youngsters who use their services. Sadly, Planned Parenthood apparently doesn't like parents very much, and it certainly doesn't trust them to know what's best for their own children.

At first glance, it appears that the aims of Planned Parenthood and traditional parents are the same: neither group wants our unwed daughters to get pregnant. Where we differ, it seems to me, is that parents believe young people can be taught to exercise restraint. Planned Parenthood, on the other hand, is convinced that premarital sex is inevitable for most boys and girls; therefore the young should be taught tolerance of all forms of sexual expression and should receive information about the legality and availability of contraception and abortion services.

Such fatalism has led Planned Parenthood into some educational adventures of dubious taste. In 1978 the Marin County (California) Planned Parenthood suggested a rhyming "condom couplet" for area high schoolers. More recently, as part of its 1980 St. Valentine's Day youth activities, Planned Parenthood distributed greeting cards that contained the message "Love Carefully" and held not a red candy heart but a red rubber condom. Their enthusiasm for the tasteless "Love Carefully" message extended to posters, buttons, stickers, note paper, and even a needlepoint kit ($10), all aimed rather obviously at young people.

Does this kind of sex education, financed with federal, state, and local taxes, deductible contributions, and United Way monies, help reduce unwanted pregnancies? No, says Dr. Rhoda Lorand, author of *Love, Sex and the Teenager.* "Removal of restraints on sexual activity," says Lorand, a practicing psychotherapist in New York City, "inevitably gives rise to competition, led by the most insecure and troubled youngsters, to prove maturity and courage by engaging in it. This is especially true when the sex educators directly challenge youth."

Other Planned Parenthood material, recommended for high-schoolers, takes an almost jolly view of masturbation. In its pamphlet *The Perils of Puberty* is this advice: "Sex is too important to glop up with sentiment. If you feel sexy, for heaven's sake admit it to yourself. If the feeling and the tension bother you, you can masturbate. Masturbation cannot hurt you and it will make you feel more relaxed." Nobody today wants young people to believe, as some of our parents may have, that masturbation causes acne or blindness; but this kind of silly "me-ism" gives progress a bad name.

the failure of the new sex education

It's time for parents to take a hard look at the movement for "advanced" sex education, the kind that goes beyond biology to touchy-feely self-discovery. Does it prevent premature sexual experimentation? The hard fact of 1 million annual teenage pregnancies tells us it doesn't. Of course, the proponents of sex education try to explain this by saying there isn't *enough* sex education. This North Dakota parent of three doesn't agree:

> *My seventh-grader was getting sexual instruction in three classes during the same semester. He was learning facts about adult sexuality all right; but he was losing any timidity about practicing what he learned. That's not an acceptable trade-off.*

The new "discover yourself" sex education, as it is being promoted in many school districts, is a failure. Telling youngsters about contraceptives—even taking them on walking tours of local drugstores and health clinics to study prophylactics—does not guarantee that they will use them. *Newsweek* reported that an estimated 80 percent of sexually active teenagers fail to use birth control because of unwillingness. More than 98 percent of the young women receiving pregnancy counseling in one California county in 1977 stated that they were familiar with methods of contraception, but, obviously, they had chosen not to use them. "Since the new sex education also informs them of the back-up availability of abortion at public expense, without their parents' consent," says author and economist Jacqueline Kasun in *The Public Interest*, "it probably encourages pregnancy risk-taking."

Parents of adolescents can understand why young people don't choose to use contraceptives, even though they have been taught at public expense to do so. The young have an ironclad sense of immunity. They simply deny that the facts apply to them as individuals. As many studies show, even those teenage girls who already have had unintended pregnancies continue to avoid contraceptives. One Planned Parenthood center found that 60 percent discontinued contraceptive use within one year.

As parents know, it's not difficult for the young to participate in adult activities; the difficulty lies in convincing them to accept adult responsibility.

how parents can fight back

What can New Traditional parents do about the push for human-potential forms of sex education? (1) Insist that your school district return sex education to the biology or science classroom where the instructor is qualified to teach human development and reproduction; (2) Demand that teachers and school nurses not be asked to play psychosexual therapist in endless student "self" encounters in the classroom; (3) Object loudly when your family privacy is invaded in "feelings about your family" games; (4) Make sure that any films or material detailing the moral aspects of sexuality are viewed by parents and children together as a basis for at-home dialogue; (5) Vote out of office any school board that insists you are not qualified to make these judgments; (6) Prohibit the participation in sex education of any organization involved in the promotion of contraceptives or abortion on the basis that it is creating a need for its own services.

Parents are grappling with the new sex education and winning. In Ocean City, New Jersey, an eighth-grade girl brought home a sex-education comic book that had been left in her classroom by a guest lecturer from the Atlantic City Medical Center's Family Planning Clinic. The comic book featured the "startling exploits of Ms. Wanda Lust and Capt. Veedee-o on Venus" and, along with crude drawings dealing with venereal disease and teenage pregnancies, showed the characters riding through space in a vehicle called "V.D. Claptrap," encountering such objects as flying condoms.

The girl's father, who did not object to sex education but was dismayed at the presentation, fired off a letter to the Ocean City school board: "The subject matter is treated obscenely and in a morally objectionable manner," he said. "The tasteless method of presentation allows and encourages youngsters to believe that what they hear on the streets is the same and the equal of what they receive from the educators.

"The presentation is not only lacking in human sensitivity but fosters a definite moral position that I, and all of the parents I have spoken to, regard as unacceptable."

School officials agreed and the comic books, which were published by Syracuse University's College for Human Development and had been approved by the New Jersey Health Department, were declared inappropriate for students. Their use was discontinued.

Parents in other communities have ousted the new sex education, in the seventies and now in the eighties. In River Forest, Illinois, parents sued the state superintendent of schools in 1980 and won a ruling that abstinence from sex be taught as an alternative method of preventing pregnancy. Also in 1980, the New Jersey Coalition of Concerned Parents forced the state school board to raise the mandatory age for sex education from kindergarten to sixth grade. And a scheme, financed by state taxes, to televise sex education to Los Angeles schoolchildren was defeated in the legislature when a parents' group called Lifeline lobbied against it.

Neil Postman, one of the preeminent educators of the last two decades, adds this in *Teaching as a Conserving Activity:* "I deny that schools know what a healthy attitude about sex is, or that they have any legitimate claim to preempt religious or family teachings in this matter."

abortion—can the supreme court be wrong?

Since 1976, the U.S. Supreme Court has held that an unmarried minor female has a right to an abortion without parental consent. The child liberationists howled about the few minor girls who were forced by "fanatic" parents to have unwanted children; but they were, and have continued to be, quiet about the tens of thousands of parents deceived in a conspiracy of silence between their daughters, the abortion deliverers, and the government.

Leaving the moral issue of abortions for adult women aside, parents must consider what a law that significantly alters the relationship of parents and children does to the family. "In the first place," says columnist Joseph Sobran, "the court holds that the girl who wants an abortion owes no obedience to her own father and mother. . . . So-called children's rights mean, in practice, increased state power over parents."

The Supreme Court of the United States is not infallible; it has been wrong many times. It was wrong in *Plessy* v. *Ferguson* in 1896, which established the doctrine of separate but equal, putting a stamp of approval on segregation of the races. It was wrong in *Gannett* v. *DePasquale* in 1979, when it denied the people's right of access to an open court. It was also wrong when it ruled, in *Planned Parenthood* v. *Danforth*, 1976, that the court knows what is best for our pregnant minor daughters and that parents will only get in the way of the child's right to privacy during the most traumatic time in her young life. It is the ultimate example of the professional child advocate's power to protect the young from parental guidance; it is the ultimate intrusion on the family. As Harvard University Professor Nathan Glazer recently remarked: "The courts have changed their role in American life. American courts, the most powerful in the world . . . are now more powerful than ever before . . . [they] now reach into the lives of the people, against the will of the people, deeper than they ever have in American history."

The controversy over abortion and over whose rights are primary, the mother's or the unborn child's, will not diminish in the 1980s. (Realistically, the deciding factor may be economic and not ethical, for abortion is big business.) But we must make a distinction between the question of abortion for adult women and for minor children with parental guardians. No government, court, or agency employee should have the right to recommend and carry out surgery on my child without my express consent. If pro-choice groups—those in favor of abortion on demand—continue to support abortion for minors, they will soon alienate parents who otherwise might have supported abortion for adult women, and the pro-choice people may well lose their fight for "freedom of choice."

For my own part, I favor, reluctantly, making abortion available on a restricted basis, in cases of rape, incest, or when pregnancy threatens a woman's life. But I certainly couldn't be pro-abortion, any more than I could be pro-war or pro-murder. There is no getting away from the fact that abortion is the taking of human life. Nevertheless, I believe that for some adult women, abortion would be the least of several evils. If that is true for my child, then I as a parent should have the right to advise and consent on such a decision—not a federally sanctioned stranger. The conventional recourse for those who disagree with the U.S. Supreme Court is the constitutional amendment. New Traditional parents like myself might support an anti-abortion amendment, again reluctantly, as the only means to regain our parental rights.

Delivering the majority opinion in *Planned Parenthood* v. *Danforth*, Justice Harry Blackmun wrote: "Any independent interest the parent may have in the termination of the minor daughter's pregnancy is no more weighty than the right of privacy of the competent minor mature enough to become pregnant." Many young girls get pregnant for these "mature" reasons: to prove their femininity; to prove their boyfriend's masculinity; or because they believe it can't happen to them. Any justice of the Supreme Court who knows so little about teenage behavior has no business making decisions about our daughters' lives.

everybody's not *doing it*

The new sexual morality could be cancelled if it were not hyped. Media emphasis on adolescents who are sexually active gives an overwhelming impression that everybody's doing it. While no one can deny that sexual adventurism, especially among young girls, has risen sharply since 1960, there are still more of our daughters who don't than do. Researchers Melvin Zelnick, John Kantner, and Young Kim at the Johns Hopkins School of Hygiene and Public Health found that of every ten girls, nine do not get pregnant before age 17 and nearly eight do not get pregnant before age 19. The same study shows that four out of five girls have not had intercourse by age 16.

As it happens, this study was publicized with the pregnancy percentages up front to dramatize our teenage sex "boom," but it can be viewed from either the glass-is-half-full or the-glass-is-half-empty perspective. It is certainly more positive (and just as realistic) to look at the number of young people who are not having adolescent sexual relations than to highlight those who are. Such an approach would encourage more young people to say no and avoid early sex-related tragedies; also, it would give parents a factual, as well as a moral, basis for withstanding the "everybody's doing it" hype and establishing a strong family moral code.

The joys of the sexual revolution have gotten far more attention than research showing that younger teenage girls don't physically enjoy coitus; they may experiment once, or for a short period, and then maintain chastity for a good number of years. Dr. James Ford, a member of the National Advisory Board of the American Life Lobby who has worked on a number of such studies, says that teens who let themselves be pressured into sexual activity sometimes recognize that they are engaging in self-destructive behavior and stop. He describes it as "secondary virginity."

There are overwhelming societal pressures on the young and on their parents to regard early sex as inevitable in our social climate. A pessimistic reading of statistics can stampede us into more sex-education experiments, contraceptive and abortion way stations, and permissive (helpless) parenting attitudes. Reading between the numbers is the least that we New Traditional parents can do to get real information, pass it on to our children, and act on it in our communities.

The next time you see some form of the bold headline "Teenage Sex Booms" under which the article goes on to statistically prove just the opposite, remember that the glass is still more than half-full and that you, as New Traditional parents, can keep it that way.

talking to your child about sex

It's understandable that discussing sexual matters with your children can make you uneasy. I was prepared for How do babies get in? and How do babies get out? I talked easily to my daughter about menstruation, supplied informative pamphlets, and never used such words as "curse" or "sick." I identified all organs by their proper names. But I was like most parents, uncomfortable with talk of adolescent sexuality and contraception. Most professionals think parents fall down when they fail to give youngsters contraceptive advice. But for about half the parents surveyed, giving such information violated their consciences. A Maine mother wrote:

> *Why would I give them direction to do something I consider wrong? Neither would I tell them how to steal and not get caught.*

An Ohio father of two girls says he tried a middle road:

> *I made the mistake of telling my daughters to wait till they were ready for a serious relationship and then to please prevent pregnancy—but I didn't define serious relationship.*
>
> *My youngest girl thinks she's serious everytime the moon comes out, a rock record plays, or the guy is good-looking.*

A psychologist mother of three teenage girls approached parental sex education as a professional:

> *My girls are sexually active. I have always accepted my children as sexual beings but made it clear that along with sexual activity came the responsibility of contraception and VD control. I told them birth control was available, to use it and not become pregnant—because they would raise their child, not I. My children are comfortable with their bodies, themselves as sexual beings, as women*

who have control over their own sexual activity. This was a goal for me in raising three girls.

About half the parents I talked with had problems with this kind of intellectual approach. A mother of a 16-year-old girl had a more typical reaction:

We came home early one night from the movies and caught them in bed in our own house. I cried and her father tried to hit the boy. We haven't coped with the situation yet; we're flailing around trying this and trying that. She says she's not doing it anymore, but who knows? She wants to quit school to live with this jerk.

But most parents I surveyed, uncomfortable or not, reported dealing with their children's sex education in ways consistent with their own values. The following advice summarizes the things they believe they are doing right.

1. *Don't say too much too soon.* Wise parents provide sexual information only in response to their children's questions. If children are reticent about sexuality, forcing knowledge on them too early, according to some clinical timetable, reinforces the sexual preoccupation they see all around them.

2. *Give your children a code of sexual conduct.* Parents who maintain traditional values do not let the fear of being "old-fashioned" or of giving the wrong answer stop them. A California father told me his answer to being called out of date was to proudly tell his children, "It may be 1980 out there, but it's 1940 in here."

3. *Offer virginity as an attainable ideal.* Despite negative cultural indoctrination, many parents believe they can guide their children toward abstention and away from sexual intercourse.

4. *Teach that sex isn't "natural" in the same way as walking and talking; explain how it changes relationships.* Many parents say they try to get beyond the popular idea that sex is just another way of confirming love. Sexual intercourse is more than two bodies coming together; it also involves two complex people with different feelings, needs, and backgrounds.

Admittedly, it is tough to talk about restraint to children raised in a culture that seems to venerate hedonism. But many worthwhile things are difficult. It is difficult to get overconfident adolescents to respect such matters as family, duty, and self-respect. It is difficult to talk about responsible sexuality with children who see sex treated increasingly as a sport and illegitimate baby-making as a subsidized right. And finally, it is difficult to talk about decency and moral codes when most of our children are exposed to pornography, erotic pictures, and movies at every turn. The victims of the so-called victimless crime of pornography are the traditional family and the solid values that have contributed so much to our society for so long.

British social anthropologist J. D. Unwin studied the fall of more than 80 cultures and concluded that each followed the same sexual pattern: As morality weakened, the civilization disintegrated. "Any human society," he reported, "is free either to display great energy, or to enjoy sexual freedom; the evidence is that they cannot do both for more than one generation."

If Unwin is right, the New Traditional Family's role in holding back the forces that are invading the sanctity of the family home may be more important than most people think.

CHAPTER 15

chemical warfare: parents versus drugs

A horror facing today's parents is children stoned on mind-altering drugs or on alcohol, subject to addictions that are defended with flimsy righteousness by the "take-charge-of-your-own-body" crowd. New Traditional parents can't accept this defense. Children have no "right" to kill themselves with chemicals. Parents have every right to fight to stop them.

A drug-using child can cause terrible trauma in a family. A 16-year-old boy's mother wrote:

> *My life has been turned upside down by drugs. I never get a worry-free night's sleep. I cringe when the phone rings. My husband and I can't go away for a weekend and know all is well at home. We're not a family anymore; we're strangers waiting for a tragedy to end it for us.*
>
> *I would give five years off my life to see my son not stoned tonight at the dinner table, but I don't believe in miracles.*

This crushingly sad picture of a family almost destroyed by a drug-addicted son—a boy with intelligence, material advantages, psychiatric counseling, and loving parents and teachers—is a story I heard repeated by dozens of desperate parents. Drugs that can cripple young lives can also cause a nightmare existence for mothers and fathers.

how you are manipulated by your fear of drugs

You don't want to believe it can happen in your family, so you rationalize. A Pennsylvania mother of three tells how her fear of the truth kept her from confronting her 14-year-old daughter:

I wanted so much to trust her. When she insisted that the pills I found in her jacket pocket belonged to a friend, I believed her. I wanted to believe my little girl could never lie to me.

When her grades started slipping and she was listless and sleepy, I told myself it was just her age—a part of growing up.

When she told me her old friends were "square" and brought new friends home, I thought it was because she was mature for her age and needed older friends.

We had long talks about the bad effects of taking drugs. She told me stories about kids she knew who were "wasting" themselves. "I'd never do a thing like that," she assured me.

One day, while I cleaned her room, I found a note in one of her schoolbooks. All the fear that I had pushed down came rushing up. There was no doubt that the note was written to my daughter and that she was getting stoned on pot and God knows what else!

I felt like I'd had a sudden kick in the stomach; but in a strange way, I was glad the problem was out in the open. For so long I hadn't wanted to know it was true. I had given her more and more trust, hoping that she would grow out of it. Just hoping against hope is a helpless situation for a parent. It's a sickening feeling—wanting to protect my daughter and at the same time wanting to protect myself from dealing with something I didn't understand.

This woman's daughter was subsequently found to have experimented with cocaine and a variety of pills, including barbiturates and amphetamines. Fortunately there was no physical addiction, but the girl was deeply loyal to her peers in the drug culture. She boasted of being a "hophead." It took almost a year of firm, loving control for her family to reclaim her, to "get her back," as the mother said. They moved her to another school and her father drove her to school and back. The phone was removed from her room, forcing her to make all calls in her parents' presence. They took the locks off every door inside the home, supervised the spending of her allowance, and did not go out at night or on weekends without her. The mother even quit her part-time job so that the house would never be empty. True, these measures were stringent, and the home was not happy for a while, but the parents were caught in a kind of chemical warfare—fighting a powerful, alien enemy that is strongly supported by the culture. The father added this ending to the story:

Sure we worried that she would run away or commit suicide, like she threatened to do many times. It was a chance we had to take. She was going to be lost to us and to herself at the rate she was going. We told her that we were doing these things because we loved her and we absolutely refused to give up on her. Eventually, she saw it was true.

There are dozens of different drugs to which our children are exposed during their young lives, from marijuana to the badly named angel dust, which turns them into Jekylls and Hydes. But in this book, I'm concentrating on marijuana, since it is the drug most commonly available to youngsters and the one that the drug culture has made the most progress in glorifying.

marijuana—the drug they want us to legalize

According to the popular pot mythology—as reflected in the humor, music, and rituals of the youth drug scene—marijuana is non-addictive, harmless; indeed, "not even a drug," as one teenager told a Washington reporter; "it's just around, like blue jeans." For these reasons, our children laugh at our panic; they are even joined by some professionals who tend to take a "kids will be kids and experiment" stance, advising parents not to get so "emotionally involved" or "overreact."

Thank God for parents who do overreact! Thank God they press the panic button; they deserve a medal of honor for it. Try to tell a parent whose child is failing in school, failing at home, and failing as a person that marijuana is harmless, that it does not lead to experimentation with other drugs or alcohol. Tell such parents that marijuana does not set a drug-scene style for their children to follow.

Not enough is known about the long-term effects of marijuana for it to deserve its benign reputation, even with determinedly gullible youngsters. Just the opposite. Marijuana is both a psychoactive (euphoriant) drug and a sedative. And the marijuana that is sold on the streets is becoming stronger every year. Since 1975, levels of delta-9-tetrahydrocannabinol, or THC, the drug's major active ingredient, have markedly increased from 1 percent to 5 percent due to better cultivation and more exotic strains of the plant. THC does not dissipate with a marijuana cigarette's sweet-smelling smoke but burrows into brain and body tissues, where it accumulates with each new "joint" smoked.

Some young people look on marijuana as just an exotic herb. Some herb! It contains at least 419 chemicals, 61 of them found in no other plant. There is growing evidence from private research and ongoing studies for the Department of Health and Human Services and the National Institute on Drug Abuse that heavy pot use can alter chromosomes and produce lower sperm counts. There is speculation that the estrogenlike effect of THC can cause the enlarged breasts sometimes found in pot-smoking adolescent boys. There are undoubtedly hormonal effects on adolescent girls, too, especially those using birth-control pills; who knows how marijuana will complicate those more than 100 documented risks?

But it's not just the unhealthy physical effects of marijuana use that hurt children and families. It's the drug life-style itself that befuddles adolescents at the very time they need all their wits to tackle math and grammar and biology, to deal with body changes and strange feelings. Marijuana attacks the family's moral standards by rendering children more pliable and suggestible in a society that devours weak character. "Large amounts of marijuana," says Dr. Sidney Cohen, former head of the National Institute on Drug Abuse, "have a depressant effect upon the central nervous system. . . . [and] produce a decreased desire to work, poor performance and a blunted emotional response."

Paul Copperman says in *The Literacy Hoax* that 40 percent of students in metropolitan high schools take some form of drug several days a week during school hours and that twice that number use drugs regularly.

"I can always tell the kids on pot," a high-school teacher told me, "because they have such bad memories. They forget the beginning of a sentence before they finish it."

A physician specializing in adolescent care, Dr. Walter X. Lehmann, contends that some of these young people never make it all the way back, even if they quit smoking marijuana. "I know a lot of young people," he says, "who have broken the pot habit and seem to be doing well, but who are not likely to realize the rich potential that once was theirs."

Is this the substance some counselors and the legalize-marijuana people want parents of adolescents to accept as a rite of passage—

just experimental high jinks? This is the very attitude that perpetu-ates the problem. The justification for the movement to decrimin-alize marijuana is that everybody's doing it, so it must be accepted to keep from making criminals out of our youth. One California father had this perspective:

> *These days when we have trouble controlling something, we make it legal—like marijuana. Just sign it into law so the law isn't broken; then our statistics look better. At this rate, nothing will be illegal.*

A San Francisco-based group called NORML (National Organi-zation for the Reform of Marijuana Laws) heads the movement to make small amounts of marijuana, usually an ounce, legal for per-sonal use. Financially supported by aging Peter Pans, this organi-zation had successfully pushed for lowered penalties in ten states (California, Colorado, Maine, Minnesota, Mississippi, Nebraska, New York, North Carolina, Ohio, and Oregon) and total legalization in Alaska before the general alarm was sounded.

To be fair, NORML advocates marijuana use for adults, not chil-dren, but it is naive to think that pro-drug propaganda reaches only adult eyes and ears. The marijuana-accessory industry has become a half-billion-dollar business, with more than 15,000 "head" shops selling most of the paraphernalia associated with pot. The merchan-dise is frankly aimed at minors; examples are a Star Wars–type space gun that lights a joint and a matching container that collects mari-juana smoke and propels it into the lungs; a Christmas stocking that holds, in addition to candy, a roach clip, papers, and "practice grass"; a Frisbee-like toy with a hole in the center to hold a joint; and mag-azines that advertise T-shirts with the message "For Toddlers Who Toke."

Here's the irony: In states and communities where it is illegal to smoke marijuana, it isn't illegal to sell drug-culture accessories to youngsters. The head-shop business exists for no other reason than to act as a distribution network for equipment, literature, and ma-terials that aid and glamorize the illicit use of drugs.

Some parents are doing something about closing these gateways to drugs. When Sue Rusche, an Atlanta mother of two, began a par-ents' pressure group in 1977, there were 35 head shops in Atlanta. By 1980, there were only three. This cleanup was achieved through a forceful combination of state law, parental action against such merchants, and an effective public-relations campaign.

Across the country in the San Juan school district, California, Carla Lowe, mother of three and vice-president of the PTA, started another anti–drug paraphernalia drive simply by educating other parents, who had never heard of head shops. In 1980, she pushed for a county regulation based on a model act from the Department of Justice. Her group ran smack into tough opposition based on "the right of business to sell products no matter how they are later used." But she continues the battle. "We're not after money or fame," she says. "Most of us are working in this campaign between family, the laundry, or running to ball games and music lessons. We're just parents trying to improve the place in which we live. Isn't that a fundamental right, too?"

In Maryland, Joyce Nelepka organized parents to defeat a congressman who supported a bill to decriminalize marijuana.

These parents aren't so unsophisticated as to think their actions will make the multibillion-dollar marijuana industry go up in smoke. But it's a place to start.

Why do youngsters, some as young as 8 years old, choose to take drugs? By now, you know much of the answer. No matter how good the loving home you provide for your children, they also live in another world. It is a feel-good world—attractive and powerful. Young people find among their drug-using peers an atmosphere in which rejecting the standards of parents is "cool," where blatant musical drug messages are the drumbeat of their everyday lives, where smoking pot is a "so-what" right to use their bodies as they deem fit. Increasingly, youth are being forced into a no-win decision by their own culture.

Parents are not to blame for their children's using drugs. And I'm tired of the shabby argument that because parents legally take a drink, children have a right to illegally take drugs. I am also tired of the "you're not communicating, listening, understanding" accusation. Dr. Marsha Schuchard, a literary historian, mother, and member of an Atlanta-based parents' anti-drug group, says: "All the listening in the world won't gain anything from a child who is intensely loyal to his peer group, who would never break the 'narc' code."

Parents surveyed for this book reacted to their children's drug use in a variety of ways. One Louisiana mother of two felt helpless:

They keep telling me how harmless it is, but I keep seeing a sort of oblivion and it saddens me. They're missing so much.

A Wisconsin father wrote:

After a period of shoplifting to get money for drugs, my son has begun to straighten out. I prayed a lot.

Other parents took stern action; for example, these Ohio parents:

We found a great quantity of marijuana in our son's room recently. He was taking it back to college to sell to his friends because if you buy in quantity, yours is free. This is our budding archaeologist. We sat him down and told him if we ever hear of his using marijuana or find evidence of it again, we'll pull him out of school and he can collect garbage.

A father in Oregon also got tough:

I chewed my 12-year-old son's ass out and restricted his friend-ships. He gave me that bit about "You don't trust me," and I told him, "You're damned right. I don't trust you now. You'll have to earn it back."

All but two parents I surveyed were decidedly against marijuana use for minors. Both these parents admitted to using the drug them-selves "in moderation" and saw nothing wrong in children using it as long as it was done at home and controlled by parents.

But most parents have a gut instinct that tells them they have real reason to worry about any psychoactive, illegal drug used by their children. Increasingly, parents are being galvanized into action by a pot explosion that is reaching younger and younger children and turning some, according to California drug counselor Sonia Lamb, into "vegetables."

In Willimantic, Connecticut, parents' complaints prompted a six-month police investigation that netted 54 schoolchildren—six of them only 9 years old—and charged them with possession and sale of marijuana. "The kids," said Police Chief John P. Hussey, "were ripping off their parents' money to buy the stuff." In Naples, Florida, parents calling themselves the Informed Parents Group persuaded the sheriff to put a local school under photographic surveillance. Students were shown dealing and smoking right in the schoolyard.

Schuchard of Atlanta's anti-drug Nosey Parents Association (so named by their children) says these groups emphasize that "parents are not helpless. Parents have much more muscle, many more resources than we often realize. And the best way to find out what these resources are and how to exercise that muscle is by getting together with other parents." The parents in the Atlanta group decided to act when they learned that their sixth- and seventh-grade children were casually smoking pot and viewing it as "no big deal." These parents had been advised by experts that there was little they could do except wait it out. They couldn't—didn't dare—believe they were so helpless. This is the action they took:

1. They contacted the parents of all their children's friends and told them that parents were forming a group to find out if there was a drug problem.

2. They met to pool their information. The parents aired suspicions, rumors, gossip, and guesses, as well as known facts. "It is crucial," says Schuchard, "that parents learn what is going on, that they do not bury their heads in the sand, that they do not back off when information begins to surface." She goes on to say that parents must find out which friends are involved as users and suppliers and be ready to confront all of them *with* their parents.

3. They educated themselves on the effects of drugs and the local drug scene. According to Schuchard, "Here is where family service and drug counseling agencies can be a great help, but if the professional's attitude is cavalier, or uninterested, or passive . . . be prepared to do your own drug education research and program."

4. They committed themselves to teaching drug and alcohol facts at home. Parents shared what they learned with their children (users and nonusers).

5. They took a firm stand, clearly opposing any drug use by their children.

6. They evolved a common code of basic behavior for drugs, dating, curfews, and chaperoning. Then they presented a unified parental front and supported each other when kids tested them by claiming "so-and-so gets to do such-and-such."

7. They kept a parent-communication network open to keep up with changing problems. They recognized that their kids would fight to maintain their secure circle of friends by being sullen, defiant, and

deceptive. "A parent has to hang in there," says Schuchard, "to act out of pure faith, for a long enough time to make his child recognize his seriousness."

8. They worked hard at developing fun and constructive alternatives to drug use in the community.

What this program amounts to is parents banding together to counter youth peer pressure. When this happens, the effects of peer pressure in a class or neighborhood can be reversed.

There are at least two active ways parents can deal with their children's drug usage: Remove the child from the drug culture, as the Pennsylvania parents did; or challenge and change the culture itself, as the Atlanta and other parents have. Such actions are difficult to take and require no little parental sacrifice, but they can eventually unify a family torn apart by chemical warfare. The primary thing we parents must do is to cease viewing ourselves as helpless people. We are strong as individuals and stronger still when we unite.

Some professionals agree with what these parents are doing. Dr. Harold Voth, senior psychiatrist at the Menninger Foundation, has found that "there is only one certain way to be cured of chronic marijuana smoking. The user must be totally isolated from the drug for a minimum of three months. Only then will he become aware of the profound effects the drug has had on him and at the same time become free of its addictive effects. . . . Someone who cares must intervene totally, consistently, and with unrelenting perseverance. Efforts short of all-out efforts generally fail."

It is at this point that the Love-Machine Mother (or caring father) may balk at depriving a child of friends and social life. Here is the story of one New Mexico mother whose love could not protect her son:

> *This is a very difficult letter to write. But I'm doing it because it may help some other parents.*
>
> *What does a mother do when her teenager is picked up for shoplifting? In my case, I felt shock and then parental love. I was deeply hurt that my son would do such a thing, and then I wanted to protect him from the possible harm he might come to as a result of his actions.*
>
> *The county sheriff's office did not help the situation, because the shoplifting charge resulted in a slap on the wrist for my son. Since*

the first case of shoplifting, there were three others. My son never spent one day in detention for these offenses.

During the same period, my son developed changes in his personal behavior. This was a direct result of smoking pot.

Then I found that a check had been written for more than $300 against my account by my son. The bank wanted to press charges, but parental love made me say no.

I bought a moped so that my son could have transportation to and from work. He came home one day two months ago and said the moped had been stolen. The sheriff's office was notified and a report filed.

Shortly thereafter, I received a phone call from a young man who had purchased the moped from my son. The money from the moped was used to buy pot, as you might have guessed. At the end, I called the sheriff's office and reported my son had stolen my moped and sold it without my consent. My parental love was beginning to waver.

The court fined him $70 for filing a false report, and he was again not held accountable for his stealing.

Today my son is in jail for grand theft. How did he get there, I ask myself? Because of parental love, I think, and a court system that does not make our children pay for their crimes. Although the tears are no longer falling, I am crying just the same, for now he is having to face his troubles alone.

alcohol and adolescents

More than three-fourths (79 percent) of the parents interviewed think the legal drinking age should be returned to 21. A Florida mother of two explains why:

We got taken in by all the "if they're old enough to fight, they're old enough to drink" talk. This is fine philosophy, but it didn't help me much when my son came home drunk and vomited all over the living-room floor.

After the Twenty-sixth Amendment gave 18-year-olds the vote in 1971, 24 states lowered the drinking age from 21 to 18 in an excess of enthusiasm for the young. Hartford, Connecticut, during the following two years, experienced a 20.9-percent increase in the number of young persons involved in traffic accidents and a 15.4-percent increase in the number of drunk-driving convictions. Today, according to the U.S. Department of Transportation, 4,000 teenagers are killed and 40,000 injured every year because of drinking and driving. Many thousands more will earn drunk-driving arrest records, or at least staggering repair bills for bent fenders and grills. Of course, all of these drinkers are not 18. When the legal age was lowered, the age of illegal drinkers dropped lower, too. By 1975, 45 percent of high-school students reported they had been drunk at least once. Alarmingly, the number of adolescent girls who drink has increased at an even greater rate than that for boys.

According to a 1981 nationwide survey by the Research Triangle Institute of North Carolina, one-third of our high-school students are *problem* drinkers. The very nature of adolescence makes drinking a risky business for the immature. The onset of alcoholism can be rapid. Some youngsters have become alcoholics within six months of their first drink, and *preteen drinkers*, once unheard of, have turned up at Alcoholics Anonymous meetings.

Whatever one's moral position on alcohol, the fact remains that, when mixed with young blood, it can ruin barely begun lives and devastate families. One way to dilute its effects is for parents to support raising the drinking age from 18 to 21 nationwide. Second, parents who discover that alcohol has become the drug of choice with their child or in their community can take the same activist stance as do parents fighting marijuana use.

your right to snoop

Children's rights advocates scored a big victory in 1979 when the U.S. Supreme Court upheld a landmark California ruling that said a parent cannot let police search the personal effects of a minor living under his or her roof. This is the most explicit instance yet of placing the rights of minors above parental authority—in this case, above authority over their children's moral and health training. No matter what the good intent, this ruling, if allowed to stand, may legally stop parents from preventing criminal activity within the home. "Such a result," argues California Attorney General George Deukmejian, "clearly endangers the welfare of many minors and the stability of families as a whole."

The stage for this ruling was set when investigators found nine bags of marijuana in the room of a 17-year-old boy. The drug was discovered after his mother had gone to the police. Few parents I talked with had heard of the case, but every parent had an opinion about the subject. I asked parents: If you thought your child had drugs or alcohol in his or her room, would you think you had the right to search for it? Sixty-two percent said yes and 38 percent no, but many of the "yes" parents weren't happy at the thought. A California psychologist/parent told me:

> *I have done it, though I sure didn't like doing it. But these are my children and I have the responsibility as a parent to do what I believe is in my child's best interest.*

A Mississippi mother of three explained:

> *Once I thought I couldn't—the sacredness of privacy and trust and all that—but after searching my daughter's room, I feel no guilt about it. She wasn't being honest with me and was endangering her health.*
>
> *I used to look down on suspicious parents who locked up the liquor cabinet when they went out. Now I do.*

Other parents had no qualms at all, confident in their right to protect their children. An Ohio father, who had reported his drug-using daughter to the police, said:

> *You're damned right I search. That stuff is bad news, and if it is in my home I'm going to know about it. It's my duty to control what comes in.*

Another mother whose son was "heavy into drugs" wrote:

> *I finally had to search his room. I hadn't wanted to; I was afraid I'd find something, but the doctor needed to know what he had been messing with.*

Most parents who said they would not search a child's room, no matter what their suspicions, thought, "If I don't respect their privacy, they won't respect mine."

A funny thing about the right to privacy—children often confuse it with a right to be secret, to hide things they think parents aren't supposed to know about. It's perfectly natural to want privacy, but when drugs or alcohol are involved in adolescent secretiveness, it is all too often accompanied by withdrawal from the family. A parent runs the risk of losing a withdrawn child.

Actress and comedienne Carol Burnett, whose teenage daughter, Carrie, became involved in drugs, announces: "I was a snoop, and I am very glad I was. You *have* to know what you're dealing with. You always read, 'No, let your kids have their privacy.' Well, I say, *snoop!*"

In some instances you may have to go outside the family or outside the community of parents to get help for your child. The physical consequences of drug and alcohol abuse are problems that few parents, New Traditional or otherwise, are equipped to handle. You may even decide to enlist psychological counselors. If you do, try to find one who encourages your child to accept responsibility for his or her actions. The Anonymous programs for alcoholics and drug users, run by former addicts, discovered nearly 50 years ago that the first step toward recovery is the admission of culpability.

CHAPTER 16

parent abuse:
the dark secret in the family closet

In South Carolina, a sixth-grade boy goes off to school screaming at his mother, "I hate your guts!"

In Ohio, a 17-year-old girl calls her mother "a ——ing liar" and pushes her down the steps, breaking her collarbone.

In New Mexico, a mother traumatized by verbal and emotional abuse confesses:

> My 16-year-old daughter has said about any and everything to me. I used to cry. Now I no longer listen to her. I shut her out. But she terrorizes her little sisters when I'm at work. I try to comfort them. I know it hurts so much. I've begged her to just get out and leave us alone if she is so unhappy and hates us so much. But is she going to give up a roof over her head, free clothes, meals, and someone to pick up after her and someone to take out her hostilities on? If she were ever to abuse me physically, I am afraid I would snap and do my level best to kill her. As I think now, sitting here, I gave her life; I chose to bring her into this world. If she turns on me like a mad dog, why must I be punished if I choose to take her out of this world? This is a horrible thought. I know it. But where do you go once you reach the ocean and there's no boat and you can't swim?

Battered parents—abused, heartsick, and heretofore silent. Now the story of parent abuse is beginning to emerge from the darkness of intimate terrorism.

Is it surprising that the home is the battleground it seems to be? In a culture that promotes aggressiveness, a look-out-for-number-one attitude, and the "right" to self-fulfillment—a culture that sneers at authority, maturity, and parental rights—the home has become the *most* likely place for conflict.

246

I asked the parents of my 402 families about parent abuse: emotional, verbal, and physical. Their answers point to the magnitude of family conflict in the 1980s. Almost all the parents (97.1 percent) acknowledged some emotional abuse, defined as their children's withdrawal of affection. Sixty percent of this number admitted that it had brought them to tears.

Verbal abuse was suffered by 92 percent of the parents to the extent that they felt it had been or continued to be a problem. Parents reported that verbal abuse ran the gamut from willful defiance to furious cursing, using foul language repeatedly for its shock and demoralizing value.

To my surprise, 14 percent of these middle-class, well-educated, caring parents had been physically attacked by their children with everything from a fist to a skateboard or a baseball bat. That such violence occurs in these families makes abnormal behavior appear almost normal.

While my sampling is not scientific by any means, it does seem near to the mark. Richard Gelles, a University of Rhode Island sociologist who has studied family violence extensively, estimates that there are 5 to 6 million minors who assault their parents—about 12 percent of all children between ages 3 and 17.

From the heartbreaking stories reluctant parents relate, a picture of the battering child emerges: These children are far more likely to abuse their mothers than their fathers; the abuse is nearly always triggered by the parent's withholding something the child wants (money, car keys, and later hours were the demands most frequently mentioned); abusive adolescent boys outnumber abusive girls two to one; alcohol or drugs are present in about half the incidents; and abusive children often abuse siblings as well as parents.

At the same time a picture of the abused parent emerges. These parents have an enormous amount of faith that they can, as if by magic, handle the next outbreak. They also have a heartfelt loyalty to their child that suppresses fear and transcends the facts of their situation. This was verbalized as, "No matter what he does, he's still my kid." I could find no correlation between abused parents and spanking; the group I interviewed was split about 50-50 between spankers and nonspankers.

My survey reveals something else. Abused parents are "guilty" parents. A mother of two in Detroit writes:

I used to be constantly deluged in guilt. I gave it to myself. My son gave it to me. I didn't realize how manipulative he was because I was too busy feeling guilty. He had the capacity to "zing in" on my weakest point.

A defeated and battered mother adds:

I guess it's my fault that I'm nursing a black eye. I must be a bad mother, or my son wouldn't hate me so.

As with so many other forms of family abuse—child and spouse—the victim is only too ready to take responsibility for the crime.

Emotionally abused parents are sad parents. The reality of beloved children withdrawing their affection, rejecting parental overtures, and shutting themselves away from family can be unbearable. Throughout history, adolescents—in a natural attempt to assert a separate identity—have tried to distance themselves from the children they once were and from parents who they think are trying to keep them forever babies.

But this normal transition is not the one many parents face today. The youth culture outside our front door tends to swallow up our young at about the time they begin to yearn for an adult identity. This is the same culture that increasingly denigrates parental intelligence, our past, our very worth to society. The result: The process of gradual separation too often becomes instant, total—even violent—rejection.

Battered parents, mothers in particular, have their own theories about their abusive children. Almost all of them say that physical abuse was the culmination of years of escalating emotional and verbal abuse. The mother of the 12-year-old, mentioned at the beginning of this chapter, who yelled, "I hate your guts!" each morning reveals that he was putting his fist through the wall by age 14 and threatening her with a gun at 16. She adds:

I don't know why I permitted him to talk to me like that. I guess I was torn with the idea that he needed to say it. The yelling, arguing, and swearing went on for years. Then when this form of explosion no longer worked (there's only so many times you can be shocked by "f——"), he went on to something bigger that did get a response.

Abused parents often report that their abusive children see *them-*

selves as abused and less loved than their siblings, a tragic turn of the old Smothers Brothers "Mom liked you best" joke. These young-sters never quite connect their violent behavior with their parents' subsequent negative response to them. This California mother of four—whose daughter has abused her in the past and at 21 is unable to leave home or hold a job—says:

> *Her perception and my perception of how she has been treated are a hundred miles apart. According to her, my other kids were always treated better. She really believes it! I used to think she was just trying to make me feel guilty by saying so, but she compares herself to the other children and always comes off worse.*
>
> *She's so full of feelings of the injustice done to her by her parents that she really can't see beyond that. She's so full of this point of view that she just cannot get a handle on her life.*

Why expose such a tragic look at family life? Because these abused parents can't bring themselves to believe they are in danger. The mother whose violent son threatened her with a gun said she never believed he'd use it. At least one sociologist, Murrary A. Straus, disagrees: "Almost one out of ten American children attack a parent each year," he says in a paper on family violence, "using methods which carry a high risk of causing injury."

why are parents abused?

A Missouri dad blames the permissive culture for parent abuse:

> *Kids treat parents badly today because they know they won't get in trouble. While they're kicking us in the heart, we're still afraid of damaging them psychologically.*

Today's parent abusers quite often get away with it simply because there is no retribution from overpsychologized parents or from a society saturated with news of child abuse. And many parents go to any lengths to protect their children from the consequences of their behavior, even denying that the most serious assaults were anything more than adolescent exuberance. For a parent, particularly a Love-Machine Mother, to admit that a son or daughter has tried to hurt her brings on such anxiety that forgetting seems to be the only antidote. A California mother whose daughter had physically attacked her says:

> *The next day my daughter acted as if nothing had happened. So did I.*

Some mothers are abused when their sons play what they think is a masculine role. A Pennsylvania mother who divorced her husband for beating her was later punched in the mouth by her 17-year-old son. "Aren't you happy now?" he asked. "You've still got me to hit you."

Daughters are usually less physically abusive, and their attacks are more often verbal and emotional. However, a North Dakota mother reports how her 15-year-old daughter lobbed groceries at her head in a supermarket parking lot:

> *She kept yelling, "I'm not your baby. You can't tell me what to do." Her father and I would not allow her to go out with a 23-year-old man and she just exploded in a place she knew would cause me the most embarrassment.*

Many abused parents lose touch with the reality of their situation. They say that as violence escalates, it takes more and more to get "the pot boiling." In other words, families simply get used to a pattern of violence. Feeling helpless and confused, these parents are not in control of their families. Adolescents are only too willing to step into such a power vacuum and become tyrannical bullies. During a recent Maryland Medical School study of families where battered parents acknowledged that the adolescent was in charge, parents were asked, "How would you like it to be?" The majority of these parents not only shied away from setting firm rules but stated that *everyone should be equal.* This is the ultimate result of the "democratic family" child-rearing attitude so lovingly fostered by children's-rights professionals. Apparently the lesson of such "democracy" was learned only by the parents, not by the children.

Battered fathers are rare among parents for the obvious reason that they do not provide a powerless target. But there are exceptions in my group. One father, a minister, describes a heartbreaking fistfight that precipitated his son's running away from home and religion. A Wisconsin mother tells me that, for a time, her son was careful not to be abusive around his father:

He knew his father would throw him out, but that I'd never get to that point. He thought I loved him so much and was so concerned with his feelings that I could never do it.

But as violence escalates, so did this situation, until the boy openly defied his father. The mother adds:

They ended up struggling on the floor. There is still a big rip in our rug that I can't fix. That's when we threw him out of the house.

the poor-kid theory

Parents surveyed for this book rarely initiated the abuse they received by acting hostile toward their children—unless saying no to unreasonable demands could be considered hostile. This conclusion was also reached by the Maryland Medical School study. Nevertheless, the attitude is prevalent that parents are basically guilty of goading their child to abuse them. In this theory, the victim makes the crime happen, not the criminal. Parents report that often relatives, other parents, and even police believe this. A California mother in a parent talkshop said:

It got awful bad before I called the police on my boy. Then this big, burly cop asks me what I'd done to him to make him hit me.

The tragedy of this situation is that parent victims who are further hurt by such accusations avoid seeking help again. One remedy for society's negative parent-abuse attitude is for more battered parents to speak out, as did these candid parents, so that other parents will know they are not unique. With such openness, painful though it may be, the public's perception will change and abused parents will get real help.

Verbal abuse by children is on the upswing, according to many parents. And it's much more than the sassiness of past generations. Parents of some adolescents tell of repeated cursing and violent threats. Bad language in good homes is an ugly outgrowth of an anything-goes culture. And when parents are urged to allow youthful disrespect and verbal defiance in the name of "democratic exchanges," the stage is set for family tragedy. In effect, the leadership of the family passes to children, authority children can't handle and don't really want.

Physical attacks, mostly against mothers, cannot be condoned on any grounds by even the most zealous of professional child libbers. It's true that very young children will sometimes strike out at their parents, who should reprimand them instantly. But while these infantile outbursts are nothing to worry about, the picture changes drastically if they become repetitive in adolescence.

Why don't battered parents call the police? Parents want to protect their children; they don't want to get them into trouble. Few of the battered parents I talked with could actually bring themselves to telephone authorities, or if they could, wouldn't press assault-and-battery charges. One abused mother, unable to bring herself to phone the police, called a family-service agency for help about her son:

> *I got to the point where I couldn't stand him any longer. I went to my bedroom and locked the door behind me. He followed me yelling to the door. Finally, he got so mad, he shoved his fist through it—just WHAM—he smashed my bedroom door.*
>
> *At that point I called family services. A social worker there told me I had waited too long. Parents like me, he said, really made him angry because we let it go on so long. Instead of giving any help, he scolded me. After that I just sort of gave up.*

Is parental protection ever misplaced? Does parental love require us to bear the blows of a child and live in fear?

Parents who haven't faced this situation tell me they would never become their child's punching bag. "I'd be all over him like ugly on a gorilla," said one father. "They wouldn't dare touch me," said a typical mother. But for battered parents, action lagged behind words, often with terrible consequences. Marriages were disrupted, as a mother of four relates:

> *When all this was going on with my son, my relationship with my husband was all off—we were both involved right up to our eyeballs. When your child is in turmoil, the whole family is in turmoil, and there's no building anything for anybody.*

Brothers and sisters suffer ambivalent agonies, as the same mother tells:

> *My youngest son was bullied and beaten by his brother until he begged us to throw the older boy out; and yet when we finally did, he was afraid his brother would be hurt.*

Physically battered parents often refrain from admitting the seriousness of their child's behavior. Even mothers wearing black eyes talk of "mistakes," "slips," or "accidents." Perhaps the first time an adolescent swings at a parent, it *could* be an accident. But the second time, parents should know they have a problem. And if it happens a third time, they should recognize that a pattern of abuse has been established.

You may decide to seek psychological counseling for your child. You'll certainly be encouraged by everyone to do so, and you may genuinely want to give it a chance as an alternative to calling the police or forcing your child out of the home. Seek a counselor who has experience with adolescents and, even more important, who believes young people are responsible for their own behavior.

What if you must call the police? The single mother who fled her home in a bathrobe in the middle of a winter's night and was afraid to go back had no other choice. Her daughter's out-of-control, aggressive impulses gave her no alternative. Heartbreaking as it is, distraught parents who cannot afford or do not want psychiatric counseling—and who can't physically force a child to leave—can ask for legal help. A few parents at the end of their rope even "divorce" uncontrollable children, giving custody to the state.

Most often, battering youngsters are forced to leave the family home after one final violent explosion. A West Virginia father of three wrote:

> *I came home from work and found him in his room in bed with two girls and some marijuana. We fought and I threw him out. When he was 16 he had quit school without my permission and for the last year was using our home as a place to party. I won't live like that.*

A mother told me that an assault forced her to pack her son's clothes and put the suitcase on the front porch while he was at work. She called a locksmith to change the front-door lock.

> *He shrieked and shouted curses at me from the front lawn until I prayed he'd go away and I'd never see him again. But when he was finally gone, it was hell. I worried that he wasn't eating right. I heard he was sleeping in his car, in trouble with drugs—all kinds of stories. It was hard to sleep at night, wondering. And yet, when he had been gone for a while, it was like a relief.*

There can be nothing so difficult for any parent. The baby you played with and rocked, the child who brought you crayon-scrawled love notes—you turn him out to fend for himself in a world that false bravado will not fool. But there are limits to a parent's responsibility to one child. Catering to the rotten apple is not only unsound but, as parent after parent told me, destructive to the whole family. Parental take-charge discipline is the best insurance against abusive children. But even take-charge discipline cannot *completely* protect families from the violent, outside, anti-parent influences on children today. Here are some positive actions based on my interviews with battered parents:

1. *Don't automatically take the blame for arguments.* It doesn't necessarily take two to make an argument—as you've always heard—if one happens to be an adolescent. Parents imbued with the feeling that every argument must be half their fault can be made helpless by undeserved guilt. Some teenagers have the ability or inner chemistry to goad themselves on.

2. *Don't allow an abusive offspring to manipulate your false guilt.* "If only you could love me as much as I need," goes the argument, "then I would no longer be abusive." As one mother put it, "I don't think there is 'enough' for him."

3. *Be constant.* Never give in or change your decisions in response to your child's aggressive act.

4. *Lay ground rules.* Make certain your child knows that abuse of any kind is out of bounds, that physical assault on your body is totally unacceptable if he or she wishes to live at home.

5. *Before deciding on total expulsion, give your child a "vacation" from the family.* Enlist a trusted relative or friend, one who will provide firm guidance, to take your abusive child for an extended visit—beyond a few days. This cooling-off period, especially with constructive direction, can give your child some perspective on his or her behavior. It also tells the child that you mean what you say. Almost every abused parent told me that their battering child did not believe the family could live without him or her.

6. *Be together.* Try to reduce the socially structured antagonism between the generations, using extended family and community supports.

7. *Say goodbye if necessary.* When your best efforts have failed, you may have to release your child. It is no use pretending that your

lives will ever be the same or that some part of you won't rebel against permanent separation. Perhaps the saddest of all abused parents are those who cannot forgive or forget what their children have done to them. "I hope God forgives him, because I can't," a Minnesota mother wrote.

8. *Know that time heals.* On the positive side, realize that for some problems there is no answer but time. One mother told a parent talkshop:

> *The hardest part of our trouble with Larry was not being sure of the outcome. Larry and I never had a pleasant word or experience when he was a teenager. It got so bad when he turned 18 that I told him, "I don't care what you do—get a job, go to college, or just bum around—but you have to leave this house every morning at eight and not return until dark, and I'll* pretend *you're working. My sanity requires you to be gone all day." At that point I didn't realize he'd be a fine young man at 26. Now raising the others is easier because I have hope.*

Parents react in diverse ways. Some withdraw from the hurt, saying, "If that's the way they want it, I don't care what they do." Others redouble their efforts. A Colorado mother of three boys refused to give up when she felt "not hated, but not cared about *at all*":

> *They hardly spoke, coming in and going out as if I didn't exist, and they backed away if I touched them. So I began to catch them unawares with a hug or kiss. After a while, I discovered they would position themselves where they knew I would surprise them. Gradually, they became tender and loving again.*

A sense of not giving up, a willingness to fight cultural influences for the affections of their children, characterizes New Traditional parents. A never-say-die strength is a vital link in the family chain that binds all our other efforts together.

CHAPTER 17

how the new traditional family works

Consider a spiderweb. You can remove one section after another and nothing much happens; but if you break one crucial strand, the whole web collapses. Like a spiderweb, society can withstand such onslaughts as inflation, famine, and savages, but it cannot survive without that last crucial strand—the family.

New Traditional parents are holding fast. We have no choice. We live in an exhausting and furious culture where parents and the family home offer the only workable answer to the anarchy of the youth culture.

The strong traditional family is what we need to form the productive, creative society for which we all yearn. It is where, to paraphrase Robert Frost, when we go there they have to take us in. Contemporary culture teaches the young how to live without family ties, but this corrosive creed is unnatural. A 1981 Harris survey found that 96 percent of adult Americans still put family at the top of their list of what is important to them. To be familial is our destiny.

There have been a great many studies about families in crisis, but little is known about healthy families and how they stay that way. In a number of interviews with those families I designate as New Traditional, I uncovered seven important factors common to all. These factors add up to a support system that strengthens these families, not only in times of crisis, but in their everyday relations.

1. *Love.* They love each other. Children are not overvalued, and parents as well as children feel appreciated. No member feels that the family exists solely to help him or her realize individual potential.

2. *Family togetherness.* New Traditional families do things together. At least one meal a day requires everyone's presence. And they generally organize their time around family needs rather than outside activities. A mother of three boys explains:

When too many outside commitments interfere, we cut down rather than take time away from the family. Last year my husband dropped out of Toastmasters and my boys had to choose between baseball and soccer leagues. Since family time has Class-A priority, we must make such choices.

3. *Family work priorities.* Children of New Traditional families learn to fit the requirements of the family, not vice versa. The family-centered family, whether or not the mother works outside, is more concerned with getting jobs done than with who does them. For example, sons may do dishes and daughters mow lawns when necessary, but most parents prefer that their children work along traditional lines.

4. *Religion.* You don't have to follow any particular religious doctrine to be a New Traditional parent, but a strong moral base makes it easier for a family to practice the principles of group loyalty. Many of the parents I define as New Traditional are either regular churchgoers or committed to a religiously based life.

5. *Tough in a crisis.* Crisis situations do not fragment the New Traditional Family—they draw the members together. Many express a sunbeams-in-the-gloom philosophy that leads them to find something positive in problems. Such an attitude helps them cope more constructively. In a crisis, these families are not loners. They reach out to extended family—even neighbors—for support. They believe that self-reliance is a good thing, but that *mutual reliance* is what builds strong families. Once we raised our children to be independent; today we must raise them to be interdependent.

6. *A sense of roots.* New Traditional families nurture a sense of their past and find that it supports them in the present. They value their backgrounds and their ethnic heritage as parts of their identity. They are individual families, but each also belongs to a larger family. They have a surer grasp of where they came from and who they are. These families have strong kinship bonds, especially with elder members. The four-generation family is not uncommon, not necessarily living together but usually with access to one another at some time. Grandparents and great-grandparents provide these families with memories that build family loyalty and cohesion.

7. *Celebrations.* Almost all the families have special ways of commemorating traditional holidays, personal celebrations that vary lit-

tle from year to year. These are rituals all family members can count on. They build bridges of continuity from one year to the next. However, ritual is not a static thing with most New Traditional families. New celebrations can become rituals when they provide significant and enjoyable experiences that families want to repeat. Celebrations also can be pleasant learning experiences. When family life is difficult, the members know that there can be happy times. Memories of these special days are a kind of "strength insurance."

Two elements are at work in these strong, healthy families: A requirement that children be responsible members of the family, and a commitment from each member to give time, sometimes even overtime, to promote the family good. These families are committed to themselves. They have connections with other families; with church, school, and community; but they find their ultimate support with each other.

All families run into times when the most carefully built internal supports fail. Even the staunchest New Traditional families must sometimes seek shelter from an anti-parent, anti-family tornado. Some parents find that a growing parent movement offers them the shelter they need.

The recent blossoming of self-help parents' groups attests to the growth of the parent movement. These parent groups gather to share common concerns about drug and alcohol addiction and to help each other cope with the terrible stresses of parenting in the 1980s. These are parents with a distrust of professional helpers, whom they see as too expensive, too uncaring, and too permissive.

do you need a parent peer group?

When I first brought parents together in talkshops, I encountered two negative attitudes that have kept parents apart from one another. First, some parents think the admission of negative feelings toward their young is an indictment of their parenting—proof positive that they must be bad parents. It didn't take long for most of these parents to see that the common bonds of parenthood bound them together and that by sharing feelings and problems, they could put their parenting in a more positive light. As a woman in a mothers' group of mine said:

When I saw parents were in this together, my problems didn't seem so much like my personal failure.

Second, a great many parents thought they were being disloyal to their own children—"talking out of school." But it made sense to most of them that, as I pointed out, their children's peer group is a powerful influence and would have to be countered by an equally influential group—a parent peer group.

Parent groups fit, indeed symbolize, the need of the 1980s. They fill the void created by the decline of public institutions that traditionally supported families and parents. These activist groups respond to parents' search for community after their disillusionment with social-engineering "solutions" to family problems. They are nonbureaucratic, directly accountable to themselves, and as infinitely diverse as the families they represent.

There is no more important question before America's families than How can we counter the youth counterculture? Parents are quick to see "getting together" as an answer. As one California mother of three wrote after attending a parent talkshop:

We parents do need each other. I've spent this past week feeling a lot better about being a parent. I've changed my old attitude that whatever goes wrong with my family is my fault. Just as my child needs friends to develop, I can use the help of other supportive parents. If we parents have to go to the trenches, if it takes a revolution, we will just have to fight all these destructive forces together.

Many parents voice the feeling that the best help they receive from parent groups is to find "I am not alone."

Another plus for parent self-help groups, says pro-parent psychologist Robert D. Hess of Stanford University, is that they may constitute the best possible program of parent education. "The wisdom and experience of other parents may be the major resource available for developing [parent] competence," he says in a paper on parent education. "Groups of participating parents might themselves identify, through discussion of their own personal experience, the problems that they face and their techniques for dealing with them. There is an authenticity that comes from having shared an experience; to realize that another parent has been through the problem gives a sense of confidence in their judgment and advice."

Hess says such mutual-support groups assist parents in another way. The realization that other parents, like them, have problems that are difficult to solve carries a unique reassurance. "Parents who are unable to deal with a particular problem, or who find they have feelings of guilt or anger about their role, or about their child, often experience a great sense of relief when they discover these feelings are shared by other parents. The fear that one is uniquely incompetent is dissipated by the knowledge that others have similar struggles."

The Stanford professor also believes that such parent groups suggest alternative ways of dealing with child-rearing situations. These group exchanges, he adds, also help parents realize that each family is in some ways unique. Therefore, a tactic that is successful for one family may not be the best for another. This says to parents that there is more than one way to be effective—and not an "official" method.

Who would recommend that parents be isolated from a peer system? Parent segregation is part of the reason that our role in society has become de-emphasized and that our collective mental health is near the burnout point.

parents who help parents

The most widespread of all the parent groups is Families Anonymous (FA). This self-help organization, established in 1971, is loosely modeled on Al-Anon, the Alcoholics Anonymous offshoot for families. FA is based on the principle that when your child is in trouble, you as a parent are also in trouble and you need help—best given by other parents. Some parents join FA before their problems reach the tragic stage, when living with their children has become almost intolerable. Other are parents of chronic truants, runaways, and drug dealers and users. FA encourages parents to put some emotional distance between themselves and the turmoil caused by their children.

Meetings are held in local community centers or churches. No dues or fees are assessed, but each person can make a free-will offering to help cover expenses. As with all Anonymous groups, only first names are used to protect the individual's privacy. There is usually a group discussion on a particular topic, followed by a question-and-answer period for new parents. Offering specific child-rearing advice is discouraged; instead, members are urged to be sympathetic and to share their own experiences. There are no professional social workers directing the meetings. An FA member told me why: "The success of the FA program in dealing with family illnesses is felt to lie in the fact that we are not professionals. We do not advise, pass judgment, or in any way add to the terrible feelings of guilt that plague the newcomer to FA."

Although FA is not a religious organization, it is based on spiritual principles called Twelve Steps. This is the Alcoholics Anonymous model of turning troubles over to "a power greater than ourselves." For those parents who don't fit into the spiritual structure of the Anonymous groups, there are other models to follow.

The Parent Place in Seattle is a drop-in talkshop for parents. It was founded by Sharon Stitt, a mother of four, who says the time came when she "had to have a place to run away to." Since 1976, the Parent Place has been a center of parent activity. They have a Parent Line to provide immediate, warm response to a crisis situation or to just everyday troublesome questions. They publish a monthly tipsheet called the *Postpartum Stress Press.* Talk sessions give parents a chance to gain respect as parents, learn parent assertiveness, and discuss destructive parent-child power games and how to stop them. These parents have not lost their sense of humor. Some of their sayings are well known in Seattle: "Children need guidance or they would have been born adults"; "Adolescence is a self-limited disease"; and "Parents need a place to maintain their sanity while their kids are losing theirs."

Numerous social-service agencies throughout the country are geared to the needs of youth; these agencies primarily teach parents how they can do more for their children. The Parent Place says family stability comes through the parent, not the child.

Parent groups can give parents tremendous release. Here's what one Parent Place mother says about her experience:

> *The biggest thing for me was realizing my problems were the children's, not mine. I told them, "I have molded you, I've put everything I have into you, now it's up to you!" I am free of feeling guilty.*

Parents Who Care (PWC), founded in Palo Alto, California, is another grass-roots group. PWC started after a mother was shocked to learn that peer pressure was being exerted on her teenage daughter to drink alcohol and smoke pot. The mother invited other parents to come to her home to talk about what she had discovered. Together they decided to attack the social acceptability of drug and alcohol use in their children's environment.

Says PWC member Joann Lundgren: "We decided the solution had to start with families working together to create the kind of atmosphere where the 'norm' for teenagers is to develop their talents to the fullest." Through a series of kaffeeklatsches held at a local high school and by word of mouth, more than 500 parents were reached. Together they developed a set of guidelines for parents who wanted to gain more control and provide a healthier atmosphere for their adolescents. Here's the PWC list:

1. Teenagers will stay home on school nights, except for school or community events. No more running the streets or driving around aimlessly looking for fun.

2. Weekend curfews for ninth-graders are 11 p.m. and 11:30; for tenth-graders, 11:30 and midnight; eleventh graders, midnight and 12:30; twelfth-graders, midnight and 1 a.m. (Palo Alto is a relatively quiet college town; other areas might require earlier curfews.)

3. When your child's friend gives a party, feel free to call the host parents to make sure there will be adult supervision and that no drugs or alcohol will be permitted.

4. Be visible at your own children's parties. Children who behave unacceptably or who have drugs or alcohol should be immediately asked to leave, after which their parents should be called. Parents should not allow young guests to leave and return—this too often signals the introduction of drugs into the party.

5. When children go out, they must leave telephone numbers where they can be reached.

6. Assure dating teens that you will provide transportation if they need it, at any time.

7. Be awake when your youngster comes home.

8. Get to know your teens' friends and their parents.

PWC parents report much less arguing over rules, better cooperation, and a great deal of parental relief. "This is a sign that parents desire to have more of a direct hand in guiding their teens' experience," says Lundgren. "It tells teenagers that their parents care, and the children do respond."

Members of PWC are not just fun-spoiling naysayers. They've developed a workshop for high-school youngsters called "How to Give a Successful Party," showing youngsters that they can have real fun without drugs or alcohol as the primary "entertainment."

All of these parent groups have guidelines that will help you break the stranglehold that the Peter Pan environment has on your own children. But you may find that you want more direct contact with other parents or that you want to begin to make changes in the atmosphere outside your front door, both for your family and for society.

you can start your own parent talkshop

When I decided to write this book and set about finding out what parents were really thinking, I discovered that I was a novice at group organization. True, I had chaired dozens of meetings, served on a board of directors, and knew *Robert's Rules of Order;* but I had never dealt with groups of people whose personal involvement in the subject of the meeting was at such an intense level. It did not take long to learn seven ground rules that helped my parent talkshops function constructively and smoothly:

1. *Keep like people together.* Although there are always individuals who fit in anywhere, I found that husband-wife teams had more in common with other couples, single parents with other single parents, divorced with divorced, remarrieds with remarrieds, parents of adolescents with similar parents, and so forth.

2. *Focus on a single topic.* Although every group needs a break-the-ice meeting where everyone gets acquainted, and an occasional freewheeling session can stimulate a lagging group, most regular get-togethers, on balance, should deal with one topic announced in advance. If every meeting is "open," too often verbal anarchy reigns, little is accomplished, and parents become frustrated. Discussion topics are easily elicited from parents; these usually center on such questions as discipline, sibling rivalry, parent feelings, dating behavior, school problems, or peer pressures.

3. *Choose a new discussion leader for each meeting.* No parent should be "better" than another, so rotate the chair. Let each discussion begin with the leader offering personal examples on the topic from his or her own life. This establishes commonality.

4. *Talk only about your own experience.* Amateur psychologists abound, and no one is more smitten with behavior analysis than a dedicated parent. Censuring other people's parenting is a negative experience for the group. When each parent honestly shares only personal experiences and feelings, other parents will feel free to silently accept or reject, according to their own circumstances. This is the very best way parents can learn from each other. As Larry Porter, author of a book on group dynamics, says: "A defensive crouch is not the best learning posture."

5. *Don't force a parent to talk.* Although every parent present should have an opportunity to contribute, it's best not to prod parents to talk if they don't want to. Some people take a little longer to warm up than others. They usually lose their inhibitions when they feel the group enthusiasm and begin to recognize that they have a common ground with others who really do understand.

6. *Wait 24 hours before putting a new child-rearing idea into effect.* At one meeting a father thought he had heard a perfect solution to a problem he was having with his son. Without thinking, he rushed home to lay down the law, with some unpleasant consequences for the family. We found it wise to suggest a 24-hour cooling-off period for parents to give them a chance to think about any new idea.

7. *Don't repeat what you hear.* Parents must be able to trust that what they say to the group will go no further.

After a few months of meeting together, your group may decide to reach out for other parents—even start a parent center. Any of the self-help parent groups mentioned earlier will help you with start-up information, usually for a small materials fee. But all you may want is to muster a little support and understanding from a few fellow parents, and that's all right, too. There's little enough of this precious help for parents today.

In a time when the adult portion of the population is beginning to reassert its rights, groups aimed solely at catering to parenting needs are gaining momentum. As increasing numbers of parents learn to seek their peers, a traditional strength will return to the family network. It has always been recognized that young people need friends to help them in the socializing process, but since the psychological age parents have been encouraged to isolate themselves and to rely only on professionals. Parental talent and experience have been made to count for nothing. Parent groups are changing that with their organized efforts to exchange information and skills in pursuit of a tangible goal: building the New Traditional Family.

family encounter

To belong to the family, our children must participate in family life—all of it. It is not enough for them to come around at allowance time, meal time, or holidays. They have to share family time with us to keep the bonds of affection and understanding pulled taut. Too often, meaning well, we've let them off the hook with: "Well, you know young people; they're so busy with their friends." But now it's time for parents to take charge of families; it's time—past time—for this generation of youngsters to grow up to their responsibilities. We parents can help them by insisting that they owe a portion of their time to their families and that this time be "prime" time, not thrown in at convenient moments.

In some families this won't be easy. Some of us have watched our children become ghosts, briefly visible while en route from their cars to their rooms; or just disembodied hands, reaching for money, car keys, or some other adolescent perk.

Sometimes the transition from child-centered family to family-centered family can be sudden. An Ohio mother of three, taking a leaf from the therapist's handbook, describes what she calls a "family-encounter" week that turned her family around:

> *My husband and I had been on a church retreat for married couples that helped us resolve some long-standing problems, so we thought something similar might help our whole family.*
>
> *Our children had grown more and more hostile and distant as they became teenagers. At first we thought it was just a part of growing up in today's world. We made all kinds of excuses for them. They were "seeking their identity" and all that. But finally we had to admit that "divorce" was a real possibility—if they didn't straighten up, we might have to divorce them.*
>
> *One night we told them we were all going to go away together for a week. They threatened to run away, flat out refused to go; they were furious, but we stuck to our guns. We also told them they couldn't take portable radios or television sets.*
>
> *My husband borrowed his boss's hunting cabin in West Virginia;*

we packed bedrolls and enough food for an army. The night we got there my husband removed the distributor cap from the car because we were afraid our oldest son would take off in the night.

We made a few rules right off. One was "If you don't help, you don't eat." I wasn't going to spend a week under primitive conditions waiting on three kids.

My husband and I thought the schedule we had known at our retreat would work for the family and that's pretty much what we followed. In the morning everybody did what he wanted to do by himself—it was our alone time; in the afternoon we all did something together, like hiking or cleaning up around the place; and in the evening we talked together. We all did a lot of talking and listening—we had to because there was no place to run.

I won't say we haven't had problems since that time, but we got our family working again that week. That's all we wanted.

Although some family counselors look askance at the idea of a family encounter without a professional to guide it, I believe it can be a positive experience for several reasons. First, there's an expectation on the part of everyone that something is going to happen, and so something is more likely to happen. Second, when parents make the effort, it demonstrates to children that the family is important. Third, it gives all family members a chance to get beneath the anger and see each other as human beings.

This third point is extremely important because the family spends so much time in "maintenance talk." Parents and children talk about endless things that go into everyday living, such as "Johnny, pick up your clothes," or "Mom, where are my skates?" Taking the family out of the family environment can cut down on maintenance talk and open the door to better understanding.

An encounter such as the Ohio family's may not be needed for the entire family. One father "kidnapped" his 14-year-old son when he felt that the boy was headed for real trouble and was pulling away from family and religious values. This parent was not going to let it happen. The father packed for himself and his son one day. When the boy came home from school, the father asked him to go for a drive. Here's what happened:

We drove for an hour or so, saying nothing. Finally my son asked,

"Where are we going?" I told him I didn't know, but we weren't going home until we got to the bottom of our problem.

That night we pulled into a motel and the next morning we started off again. I didn't even look at a map; I didn't care where we were going. That day my son said, "You can't fool me. You'll have to go back to your job or they'll fire you."

I told him I didn't care, that our relationship meant more to me than my job or anything.

On the fourth day, father and son returned home—talked out, exhausted, but with a "fantastic relationship." The experience, drastic as it was, was so successful that this father since has spent time alone, away from home, with each of his children.

Not every parent can manage such a dramatic encounter, but every family can manage a once-a-week family night. The idea came up in a parent talkshop that included a Mormon couple. It was apparent during the evening that their family had a great deal of unity that was the result, in part, of a practice they call Family Home Evening. The father explained:

Our church has set aside Monday evening for families to be together. It can be formal or informal; we can study a published Bible lesson or we can watch a football game.

We are very strong on teaching the moral aspect of life on these nights. From an early age we encourage our children, boys and girls alike, to be morally clean, and they know what we mean. We also reinforce our belief that the family is eternal; that we will be together forever. This brings a tremendous closeness to our family. Once a week we all realize that the family is the most important thing.

The next day the father brought me the book of lessons his church issued for Family Home Evening. I was struck by one passage in the introduction: "Great blessings will result," it said. "Love at home and obedience to parents will increase . . . and [your children] will gain power to combat the evil influences and temptations which beset them."

"It's too bad," I told my husband, Gene, that night, "that we didn't know about this years ago."

He asked, "Why can't we start our own form of Family Home Evening this week?"

I thought it was too late for us. Our daughter was over 16 and seemingly past any desire for family togetherness. "It can never be too late," said her father.

And so we started. We set aside Sunday night, calling it our Family Night, and decreed that it was to begin with a family meal, sometimes with grandparents or aunts and uncles invited. Later the three of us did something together, each of us taking a turn selecting the family activity. In the beginning, when it was my turn, I wanted to reestablish affectional ties and rekindle memories of a time when we were a happy family. I ran all our old home movies—something we hadn't done in years—which showed us as smiling parents with a loving child. We pored over old vacation photos, recalling a story for each one, and one night we rearranged the family album. My husband sometimes bought chestnuts and marshmallows for roasting in the living-room fireplace. Our daughter usually chose favorite games to play and, over a period of time, developed into a crackerjack poker player.

Our Family Nights weren't always prime examples of sweetness and light. In the beginning, our daughter thought the whole idea was "dumb," "boring," and "undemocratic" since we gave her no choice about attending. And, frankly, there were nights when my husband and I believed the effort was a failure. We hung on because there were also those nights when we all felt a closeness—like family.

One day, as my daughter was approaching her eighteenth birthday, a college career and adulthood looming ahead, I discovered what Family Night had come to mean to her. "Mom," she asked, "when I leave home and move to my own apartment, will we still have Family Night?"

I believe what author–social commentator George Gilder has written in *Sexual Suicide:* "The family is the only agency that can be depended upon to induce truly profound and enduring change in its members. The family is the only institution that works on the deeper interior formations of human character and commitment."

At one time I thought these profound changes would come about through democratic family principles. The idea was so appealing to me that I wrote an article about "shared power," which *PTA* magazine featured on its cover. "In order to carry out the democratic family concept," I wrote, "many families hold weekly council meetings. This gives every member a chance to express himself freely on all family matters. Parents are cautioned not to preach or try to impose their will."

Such child-centered ideas, sincerely held and scrupulously applied, nearly ruined my family. I firmly believe that family-centered ideas such as our Family Night have saved it. Families are not legislative bodies, meeting to do lofty business—they are often models of contradiction and adamantly opposing views. Someone has to be in charge for the good of all. It may jolt the permissive establishment, but I vote *un*selfconsciously for the right of parents to lead families. Such a commonsense, cause-and-effect view almost goes without saying, but there will be those child experts who see parent "uppityness" as their own call to arms. They are an effective political lobby. So must we be.

new traditional parents as a potent political force

Why can't we depend on our legislators to live up to their favorite stump speech, the one in which they put the family ahead of flag or Mom's apple pie? Because the politicians generally delegate the work to professional social activists who see parents, not government, as the main threat to families. The White House Conference on Families seems to be the government's idea of getting parental input on matters that concern them. These gaudy decennial affairs, which produce what columnist James J. Kilpatrick calls "cotton-candy resolutions, spun of good intentions," do little to stop the systematic intrusion of all branches of government into family affairs. Author Jonathan Kellerman writes in *Newsweek* that only a "self-reliant, assertive challenge to government . . . by parents [will] stem the tide of encroachment." Unless parents develop a political identity, Kellerman adds, and translate it into demanding a phase-out of government interference, the family of the 1980s will be in trouble.

Parents are a potent political force. Without our support, no legislator could be elected. It is up to us as individual parents to let our representatives know that we are aware of government's impact on our families. We want a voice in any policy that affects family unity and stability, including such divergent issues as inflationary government spending that wipes out our savings; the destruction of family farms and business by confiscatory death taxes; or the repeal of daylight saving time, designed to save energy, that sends children off to school in the dark. (This last regulation was revoked because parents simply would not stand for it.)

In the past, the crucial question of how a government policy affects families has seldom been asked. Parents in the 1980s can use their political muscle to insure that family issues win as much legislative care as the environment did in the 1970s. Environmental-impact reports are routinely required before any legislation is passed. Why not a *family-impact report* so that regulations and laws will be viewed as to their potential benefit or harm to families?

let's have an american family day

In my family, Mother's Day has always been a big day because my maternal grandmother was a Jarvis, first cousin to Anna Jarvis, who founded Mother's Day in 1913. But in recent years Mother's Day, Father's Day, and even the Children's Day celebration started by one family I talked with provide more benefits to commercial business than to families.

Just as families need to turn their thoughts inward to grow stronger, so the nation of families has to focus attention on the institution of family. I believe this can best be done by creating a special day for families called the American Family Day.

American family morale has reached a low ebb. I believe that taking one day to recognize the family as the nation's cornerstone of strength certainly couldn't lower family esteem; it might, in fact, go far toward raising it.

I hope New Traditional families will celebrate their own specialness on the second Sunday in August and will lobby to make American Family Day a recognized holiday. Let's not just bemoan the fact among ourselves that such a day is necessary. The time is right, and we have the political clout to make it happen.

a vindication of the rights of parents

Today, parents need to listen to their own questioning voices and reject the permissive imperative that tells them that children are more important than parents and that families are not important at all. This need is nowhere more clearly stated than in this Parents'

Bill of Rights that I asked parents to draw up. Here's what they wanted in order of importance:

1. The right to respect
2. The right to impose discipline
3. The right to make mistakes without undue guilt
4. The right to be an individual
5. The right to educate as we see fit
6. The right to privacy
7. The right to be loved
8. The right to require participation in family activities
9. The right to be listened to
10. The right to freedom from excess worry

It is no wonder that parents may think they've lost these rights, for although they have the responsibility for their children's lives, they have been encouraged to think that they are powerless. Parents are not powerless. The sad part of their Bill of Rights is that every right they ask for they already have—they only *think* they don't.

Since the 1960s, parent-rights advocates have been viewed as oppressors of children when, in reality, the child liberators have been the oppressors. They have harmed children because they have failed to understand their crucial need for a stable family and because they have failed to define stability as a right-side-up, parent-in-charge family. The result has been the Peter Pan generation, a stunning indictment of permissive efforts to free children from their familial bonds.

In another time, when general society was more supportive of parents, misguided intrusions into family life might not have rocked family foundations. But today our children must be rescued from a never-never land of danger and fantasy. We must, like Wendy, offer our children a chance to return to the real world. That chance is embodied in the New Traditional Family, where ties bind parents and children with a knot no professional can undo.

Realizing that family renewal will benefit everyone is like rediscovering the wheel or some even more ancient fact. There is evidence that earliest man discovered the benefits of monogamous, child-rearing families. Where would we be today if our furthest ancestors had opted for "life-styles" instead of life-giving? It's not a lesson we should have to learn again.

In the 1980s the New Traditional Family hasn't only emerged—it has arrived, taking center stage. Many parents are embracing the family-centered ideal; the sense of change is everywhere. What can parents do to make these changes work for themselves and their children?

First and foremost, we must believe in ourselves again. We are good and decent parents and we *do* know what's best for our children. Second, we must begin to behave as if we believed in ourselves. Next, we must agree on some basic goals for building our families and our society. If the American dream has gone sour, we must provide the sweetener. Where we have looked routinely to others for answers and help, let us now make our own decisions. And we'd better make room for old-time morality in our lives and rid ourselves of some of the social "enlightenment" foisted on us by permissive manipulators.

Every period of crisis may be a prelude to either disaster or growth. We have come through a critical period during which it was argued that all of society's needs had to be accomplished before family stability could be achieved. That argument is wrong. Family stability is the starting point for society, not its ending point.

I hope that this book will energize you to engage in a great movement of support for the New Traditional Family. But hope is mere longing if it is not tied to possibility. During the 1980s, an estimated 10 million new families will join the almost 60 million already in existence. If the majority of these new families are New Traditional families, the erosion of family life can and will be halted. "It takes time to ruin a world," Bernard de Fontenelle once said, "but time is all it takes." There is no time left. Action is demanded of parents who care.

The family is at a turning point. Which way will it go—to alienation and weakness, or to stability and effectiveness? Taking the latter course won't be easy; meeting challenges seldom is. But if we New Traditional parents are steadfast in our aim, society will have nothing to fear and everything to gain from the coming parent revolution.

AFTERWORD

I have been looking at families in general, and my own in particular, since 1978. I have been changed by the process of looking; I am not facing in the same direction as I then was. My total involvement with this book has given me a firm ideology of the family. Thus armed, I may not always be right but I am not often uncertain.

This book was barely begun before I realized that my seemingly major child-rearing problems were minor compared with those of some parents. My child responded to determined discipline, a new priority on family togetherness, and her own growing good sense. As this book is being published, she is beginning her adult life, a college student aiming for a career in law enforcement. My husband and I are proud she is our daughter.

For parents interested in forming parent groups
the addresses of the following organizations are included:

Families Anonymous, Inc.   Parents Who Care
P.O. Box 344   c/o Gunn High School
Torrance, California 90501   180 Atastradero Road
(enclose $1 for material)   Palo Alto, California 94306

Parent Place
1608 NE 150th
Seattle, Washington 98155

A Note to Parents

How is the New Traditional Family
working in your home? What are its problems and
pleasures? I'd like to hear about your experiences
as parents in our changing society. Please address
your letters to Jeane Westin, P.O. Box 22194,
Sacramento, California 95822.

BIBLIOGRAPHY

Burt, John J., and Meeks, Linda B., *Education for Sexuality: Concepts and Programs for Teachings.* 2d ed. Philadelphia: W. B. Saunders, 1975.

California, State of. Office of Statewide Health Planning and Development. "Issues in Planning Services for California's Children and Youth." Sacramento: California Department of Finance, 1980.

——. "Teenage Parents in Sacramento County: A Study of Needs and Services." Sacramento: California Department of Finance, 1980.

Church of Jesus Christ of Latter-Day Saints. *Family Home Evening.* Salt Lake City, Utah: Church of Jesus Christ of Latter-Day Saints, 1978.

Coons, John E., and Sugarman, Stephen D. *Education by Choice: The Case for Family Control.* Berkeley: University of California Press, 1978.

Copperman, Paul. *The Literacy Hoax: The Decline of Reading, Writing, and Learning in the Public Schools and What We Can Do about It.* New York: William Morrow, 1978.

Crosbie, Paul V. "Sex Education: Another Look." *The Public Interest*, Winter 1980, pp. 120–129.

Didion, Joan. *The White Album.* New York: Simon and Schuster, 1979.

Dobson, James. *Dare to Discipline.* New York: Bantam, 1977.

Ebel, Robert L. "The Failure of Schools Without Failure." *Phi Delta Kappan*, February 1980, pp. 386–388.

Erikson, Erik H. *Childhood and Society.* New York: W. W. Norton, 1964.

Gaylin, Willard. *Feelings.* New York: Ballantine, 1980.

Gilder, George. *Sexual Suicide.* New York: Quadrangle Books, 1973.

Heritage Foundation. *Family Protection Report.* Washington: Heritage Foundation, 1979.

Hess, Robert D. "Experts and Amateurs: Some Unintended Consequences of Parent Education." Draft of unpublished paper, 1980.

Hitchcock, James, et al. *The Family: America's Hope.* Rockford, Illinois: Rockford College Institute, 1979.

Holt, John. *How Children Fail.* New York: Pitman Publishing, 1964.

Jacobson, Ulla. *A Child's Rights.* Stockholm: Askild & Kärnekull, 1978.

Johnson, Paul. *Enemies of Society.* New York: Atheneum, 1977.

Kasun, Jacqueline. "More on the New Sex Education." *The Public Interest*, Winter 1980, pp. 129–137.

Kellerman, Jonathan. "Big Brother and Big Mother." *Newsweek*, 12 January 1981, p. 15.

Kiley, Dan. *Keeping Kids Out of Trouble.* New York: Warner Books, 1979.

Kohl, Herbert. *36 Children.* New York: W. W. Norton, 1968.

Kozol, Jonathan. *Death at an Early Age.* Boston: Houghton Mifflin, 1967.

Langman, L., and Block, R. "The Intergenerational Transmission of Values." Rockville, Maryland: National Institute for Mental Health, 1978.

Larkin, Ralph W. *Suburban Youth in Cultural Crisis.* Oxford: Oxford University Press, 1979.

Lasch, Christopher. *The Culture of Narcissism: American Life in an Age of Diminishing Expectations.* New York: W. W. Norton, 1978.

———. *Haven in a Heartless World: The Family Besieged.* New York: Basic Books, 1977.

Leman, Kevin A. "Pull the Rug Out and Let the Little Buzzards Tumble." *Frontier,* September 1980, pp. 6–15.

Malcolm, Henry. *Generation of Narcissus.* Boston: Little, Brown, 1972.

Meyer, Karl E. "The Beast in the Box." *Saturday Review,* 15 April 1978, p. 42.

Partridge, C. R. "Unspoiling the Spoiled Child." *Today's Education,* September 1977, pp. 67–69.

Peirce, Neal. "Reform in Federal Bureaucracy Is Not on Horizon." *The Washington Post,* November 1979.

Porter, Larry. *The Reading Book for Human Relations Training.* Arlington, Virginia: NTL Institute, 1979.

Postman, Neil. *Teaching as a Conserving Activity.* New York: Delacorte Press, 1979.

Rosemond, John. "The Last Oppressed Minority." *Chicago Tribune,* October 1979.

Rosenbaum, Ron. *Rebirth of the Salesman: Tales of the Song & Dance Seventies.* New York: Dell Publishing, 1979.

Stein, Ben. *The View from Sunset Boulevard.* New York: Basic Books, 1979.

Westin, Jeane. "Let's End Family Warfare." *PTA Magazine,* November 1973, pp. 14–17.

Winn, Marie. *The Plug-In Drug: Television, Children, and the Family.* New York: Viking Press, 1977.

Wynne, Edward A. "Schools That Serve Families." *National Elementary Principal,* July 1976, pp. 6–15.

Zahn-Waxler, Carolyn, and Radke-Yarrow, Marian. "Child Rearing and the Development of Children's Altruism." Rockville, Maryland: The National Institute for Mental Health, 1979.

INDEX

ABOUT THE AUTHOR

A professional writer, Jeane Westin has produced
more than 250 magazine and newspaper
articles on family and marital relations
and education. She is the author of five
books, among them *Making Do: How Women
Survived the 30s* and *Finding Your Roots*.
She and her husband, Gene, and their teenage
daughter live in Sacramento, California.